Voices of the New Arab Public

Voices of the
New Arab Public

IRAQ, AL-JAZEERA, AND
MIDDLE EAST POLITICS TODAY

Marc Lynch

Columbia University Press   New York

Columbia University Press
Publishers Since 1893
New York   Chichester, West Sussex
Copyright © 2006 Columbia University Press

Library of Congress Cataloging-in-Publication Data
Lynch, Marc, 1969–
Voices of the new Arab public:
Iraq, Al-Jazeera, and Middle East politics today /
Marc Lynch.
p. cm.
Includes bibliographical references and index.
ISBN 0-231-13448-7 (cloth : alk paper)
1. Political culture—Arab countries.
2. Mass media and public opinion—Arab countries.
3. Al Jazeera (television network)
4. Mass media—Political aspects—Arab countries.
5. Iraq—Foreign public opinion, Arab.
I. Title.
JQ1850.A91L93   2006
306.2'0917'492709051—dc22
2005049677

∞

Columbia University Press books are printed
on permanent and durable acid-free paper.
Printed in the United States of America

c 10 9 8 7 6 5 4 3 2 1

References to Internet Web sites (URLs) were accurate
at the time of writing. Neither the author nor Columbia
University Press is responsible for Web sites that may
have expired or changed since this book was prepared.

for Sophia Faith and Lauren Elisabeth

Contents

Tables

Acknowledgments

On September 11, 2001, I was more than halfway finished with a book about the sanctions on Iraq. As the world changed around me, I became increasingly fascinated by the role of the Arab media in the evolving political struggles. I was particularly affected by a research trip to Jordan, Egypt, Syria, and Lebanon in April to June of 2002. The dramatic increase in anti-Americanism in Jordan and Egypt, and the dramatic impact of al-Jazeera on political discussions, struck me as something genuinely new and important. An attention to the Arab media and public opinion was less a departure for me than an intellectual homecoming. My first book, *State Interests and Public Spheres*, had explored the impact on identity politics in Jordan of a media opening, and then slowly and steadily closing down. That book, written during the mid-1990s, had not paid great attention to television, since Jordanian TV remained tightly controlled by the government and satellite television had yet to make a significant political impact. By 2002, this situation had clearly changed.

What had originally been a single chapter about the role of Arab public opinion therefore took on a life of its own. I presented my first thoughts on the subject at the 2000 annual meeting of the Middle East Studies Association in Orlando, where I received useful feedback from Michael Hudson, Dalia Kassem Kaye, and Ibrahim Karawan, among many others. A version of that article was eventually published by *Politics and Society,* under the title "Beyond the Arab Street." Working with that journal's editorial board was a real pleasure, and their comments definitely improved both that article and this book.

Writing this book has been a genuinely interactive process. I have been blessed by the support and advice of numerous exceptional editors along the way. Chris Toensing of the Middle East Research and Information Project (MERIP) has been a constant intellectual companion over the last few years. He published my first writings about Iraq, and stayed with me as my focus shifted, publishing several articles on Jordan that helped me frame some of the arguments in this book. And last, but by no means least, Chris read this entire manuscript in a very early form, offering his typically insightful and constructive commentary along the way.

My shift into the realm of the Arab media was solidified by a timely invitation by Gideon Rose, managing editor of *Foreign Affairs*, to write an article for that august journal. Writing this piece, which became "Taking Arabs Seriously" (September 2003), forced me for the first time not only to put together a systematic critique of the American approach to Arab public opinion, but also to offer the beginnings of a constructive alternative. Gideon has continued to be a skeptical and immensely constructive reader of my work, and this book owes a lot to his interventions. Perhaps this book will convince even that most hardened of realists of the need to take the Arab media seriously!

The *Foreign Affairs* article propelled me into policy circles for the first time, as I became involved in some important debates swirling around Washington about the appropriate form and strategy for American public diplomacy. I first had the opportunity to present some thoughts on the topic at the United Nations, thanks to the Public Relations Society of America. I then had the good fortune to be invited to a forum at George Washington University organized by the Public Diplomacy Institute. At that forum I met Ambassador Bill Rugh, who has since become a trusted and valued colleague. I have benefited enormously from Bill's vast experience and deep insight into the Arab media and public diplomacy. Bill read this entire manuscript, and helped improve it dramatically.

Many other scholars and colleagues offered helpful suggestions along the way. Dale Eickelman read the entire manuscript and offered exceptionally useful advice and suggestions. Shibley Telhami has been unfailingly supportive, generous both with his time and with his unparalleled data on Arab public opinion. Finally, I wrote two articles for the *Arab Reform Bulletin* that were enriched by Amy Hawthorne's keen editorial suggestions, which in turn helped to tighten and focus this book's arguments. Mustafa Hamarneh and the staff of the Center for Strategic Studies at the University of Jordan were gracious and generous in their help, as always. At the risk of forgetting someone, I would also like to thank Asaad AbuKhalil, Hawyard Alker, Michael Barnett, Neta Crawford, Gregory Gause, Charles Hirschkind, Peter Katzenstein, Robert Keohane, and Lisa Wedeen. I am also deeply grateful to dozens of Arab journalists, politicians, and activists who shared their thoughts and experiences with me; although some of them must remain anonymous, others are quoted freely in the text that follows. And last but not least, I owe a particular debt of gratitude to the infamous "Jordan mafia": Curtis Ryan and Jillian Schwedler. No part of my academic life, or my life in general, would be the same without their companionship and support over the years. I can only hope that Sean, Nick, and Jake will allow that to continue!

Williams College has offered a supportive environment since I started teaching here in 1998. I would like to thank the Oakley Center for hosting my assistant professor leave in 2000–2001, and the World Fellowship for funding several crucial research trips to the Middle East and London. The Political Science Department's faculty and students have been a constant source of intellectual stimulation and support. Sara Schwanke provided very helpful research assistance. By far my greatest debt at Williams College goes to James McAllister, my colleague in the subfield of international relations and my closest intellectual sparring partner over the years. James has been a tireless discussion partner over countless cups of coffee, an indefatigable critic, and a perennial one-man reality check. James read the entire manuscript, and his critical perspective significantly strengthened the book's arguments and conclusions.

Finally, I would like to thank my editor at Columbia University Press, Peter Dimock. It has been an enormous pleasure getting to know Peter over the course of developing this book. I have learned an incredible amount about publishing, editing, and the value of writing from Peter, and hope to continue the dialogue for many years to come. Peter showed unwavering faith in this manuscript, and intervened at appropriate times to spur me to finish a book that might otherwise have continued its evolution for far longer.

Many of the ideas in this book were developed and initially presented on my pseudonymous blog, Abu Aardvark (http://www.abuaardvark.com/). I began blogging in late 2002, and quickly found the Aardvark's reputation and influence surpassing my own. I will never forget the first time that a colleague unknowingly quoted the Aardvark as evidence against me in an argument. I maintained my pseudonymity until May 2005, when I participated in a week-long on-line debate at the *Washington Monthly*. I have developed a great appreciation for the blogging format. It rewards clear writing and quick thinking, while inviting comments from a wide range of readers of astonishingly diverse intellectual and political backgrounds. Abu Aardvark allowed me to develop my ideas in real time, while also keeping a useful record of those thoughts and the supporting documents. It also gave me a kind of direct access to public debates that many scholars lack, especially as some intrepid journalists used the blog either directly or indirectly by getting in contact with me. Readers of this book are invited to check Abu Aardvark for ongoing commentary and discussion of these topics.

Which leaves me with my greatest and deepest thanks, which go to my wife, Lauren, my daughter, Sophia Faith, and my son, Alexander Reyes. They make life worth living.

Williamstown, MA
February 3, 2005

Voices of the New Arab Public

1

Iraq and the New Arab Public

At the end of August 2003, the controversial al-Jazeera talk show host Faisal al-Qassem introduced the topic for the night's live broadcast of *The Opposite Direction*: do the Iraqi people have the right to demand an apology from the Arabs for their support of Saddam Hussein over the years? With Abd al-Bari Atwan, editor in chief of the Pan-Arabist newspaper *al-Quds al-Arabi*, facing off against Entifadh Qanbar, spokesman for the Iraqi National Congress (INC), Qassem framed the show—as he always does—by posing a long series of questions. The first dozen questions offered a strong defense of Arabs against their accusers: "Do Iraqis have the right to demand an apology from the rest of the Arabs? Should the Arabs actually make such an apology, or should the Iraqi people extend their thanks to the Arab regimes who did terrible things to the departed regime? Aren't they the ones who conspired against [Saddam] and allied with the occupiers against him? . . . Do they want an apology from the Arab regimes which enforced the embargo? Why don't we hear the Iraqis demanding an apology from the Americans and British who starved them and blockaded them and enslaved them? . . . Who is the real traitor to the Iraqi people: the one who minimized Saddam's crimes or the one who rode American tanks to occupy Iraq? Aren't those who opposed the invasion of Iraq worthy of praise?"[1]

In the popular stereotype of al-Jazeera, Qassem's questioning would have ended with this defense of the Arabs and attack on their critics.

But it did not. Instead, Qassem pivoted 180 degrees and posed a series of sharp questions to his Arab audience: "But on the other side:
why were the Arabs silent politically and in the media for years about
the horrors of the Iraqi regime? Aren't all of those who defended Iraq
in the past now free to apologize to the Iraqi people after seeing the
mass graves? Doesn't the revelation of the mass graves give Arab states
some moral responsibility for the crimes of the old regime? Why did
Arab rulers and information ministers and editors in chief of newspapers and television stars incline toward Saddam and not toward the
people? . . . Why do some use the question of the relations between the
Iraqi opposition and the Americans to justify their refusal to condemn
the repression faced by the Iraqi people under Saddam? . . . Was there
a single Arab government which issued a statement condemning the
massacres of the Iraqi people? Isn't it the right of the Iraqi people to ask
for an explanation for the Arab silence?"

Qassem's framing of the arguments to come is remarkable in part
for not being remarkable. Such open arguments over the most sensitive issues, involving strong representatives of both sides of the dis-
pute, represent the hallmark of al-Jazeera's approach to Arab politics.
Where Arab public life had for decades been dominated by the voice
of the state, al-Jazeera ushered in a new kind of open, contentious public politics in which a plethora of competing voices clamored for attention. Rather than imposing a single, overwhelming consensus, the
new satellite television stations, along with newspapers, Internet sites,
and many other sites of public communication, challenged Arabs to
argue, to disagree, and to question the status quo. These public arguments, passionate in their invocation of an aggrieved Arab identity,
sometimes oppressively conformist and sometimes bitterly divisive,
sensationalist but liberating, defined a new kind of Arab public and
new kind of Arab politics.

What I call the *new Arab public* is palpably transforming Arab
political culture. It has already conclusively shattered the state's monopoly over the flow of information, rendering obsolete the ministries
of information and the oppressive state censorship that was smothering public discourse well into the 1990s. The new public rejects the
long, dismal traditions of enforced public consensus, insisting on the
legitimacy of challenging official policies and proclamations. This has

created an expectation of public disagreement, an expectation vital to any meaningfully pluralist politics. The new public has forced Arab leaders to justify their positions far more than ever before, introducing a genuinely new level of accountability to Arab politics. By focusing relentlessly on the problems facing the Arab status quo—social, cultural, and political—it has generated a sense of urgency for change that had long been lacking. And by placing political developments both positive and negative into a common Arab narrative, treating protests demanding political change in Egypt alongside mass demonstrations against the Syrian occupation of Lebanon and elections in Iraq and unrest in Saudi Arabia, the new Arab public has made it impossible for any Arab state to set itself apart from these demands. While this new Arab public cannot alone substitute for electoral democracy, it is doing something in many ways more important: building the underpinnings of a more liberal, pluralist politics rooted in a vocal, critical public sphere.

This new public was highly self-aware of its own role in challenging the status quo, giving it a self-defined sense of mission that sometimes sat uneasily with the standards of objective journalism. And challenge the status quo it did, with a fierce drive toward internal reform and foreign policy changes that led Arab governments and the West alike to regard it with great suspicion. This new public emerged in something of a cocoon, with a sharp contrast between its internally extraordinarily public politics and its general isolation from wider international debates and concerns. Its arguments took place within a common frame of reference, an Arab identity discourse that shaped and inflected all arguments, analysis, and coverage. Together, these three elements produced a distinctive kind of political public sphere, an identity-bounded enclave, internally open but externally opaque.

Whether such a populist, identity-driven, enclave public could be the foundation for reform and liberalization—at a time when neither Arab states nor the most powerful popular movements such as Islamism offer such a foundation—represents one of the most urgent problems facing the Arab world today. The centrality of identity politics to the new Arab public, with its avowed goal of giving voice to an oppressed and long-silenced Arab political society, is rife with paradoxes. It is fueled by a determination to bring publicity to the closed, repressive

Arab political world, shattering every taboo and crossing every red line with abandon. At the same time, its politics of identity could all too easily slide into a tyranny from below, excommunicating those who disagree and demonizing outsiders to enforce internal unity.

The new media has dramatically affected conceptions of Arab and Muslim identity, linking together geographically distant issues and placing them within a common Arab "story." In a 2001 survey, Shibley Telhami found that watching Arab television news made 46 percent of Saudis feel more sympathetic to Arabs in other countries, a sentiment shared by 87 percent in the United Arab Emirates and 75 percent in Kuwait.[2] Even more striking, large majorities in the Arab countries he surveyed ranked the Palestinian issue as the most important political issue to them personally. But these greater feelings of closeness capture only half of the story. At the same time, Telhami found upwards of 40 percent in each population felt that despite feeling *closer* to other Arabs, *differences* among Arabs had grown greater in recent years. Why? I argue that this seemingly paradoxical finding follows from an exceptionally important change in the way this new public conceives of Arab identity.

In the new Arab public, Arab and Islamic identities serve as a reference point, but no single set of policies or orientations necessarily follows from that identity. Arabs take for granted that Palestine and Iraq are Arab issues about which Arabs *should* agree, but they often disagree vehemently about what should be done about them. In contrast to earlier eras of Arabism, such as the "Arab Cold War" of the 1950s and 1960s (Kerr 1971), the public political arguments today throw wide open fundamental questions of what it means to be Arab. Anti-American voices routinely square off against pro-American figures, or against Americans themselves; defenders of Saddam argue with representatives of the Iraqi National Congress; Islamists argue with secularists. Al-Jazeera, in particular, thrives by pitting people who sharply disagree against one another, thereby proving by example that Arabs can disagree and still be authentic Arabs. Al-Jazeera's innovation was to open the phone lines during live broadcasts, to let ordinary Arabs into the arguments for perhaps the first time in their history. By 2005, political talk shows had become an entirely normal and indispensable part of Arab political life, with dozens of such programs broadcast by a bewildering array of satellite television stations. Virtually any political trend or position could be found by channel-surfing Arab viewers: pro-American "moderates" on the Saudi-owned al-Arabiya, radical anti-American Islamists on the Hezbollah-owned al-Manar, and all points in between. In later chapters, I present some of these exchanges in detail to show the diversity of opinions and the style of political argument that ensued.

The ramifications of a rapidly emerging public sphere for Arab politics are only beginning to be felt. Fueled by technology, by a shared identity, and by enormous frustration with the status quo, this new Arab public has already reshaped the regional and international political terrain. In what direction, however, remains unclear. Arabs can interact, argue, and mobilize in revolutionary ways, defying the attempts of states to maintain their dominance over all aspects of life. At the same time, the new Arab public offers no mechanism for translating its ideas into outcomes. Lacking effective Arab international institutions or domestic democratic politics, and feeling besieged by hostile powers and unchecked global forces, many Arabs find themselves frustrated within their new consciousness. And with that frustration, the public sphere is increasingly consumed with sensationalism and anger, which threaten to undermine its contribution to liberal reforms.

Where political talk shows have transformed the nature of Arab public opinion, the impact of the news coverage has similarly revolutionized political behavior. News coverage has inspired contentious politics on the so-called Arab street, from the fierce demonstrations sparked by al-Jazeera's coverage of the American-British bombing of Iraq in December 1998, to the intense waves of sustained popular protests over the bloody fighting between Palestinians and Israel in 2000 and 2002, to the demonstrations against the invasion of Iraq in 2003, to the wave of protests demanding political reform that swept from Lebanon through Egypt into the Gulf in the first months of 2005.

The new information environment has palpably affected American strategy in the region as well. In Operation Desert Storm (1991), the American-led coalition was largely able to control the information war, shaping the media coverage and carefully managing perceptions of civilian casualties and the course of events (MacArthur

1992; Tayler 1992). In 2003 the Americans proved unable to control the flow of information, images, or reporting from Iraq. Al-Jazeera, al-Arabiya, and other Arab satellite stations reporting live from Iraq conveyed a picture of the war dramatically different from that emanating from the coalition, one that emphasized civilian suffering and American setbacks rather than a bloodless and popular liberation. As the occupation turned uglier, the Arab media's coverage of the violence gripping Iraq infuriated the Americans, who wanted to maintain information dominance but seemed powerless to achieve it. Al-Jazeera's reporting from the besieged city of Falluja in April 2004 contradicted the coalition's narrative so graphically and dramatically that it determined the outcome of that battle. The new Arab media arguably represented the single greatest strategic difference between 1991 and 2003.

Given the magnitude of its challenge on every political front, it should be no surprise that the new Arab media has become as intensely controversial within the Arab world as it has in the United States. Many Americans view al-Jazeera and the new Arab media as a fundamentally hostile force generating anti-Americanism and complicating foreign policy objectives in Iraq, Israel, the war on terror, and more. Inside the Arab world, al-Jazeera has generated equally intense criticism, as well as impassioned defense. For its supporters, al-Jazeera represents the best hope for challenging the repressive Arab status quo and for defending Arab interests. For its critics, al-Jazeera represents a tremendously damaging cultural phenomenon, one which threatens to drag the struggling Arab world down into the abyss.

As it has risen in influence, then, the Arab media has become a topic as divisive as Iraq itself. The political war over the media raging in the Arab world resembles American battles over media bias from the left and the right in its intensity and its venom. For example, the journalist Fadhil Fudha laments that al-Jazeera betrayed its vast potential by transforming itself from an objective news station into a self-proclaimed carrier of an ideological message.[3] Abd al-Monam Said, director of *al-Ahram*'s Center for Strategic Studies, blames al-Jazeera for the failures of Arab interests; according to Said, al-Jazeera's propensities for crowd-pleasing radicalism make it too easy for Israelis and Americans to portray Arabs as radical.[4] The American-based Egyp-

tian columnist Mamoun Fandy denounces the Arab media for suc-
cumbing to sensationalism and a "political pornography" of violence,
extremism, chaos, and beheadings.[5] Mohammed Ma'wadh of Kuwait
University complains that the new media "incline to the superficial
and the sensational and they lack focused and scientific dialogue. . . .
They are dominated by accusations and settling of scores."[6] A cartoon
in *al-Sharq al-Awsat* portrays "the satellites" spooning garbage into the
heads of Arab viewers.[7] *Al-Hayat* journalist Hazem al-Amin argues
that al-Jazeera is dominated by the spirit of a dogmatically Islamic Yusuf al-Qaradawi and the legacy of former director Mohammed Jassem
al-Ali, who allegedly was on the Iraqi payroll, with the "embarrassing
comedies" of Faisal al-Qassem and Ahmed Mansour drowning out
more serious voices.[8]

Even sympathetic Arab observers wonder whether the introduction
of "Crossfire"- and "Hardball"-type talk shows could really be called
a positive contribution to a political culture. Rami Khouri, a liberal
Jordanian journalist, dismisses the new public sphere as "more of the
same vapid talk." Abdullah al-Ashal, an Egyptian writer, points out that
the political effects of the new public can hardly be taken for granted.[9]
Despite all of the real problems of the Arab order, and despite the real
need for democracy in the region, more democracy would not lead
Arabs to be more accepting of American and Israeli policies. Quite
the opposite, he argues—it is the craven and weak leaders of the Arab
world that give in to these demands, whereas a strong Arab public
would resist. It is not lost on the new Arab public sphere that many
Arab states enforced the sanctions on Iraq even as public opinion denounced them, and quietly cooperated with the American war against
Iraq even as public opinion loudly opposed it. Indeed, some of the
most vocal critiques expressed in the new Arab public sphere emphasize the hypocrisy of Arab regimes, exemplified by their failure to act
on the policy preferences that they claim to share with their publics.
It is quite striking that opinion surveys have consistently found that
those Arabs with access to satellite television consistently have more
positive attitudes toward democracy—but not toward American foreign policy (Tessler 2003).

This book presents these debates and controversies in all aspects,
both from a Western perspective and from an internal Arab view,

offering substantial evidence for assessing claims on both sides. It relies primarily on what Arabs themselves have actually said rather than on what others have said about them.[10] First, I have compiled a database of transcripts of 976 episodes of the five most important al-Jazeera talk shows broadcast between January 1999 and June 2004.[11] Second, I have compiled a secondary database of al-Jazeera programs dealing specifically with Iraq; while there is some overlap with the first data set, this one includes a number of more specialized programs, including several new programs broadcast directly from Iraq after the fall of Saddam Hussein. Third, I draw on thousands of opinion essays published in Arabic newspapers between 1992 and 2004. Fourth, I have interviewed a large number of people involved in both the Iraqi issue and the Arab media, including American, European, and Arab officials as well as a wide range of Arab journalists and political activists. Finally, I draw on additional published and unpublished public opinion surveys. All translations, except where otherwise noted, are my own.

Certain points become clear on even a cursory reading of these sources. It is manifestly untrue that the Arab media is dominated by a single perspective. On a typical day, the Saudi newspaper *al-Sharq al-Awsat* publishes translated op-eds by Thomas Friedman and Jim Hoagland alongside essays by Egyptian Islamist Fahmi Huwaydi, the pro-American Egyptian commentator Mamoun Fandy, and the more anti-American Syrian secularist Bathina Shabaan. Next to it on most newsstands is the popular Arabist daily *al-Quds al-Arabi*, which highlights voices critical of Arab governments and the United States, and heavily covers the violence and traumas of Palestine and Iraq. Al-Jazeera, as I document in the chapters to come, offers an extraordinarily wide range of viewpoints, while its live call-in programs offer an unprecedented glimpse into the concerns and passions of ordinary Arabs. Al-Jazeera's satellite television rivals offer a variety of alternative viewpoints, as do domestic television stations and other local media. American news agencies provide significant percentages of the copy used by many Arab newspapers and television stations. Where only a decade ago the typical Arabic-speaking media consumer would have struggled mightily to find serious differences of political opinion, by 2003 she would be relentlessly bombarded with political arguments across the satellite television dial.

Long before the American invasion of Iraq, al-Jazeera programs railed against the repressive, corrupt, stagnant Arab order, shattering what Kanan Makiya described despairingly as "a politics of silence" stifling Arab intellectual and political life (1995: 25). In 1999 alone almost a dozen al-Jazeera talk shows criticized the absence of democracy in the Arab world. In a January 2005 online al-Jazeera poll, almost 90 percent of some 30,000 respondents expressed their doubts that Arab governments really wanted reform. Indeed, virtually every issue that American critics claim is ignored by the Arab media has in fact been covered in these programs. Does the Arab public ignore Iraq's mass graves? Not in the May 31, 2004, episode of *al-Jazeera Platform* hosted by Jumana al-Namour entitled "The Mass Graves." Does the Arab public not question the legitimacy of suicide bombing? How then to explain the furious arguments on the May 15, 2002, episode of *No Limits* on "the future of martyrdom operations," or the June 29, 2002, *Open Dialogue* on "the martyrdom phenomenon," or the August 20, 2002, *The Opposite Direction* treatment of "martyrdom operations"? The first, and most visible, response to the revelations of sexual torture of Iraqis by Americans in the Abu Ghraib prison was Faisal al-Qassem's provocative program discussing conditions in Arab prisons.

In this new Arab public, Iraqi opposition figures argue with their critics on live television, Islamists and feminists square off over women's rights, a call-in vote resoundingly declares the current Arab state system to be worse than colonialism, Kurds openly challenge al-Jazeera on its own broadcasts over its alleged silence about Saddam's mass graves. Kanan Makiya's "wall of silence" has been broken, but by Arab satellites rather than by American guns.

Iraq and Public Arab Arguments

While several outstanding recent works have offered general overviews of al-Jazeera (Miles 2005) or Arab public opinion (Telhami 2005), this book takes a slightly different approach, using a single, vital issue in Arab politics to document the political significance of this new Arab public. Given the centrality of the question of Palestine, or the urgent concerns surrounding terrorism and radical Islamism, it is worth asking why I have chosen Iraq as my focus. In part, simply because the Palestinian dimension has been widely studied. But more important, reducing Arab politics to attitudes toward the Israeli-Palestinian conflict presents a highly misleading picture of a relatively unchanging Arab public opinion. The issue of Palestine was, without question, the area of the widest consensus in the new Arab public sphere. Support for the Palestinians against Israel was rarely, if ever, contested (although there were moments of frustration, as in Faisal al-Qassem's January 2002 program asking "is the Intifada a waste of time?"). Palestine served as a unifying focal point, one which diverse political groups could use as a common front, rather than as a point of meaningful debates. The political implications of the new Arab public are more clearly demonstrated through its engagement with Iraq, an issue on which no such clear Arab consensus exists and on which Arabs have openly argued and disagreed with each other over the right course of action.

Iraq stands out as a window into both the power and the limitations of the new Arab media. Unlike Palestine (a unifying issue about which virtually all Arabs agree) or domestic political issues (which generally interest only local audiences) Iraq in the 1990s generated both a clear sense of commitment to a collectively shared "Arab" issue and intense disagreements. Arguments about the Iraqi sanctions allowed Arabs to rebuild the sense of sharing a community of fate, as Iraqi suffering under the sanctions became a potent symbol of the suffering of all Arabs. As the influential Sudanese Islamist Abd al-Wahhab al-Affendi evocatively described it, Iraq posed "a crisis of the Arab soul [about which] silence is not an option." This crisis proved deeply divisive and generated tremendous passions. But even if divided over the nature of the problem in Iraq and the appropriate response, most Arabs agreed that it was a matter about which a collective Arab position *should* exist. Arabs defined themselves as Arabs by the act of participating in the debate, an *expressive* approach to political action whose importance cannot be reduced to strategic outcomes.

Iraq has been far more central to the new "street politics" of the last few years than is often recognized. While many observers date the "resurgence of the Arab street" to the outbreak of the "al-Aqsa Intifada" in September 2000, and others consider the 2005 protests for reform across the Arab world as something wholly novel, both share roots in the Iraqi question. As documented in chapters 3 and 4, showdowns over Iraq frequently galvanized Arab protests in the 1990s, while the growing Arab movement against the sanctions on Iraq helped build many of the techniques and networks that later agitated for political reforms. The Egyptian analyst Mohammed Sid-Ahmed attributes the nature of the Arab response to the "al-Aqsa Intifada" as beginning with the shift in Arab public perceptions of American policy toward Iraq, rather than the other way around.[12]

Iraq became central to Arab identity as a result of the intense public arguments in the new Arab media, which were characterized by visceral disagreement rather than by consensus. Just as the Palestinian issue became a part of personal identity for many Arabs, so did the Iraqi situation. The "suffering Iraqi people" became a vital touchstone for all Arab debate, a starting point of consensus rather than a point to be established. Indeed, concern for the Iraqi people became, in a very real sense, part of what it meant to be Arab in the late 1990s. Even Iraq's fiercest enemies found themselves forced to justify their support for the sanctions or for American military efforts in terms of their concern to "liberate the Iraqi people from Saddam Hussein's regime." And for growing numbers of Arabs, those responsible for the suffering of the Iraqi people dovetailed with those responsible for the suffering of Palestinians: not only Israel, but also the United States and the Arab regimes that either actively supported or did nothing to overturn the pernicious policies. The hostility to the American campaign against Iraq, so baffling to many Americans, arises out of this particular conception of identity, a narrative of solidarity and enmity that has shaped the meaning of all that happened. And the new Arab public sphere was a primary source of this identity and this narrative.

Iraq has therefore been central to the meaningful debates *in* the new Arab public sphere in the last decade. It has also been central to the debates *about* the new Arab public sphere, with the Iraqi opposition taking the dominant Arab position toward Iraq as the main evidence for Arab corruption, failure, and self-deception. The most important book on the failures of the Arab public sphere, Kanan Makiya's *Cruelty and Silence* (1995), is primarily about Iraq, and Makiya himself was an important intellectual figure within the Iraqi National Congress. Fouad Ajami's widely read *Dream Palaces of the Arabs* is framed around a gripping account of the 1996 death of exiled Iraqi poet Buland Haidari, and Ajami places Iraq under Saddam Hussein at the center of his reflections on the degradation of Arab political culture (1998: 173).

Unlike the issue of Palestine, which has tended to produce an unchallenged consensus unifying different sectors of Arab opinion, Iraq tended to exacerbate differences and to bring real disagreements into the open. Where Israel produced mobilization and an artificial consensus through which any politician could score easy points, Iraq produced real arguments. These arguments themselves demonstrated the possibility of disagreement, the simple and essential lesson that policy disagreements need not *necessarily* mean excommunication from a community of identity. Certain Iraqi opposition figures (those who declined to cooperate with the United States) appeared frequently in *al-Quds al-Arabi*, the most Arabist of Arab newspapers. The debates, by virtue of their heat and passion, focused the attention of audiences on arguments that could make a difference, on an issue where change seemed possible. From the first Gulf War to the growing dissension over sanctions, from Desert Fox to the American campaign for war, Iraq repeatedly took center stage. And unlike in Palestine, where Arab states seemed hopelessly stymied, Iraq—at least in the eyes of the Arab public—was an arena in which Arab states could actually do something if they really wanted to: stop complying with the sanctions, support or oppose the war, support or oppose regime change attempts, allow or refuse the reintegration of Iraq into Arab institutions.

These hot debates spanned nearly a decade and a half, the entire life span of the new Arab public sphere. As a historical trauma and ongoing issue about which endless argument seemed possible, Iraq served as a focal point for private Arab debates after 1990. It is not obvious that it should have become such a vehicle. Iraq's invasion of Kuwait shattered Arab norms against inter-Arab warfare; the dissension at the Cairo Summit of 1990 decimated the official Arab order; and the intense divisions between popular support for Iraq and official support for the coalition in many Arab states exacerbated domestic tensions. In contrast to Palestine, about which regimes often encouraged popular mobilization in order to deflect domestic criticism, Iraq was seen by most Arab regimes as an issue to be avoided. The Iraq issue intensified the political differences of Arab states, while simultaneously helping to reconstitute and to mobilize an Arab public critical of the failure of the Arab order to deal with the problem.

The collective trauma of the first Gulf War, and the failure of the Arab order to deal with it, opened up the field for public argument. Indeed, the sense of general crisis almost demanded it. This potential remained tentative and untapped for several years, however, because of the absence of an appropriate media. Writers did debate the Iraq issue in the elite newspapers, which arguably had some limited influence on Arab state policies, but in general this represented a quiet, internal dialogue within clearly defined red lines. Over the course of the 1990s, however, popular movements from below, often led by social activists working beneath the radar of the official media, forced the Iraqi issue onto the agenda. The Iraqi regime encouraged these activists in a number of ways (described in chapter 3), but they did not create out of nothing the anger and outrage felt by Arabs who deeply identified with Iraqis visibly suffering under sanctions. Palpable public anger over the sanctions and over American bombings of Iraq undermined the pragmatic inclinations of the Arab regimes, forcing them to address the issue at least rhetorically.

With Al-Jazeera's explosive coverage of the December 1998 "Desert Fox" bombing campaign, this new Arab public sphere finally found its voice. Al-Jazeera was virtually the only network operating in Iraq by the end of 1998—just as it was virtually alone in Afghanistan in the fall of 2001. Personnel of al-Jazeera themselves "regard this as the milestone event that brought it to the international attention of many Arab viewers" (Rugh 2004a: 217). After watching the massive street protests against the bombing of Iraq in December 1998 on al-Jazeera, one Arab writer declared that "as the night does not resemble the morning, the winter of 1998 cannot resemble the summer of 1991. . . . Where the Gulf crisis divided the Arabs, these attacks united us."[13]

That Arab opinion changed over time cannot seriously be doubted. A number of major Arab states, including Egypt, Syria, and Saudi Arabia, joined the American coalition against Iraq in the 1991 war, with that campaign authorized by an Arab League resolution (albeit a contested one). An early study of elite public opinion in the Gulf found that as late as January 1991 some 86 percent agreed that Saddam Hussein bore primary responsibility for the crisis (Ismael and Ismael 1993). Seven years later, in February 1998, 94.1 percent of Palestinians supported Iraq in its confrontation with the United States. By April 2002, only 3 percent of Egyptians favored an American attack against Iraq and 84 percent were against; 7 percent of Lebanese for and 84 percent against; 11 percent of Saudis for and 80 percent against; 13 percent of Kuwaitis for and 61 percent against.[14]

A Zogby poll in early 2003 found that 95 percent of Saudis, 58 percent of Jordanians, and 74 percent of Lebanese believed that the war would create less rather than more democracy; 97 percent of Saudis and 78 percent of Jordanians believed it would create more terrorism. A BBC poll in Jordan in February 2003 found that 68 percent of Jordanians believed that the American motivation for attacking Iraq was to secure oil supplies, while only 4 percent thought that it was to prevent another 9/11 and only 16 percent thought it was to depose Saddam.[15] 64 percent thought that removing Saddam would not make Iraq better off, and 22 percent thought that it would.

State policies followed these changes in public opinion, rather than creating them. At the time of the Gulf War, the entire Gulf Cooperation Council (Saudi Arabia, Kuwait, Bahrain, UAE, Qatar, Oman) took strong positions against Iraq, as did Egypt, Syria, Morocco, and Lebanon, in spite of often pro-Iraqi public opinion. By the mid-1990s, only Saudi Arabia and Kuwait remained strongly supportive of American policy toward Iraq in public, even if many Arab leaders continued to support the containment of Iraq privately (Ebert 1992). By the end of the 1990s, most Arab leaders opposed the sanctions in private as well as in public. The first full Arab summit in a decade, held in 2000 in response to Arab popular anger over the Intifada, pointedly included Iraq, signaling the linkages between these two key Arab issues. In March 2002 an Arab summit in Beirut finally brought about a public Arab consensus on restoring Iraq to the Arab order, while a succession of Arab leaders pointedly rejected American vice president Dick Cheney's suggestion that they privately supported the American agenda of war against Iraq.

This change in attitude did not take place naturally, nor did it reflect some pre-rational emotional bond with fellow Arabs. On the contrary, the invasion and occupation of Iraq in 2003 came at the end of a long, tortured public Arab argument. The antiwar consensus produced by these arguments was deeply rooted not only in Arab interests but in this newly constructed Arabist identity. Opposition to the invasion of Iraq merged with a general anger with American policies, as well as disgust with actors viewed as American proxies in the region—from Israel to the Iraqi opposition and Kuwait. The sympathy with the Iraqi people, embodied in the demand to lift the sanctions and opposition to military action against Iraq, emerged through a complex and sustained public argument in the new Arab public sphere. This new public prioritized questions of Arab identity, searching to define Arabness in new ways and to challenge the stagnant and repressive status quo.

Saddam, the Iraqi Opposition, and the Arab Public

Saddam himself enjoyed little popularity by the late 1990s. In a February 1998 survey of Palestinian opinion, for example, 72.4 percent supported Iraq against the United States because of their sympathy with the Iraqi people and only 28.9 percent because of their support for Saddam Hussein's regime. The collapse in support for Saddam personally came partly because of deep frustration with the endless crisis, but also in no small part because the horrors of his regime were far more widely aired in the new Arab public sphere than they had been during the 1980s, when Saddam's Iraq had been the Arab champion against Islamic Iran and Saddam himself had been lionized in the Kuwaiti and Gulf media. While the sanction-induced suffering of the Iraqi people became a core shared point of Arab identity over the course of the 1990s, however, most commentators carefully distanced themselves from overtly glorifying Saddam's regime. For many critics, such a distinction was untenable: protests against the sanctions strengthened Saddam's hand in negotiations with the United Nations, regardless of the sympathies of the protestors. Such criticism became more influential, and more poignant, after the fall of Baghdad allowed many Iraqis to vent similar frustrations with the Arab public.

As early as 2000, Kuwaiti officials worried that "Saddam Hussein has begun to penetrate [through al-Jazeera] the Gulf positions."[16] The relationship between al-Jazeera and Saddam's regime was intensely controversial, fueled by incendiary allegations of penetration of the station by Iraqi intelligence, which in April 2003 led to the resignation of station manager Mohammed Jassem al-Ali (see chapter 4). While it had always covered the humanitarian side of the sanctions—perhaps because of the emir of Qatar's interest in initiatives to end them—after Desert Fox al-Jazeera's coverage of Iraqi suffering increased dramatically (el-Nawawy and Iskander 2002: 36, 58). After this, al-Jazeera enjoyed privileged access to senior Iraqi leaders, not because of a preexisting relationship with Saddam's regime but because Saddam recognized the value of a good relationship with the most popular and influential Arab television station (Miles 2005). Intense popular interest in Iraq was not created by al-Jazeera, nor was al-Jazeera's coverage dictated by Iraqi intelligence.

The Arab public was not mindlessly supportive of Iraqi policy, and indeed was often quite critical of Saddam's tyrannical regime—in chapters 3 and 4 I present considerable evidence against the conventional wisdom that the Arab media ignored or downplayed the nature of Saddam's regime. This was a genuine argument, in which contrarian voices were widely heard, if not widely accepted. Kuwaitis and the Iraqi opposition were well represented in the new Arab public sphere, with regular access to opinion columns in the major Arab newspapers and to the talk shows on al-Jazeera and other satellite television stations. These opponents of Saddam had access to the public sphere, and substantial political and economic resources behind them—and yet they conclusively lost the argument.

Claims that the Arab media's coverage of Iraq over the years represented "not only the denial of mass graves, but a crisis of the Arab soul" should not be taken at face value, no matter how poignant.[17] Hundreds of articles appeared in the major Arab dailies—written by Iraqi opposition figures and regime sympathizers as well as non-Iraqi Arabs—discussing the possibilities for change in Iraq and proposals for post-Saddam structures. Saudi influence over much of the Arab media ensured a prominent voice for defenders of the sanctions and critics of Saddam. Kuwaitis and Iraqi opposition figures regularly appeared even on al-Jazeera, if for no other reason than that their unpopular positions guaranteed good television. The chief editor of a leading Arab paper once wrote that Saddam Hussein was personally responsible for everything that had gone wrong in the Arab world for two decades. And hardly any al-Jazeera program on Iraq lacked at least one representative of the opposition or numerous phone calls from their sympathizers.

It is therefore wrong to claim that Iraqi opposition voices were excluded from the new Arab public sphere. Despite their heavy presence in the elite media, however, Saddam's critics largely lost the Arab public debate—until their fortunes were reversed by the brute force of the American military. The survey evidence above, as well as the overwhelming weight of public discourse and the protests in the streets, suggests that they failed to persuade the vast majority of Arabs to support their cause. More than that, these voices favoring the sanctions and supporting a military action against Iraq sometimes came to be defined not only as wrong, but as non-Arab. The Iraqi opposition, therefore, more than almost any other group within Arab politics, felt keenly the sting of the politics of authenticity and identity.

The bitter experience of the Iraqi opposition members within the Arab public sphere fueled their anger against the Arab order as a whole, while the close alignment of some parts of the Iraqi opposition with the United States intersected with and contributed to the growing anti-American sentiment in the region. When the formerly exiled opposition came to dominate the post-Saddam Iraqi government, this struck much of this new Arab public as an imposition of power over reason, with the losers of open debate imposed by force as the winners in the new Iraq. Arabs bitterly resented that the losers of the argument had been catapulted to the top not by the power of their arguments, but by the military power of a foreign army. A substantial portion of the Arab hostility to the invasion of Iraq and the new Iraqi regime—as well as the visceral anger expressed by many of the new rulers of Iraq—stems from this reversal of fortunes.

The Iraqi opposition reciprocated this resentment with the metaphoric fury of a woman scorned, lashing out at the Arab media with criticisms tailored to fuel the American critiques and to draw American power—so useful against Saddam—against their other enemies. Once in power in postwar Iraq, the former opposition leaders continued to harbor resentment, and to treat the Arab media with suspicion. One of Iyad Allawi's first moves after his appointment as temporary Prime Minister in June 2004, for example, was to close down the al-Jazeera offices in Iraq, while other members of his administration (especially Defense Minister Hazem Sha'alan) repeatedly accused it of indirectly or even directly supporting the insurgency.[18]

The role of the Iraqi opposition in shaping official American views of the Arab media has not often been appreciated. Just as Ahmed Chalabi and the INC contributed significantly toward misleading Americans about the extent of the threat posed by alleged Iraqi weapons of mass destruction programs, and badly misled Americans about their likely reception as "liberators" by flower-throwing Iraqis, so did they also transmit their own intense hostility toward the Arab media to their American allies.

The greatest absence from Arab public debates was not the Iraqi opposition, but rather the voice of the Iraqi people themselves. The Iraqi regime hardly counted as a legitimate spokesman for their interests. The Iraqi opposition, particularly the exile groups favored by Washington, had little real influence inside Iraq and were discredited within Arab public spheres by association with the United States. A small number of Iraqi dissidents who maintained their independence from those groups were published in the Arab press and appeared on Arab television, but even these individuals could not claim to speak for the Iraqi people living under Saddam's rule. In short, the Iraqi people were endlessly invoked by all sides in the debate—by sanctions critics mourning for the "suffering Iraqi people" just as by Iraqi opposition figures claiming to defend "the oppressed Iraqi people" from Saddam—but they remained objects rather than subjects in the great debates about their own future. Almost immediately upon the fall of Baghdad, al-Jazeera and other Arab media outlets rushed to bring these Iraqi voices to the Arab public. As discussed in chapters 5and 6, the anger expressed by many of those Iraqis toward Arabs for their failure to act against Saddam stunned Arabs, whose very identity had been defined by their deep sympathy for the Iraqi people.

American Misreadings of the New Arab Public

Al-Jazeera has become the most powerful ally of terror in the world— even more important than Saudi financiers. We're foolish if we do not recognize it as such.

—Ralph Peters[19]

September 11, the American war on terror, and then the move to war with Iraq brought the Arab media firmly into the center of American foreign policy debates. What had been seen as a force for democracy and modernity now struck many Americans as a potent enemy, spreading hostility and dangerous ideas to a credulous audience. Dire warnings about "Arab hate TV" filled the American media, while Secretary of Defense Donald Rumsfeld, National Security Advisor Condoleeza Rice, and other senior administration officials lashed out at the Arab media with growing frequency.[20] These reports took on even greater urgency as evidence began to filter in of unprecedented levels of hostility to the United States in the region, with tracking polls demonstrating stunning shifts from high levels of pro-American sentiment to near-universal hostility. The Bush administration responded in a variety of ways, including launching an ill-conceived American-run Arab language satellite television station and radio station of its own (Rugh 2004b).

The criticism of al-Jazeera specifically, and of the Arab media in general, has become almost doctrinal in much of American public discourse. In this view, what passes for an Arab public sphere is little more than a "wall of lies," a nightmarish panoply of censorship and self-censorship, propaganda, conspiracy theory, self-pity, and empty rhetoric (Rubin 2002; Ajami 2001). Where signs of life are recognized in the Arab public sphere, they generally take the form of manufactured demonization of foreign enemies—the West, Israel, imperialism—as a way of deflecting popular anger from the regimes themselves. Arab public opinion does not exist in any recognizable form; instead, cynical and repressive regimes monitor, control, and manipulate a dangerous and unpredictable, and ultimately irrational, Arab street. Barry Rubin, for example, dismisses the Arab media as "usually—with rare exceptions and slight variations—act[ing] as a wall, reinforcing unanimity, shutting out the kind of discourse that has become dominant almost everywhere in the world" (2002: 259). Al-Jazeera, in this view, "reinforced rather than undermined the existing system of ideas . . . [using] 'free speech' as one of the most effective forces combating the possibility of real free speech or democratic reform." For Benjamin Gilman, Republican chair of the House International Relations Committee, "the fanatical anti-American and anti-Semitic incitement that has permeated the Arab world . . . constitutes a real threat to long-term interests in the region."[21] When Gilman looks at the Arab media, he sees little but "nonstop incitement." Like many others, Gilman blames this incitement on the interests of powerful authoritarian states: "useful as a smokescreen for their nations' many problems, their internal corruption, their lack of legitimacy, the oppression of their own citizens."

This consensus transcended partisan lines. In Congressional testimony as late as 2002, Martin Indyk, a leading Middle East policy-maker under Bill Clinton, complained that American peace-making efforts "were dogged every step of the way by a hate-filled environment in which official organs of the Arab states, as well as other means of communication, were pouring out a litany of incitement."[22] Indyk complained that Iraqi propaganda had persuaded Arab public opinion of American responsibility for the deaths of Iraqi children and that "nothing we could do could change the impact of the images and the rhetoric that were being spread throughout the Arab world." Al-Jazeera may have given "voice to a broad range of opinions," but "most of them [were] extreme in their anti-American and anti-Semitic sentiments." There is no point trying to "win the hearts and minds of the Arab world," because Arab leaders find it too useful to deflect hostility outwardly. David Hoffman similarly describes

Arab news as "obsessively anti-American," and mirrors Indyk in calling for pressure on Arab states to exert more control over "this kind of hate propaganda."[23] And Fareed Zakaria complains that al-Jazeera "fills its airwaves with crude appeals to Arab nationalism, anti-Americanism, anti-Semitism, and religious fundamentalism" (2004: 3).

The burden of this book is to offer a more realistic assessment of the content, quality, and political impact of this new Arab media, one which neither exaggerates nor glosses over its troubling qualities. American observers have misunderstood and misjudged the Arab public with an impressive consistency. First they overemphasized the risk of violent uprisings against friendly regimes, and then under-appreciated the depth of hostility to American policies. American officials blame the "poisonous" Arab satellites for American problems in the region. But these claims are far more problematic than is generally assumed. Anti-American sentiment exploded throughout the world during the run-up to the invasion of Iraq, in places far from the range of the Arab media, such as Europe and Latin America. Public support for the United States collapsed in non-Arabic speaking Muslim countries such as Indonesia and Pakistan, where al-Jazeera again had no impact. Furthermore, al-Jazeera rose to dominance in the Arab political arena in the late 1990s, but hostility to the United States only shot skyward in 2002. In the words of Abdallah Schleifer, the Arab media became "a convenient scapegoat for profound U.S. policy errors."[24]

The New Arab Public

Al-Jazeera has received increasing attention from academics, policy-makers, journalists, and even movies (*Control Room*, a documentary about al-Jazeera, was a surprise hit in 2004). But the new Arab public is more than just al-Jazeera. It is defined by the rapidly expanding universe of Arabs able and willing to engage in public arguments about political issues within an ever-increasing range of possible media outlets (Salvatore and Eickelman 2004; Anderson and Eickelman 1999). It is made up of dozens of competing satellite television stations, independent newspapers, state-backed official media, and even on-line news sites. It comprises Islamic networks and mosques, NGOs and transnational organizations, and prominent public figures and intellectuals. It includes a vast Arab diaspora that is increasingly able to maintain contact with and actively engage with the politics of the Arab world through information and communications technology—whether by watching al-Jazeera in San Francisco or by emailing friends from Denmark. The new Arab public is actually composed of multiple, overlapping publics that should be defined not territorially but by reference to a shared identity and a common set of political arguments and concerns. Ironically, perhaps, the Arab world has achieved something of which European enthusiasts only dream: a transnational public sphere united by a common language and a common news agenda (van den Steeg 2002; Calhoun 2004).

While chapter 2 explains what I mean by a "public sphere" and presents the history of the Arab public sphere in more detail, a brief overview here may be useful. In the 1950s, radio broadcasting created a distinctive kind of adversarial, competitive political argument that crossed national borders. In the 1970s and 1980s, Arab states asserted their power over national and transnational publics alike, shutting down public debate beneath a stifling hand of censorship and repression. In the late 1980s, however, a renewed Arab public sphere began to emerge. In the early 1990s, a number of states began to allow some media freedoms as part of defensive strategies of partial liberalization. These tentatively emerging domestic publics emphasized domestic political issues, and the primary carrier of political debate tended to be the press as states retained a tight grip over television (Lynch 1999). When Arab satellite television stations began to be launched after the first Gulf War, they focused on entertainment and offered no real political transformation.

What has been called the "al-Jazeera Era" extends from 1997, when the Qatari station exploded onto the media scene, through early 2003 (Miles 2005; Rugh 2004a; el-Nawawy and Iskander 2002). Unlike the earlier satellite stations, it emphasized politics and open debate, and quickly assumed a dominant, near-monopoly position within Arab public discourse. Its coverage of the December 1998 American-British attacks on Iraq, and then its coverage of the outbreak of the Palestinian uprising beginning in September 2000, cemented its status. It was the one station that virtually everyone watched—and that everybody knew that others had seen—creating a real sense of a single, common Arab "conversation" about political issues.

By 2003, greater market competition and the fragmentation of the media market—particularly with the February launch of al-Arabiya—challenged al-Jazeera's dominance. Whether that competition will lead to homogenization—either in a more radical direction or in a more centrist direction—or to market segmentation remains unclear. Pierre Bourdieu argues that "competition homogenizes when it occurs between journalists or newspapers subject to identical pressures and opinion polls, and with the same basic set of commentators" (1998: 23). That al-Arabiya initially imitated al-Jazeera's coverage of Iraq in order to gain market share supports that thesis. On the other hand, several Arab satellite television stations have sought to differentiate themselves from al-Jazeera by offering more staid, muted coverage or by appealing to specific markets. After the Iraq war, al-Arabiya hired journalist Abd al-Rahman al-Rashed to revamp its coverage in a more pro-American direction in order to appeal both to the United States and to Arab elites threatened by al-Jazeera's powerful critiques (Shapiro 2005). Abu Dhabi TV did surprisingly well with its restrained coverage of the Iraq war. The American station al-Hurra and a proposed BBC Arabic language satellite television station, as well as the radical propaganda of Hezbollah's al-Manar and many others, constituted a far more complex media environment even as al-Jazeera retained its overall market leadership.

The American-led invasion, and subsequent occupation, of Iraq coincided with this shift in the market structure of the Arab media, as al-Jazeera came to face intense competition and other media platforms competed for the same market segments. This market competition had curious, sometimes cross-cutting ramifications: sometimes pushing toward radicalism, other times pushing toward moderation. But what is clear is that this new Arab public sphere fundamentally shaped the Arab response to the Iraqi crisis and its aftermath, and will continue to play a key role for the foreseeable future.

Arguing the New Arab Public

Haven't the Arab satellites succeeded in forming an Arab public opinion probably for the first time in modern Arab history?
—Faisal al-Qassem, *The Opposite Direction*, al-Jazeera, October 3, 2000

Why does nothing remain in the Arab arena except for some croaking media personalities? Why does a loud television clamour suffice as an alternative to effective action, and compensate for weakness?
—Faisal al-Qassem, *The Opposite Direction*, al-Jazeera, March 7, 2003

Egyptian analyst Mohammed al-Sayyid Said points out that "it is easy to exaggerate the amount of change in Arab politics, but at the same time ... there is real change in the intellectual habits of viewers and listeners, and in Arab political culture."[25] Enthusiasts for the new Arab media correctly emphasize the novelty and importance of a transnational television political public sphere that is both independent of and harshly critical of the status quo. But against this must be set a political context of fiercely defensive and powerful states determined to resist any threat to their interests. Nor have the enthusiasts taken into full account the less normatively desirable potentials of such a public sphere, whose particular incentive structure might well push away from rather than toward rational critical debate or political moderation. The new media might push toward democracy, but could also drive an identity-fixated, defensive populism. While chapter 2 explores these questions in detail, it is worth previewing here some of the most important issues at stake.

The new Arab public sphere is defined by a particular set of incentives, which have rapidly shifted in response to developments both internal and external, both political and technological. The incentive to reach out to a larger regional rather than local audience is driven by a competitive drive for market share, by the technological realities of satellite broadcasting, and by conceptions of an Arabist political identity (Telhami 2005). The issues that have dominated the new Arab media span the major areas of Arabist political concern, from foreign policy to systemic areas of domestic concern such as the absence of democracy or governmental inefficiencies. Issues of wider appeal tend to dominate issues of purely local concern: Palestine, Iraq, and Arab reform at first, and then increasingly the war on terror, Islam, and the United States.

The new media has asserted a claim to represent the authentic Arab voice—to be the one free voice with the ability and the courage to speak out on behalf of the Arabs against both American power and against corrupt Arab regimes. This is a claim to authenticity, to identity, and ultimately to a very real political power. Mohammed Krishan of al-Jazeera argues that "our target is public opinion, the masses . . . to win the confidence of the people in this station, even at the expense of the anger of the official Arab institutions and the United States."[26] The deep unpopularity of most Arab regimes and their intolerance of domestic critique creates powerful incentives for the new Arab media to push an independent and critical line. On the other hand, the Arab self-conception of being dominated, threatened, and encircled by Western powers has empowered a fiercely oppositional mentality and a demand to prove authenticity and independence. The incentive structures of the new Arab public sphere, in other words, point toward confrontational and oppositional argument. But these incentives are malleable, and should not be misrepresented as either fixed or hopelessly rooted in culture, pre-rational hostility, or civilizational envy.

For all its newfound prominence, the Arab public sphere remains almost completely detached from any formal political institution. The political significance of a transnational public sphere disconnected from any effective democratic institution has hardly begun to be theorized. Can what Mihna al-Habil called "The Democratic Republic of al-Jazeera" really stand in for genuine representative liberal democracy?[27] Even where these voices hold genuinely democratic convictions and impulses, the Arab public sphere cannot be democratic in any institutional sense of the word. It is not clear who this media represents, which voices dominate, or how it can act. The public arguments and debates are disembodied from any grounded political activity, and cannot easily be translated into political outcomes. And intense market competition can make it appear that the satellite stations follow mass opinion as much as they shape it.

In the face of entrenched and repressive regimes, as well as American power, the new Arab public reached the limits of political possibility. Its limitations derived from the very conditions that gave it strength. As a disembodied international public sphere, it had the unique ability to serve as a platform for political dialogue and debate that could challenge the stagnant Arab political status quo. It had the ability to crystallize an Arabist identity and background ideas that transformed the incentives for political actors in the region. It could even make a claim to speak for this disenfranchised Arab public opinion, for a while, and could point to the "movement of the Arab street" as evidence of its claims. But ultimately, the Arab public sphere lacked any mechanisms for translating its energy, its consensus, its symbolic power into concrete political outcomes. It remained a "weak public sphere," severed from any institutional capability and not grounded in any concrete civil society. As its failure to produce political outcomes became clear, frustration set in tangibly. By the summer of 2001—even before the 9/11 attacks and the beginning of the American war on terror—the tone of al-Jazeera's discussions had palpably begun to change. Coverage became coarser, angrier, more emotional, with the arguments taking on a fiercer edge. This shift, I argue, reflected the frustration and sense of impotence felt by a public that had so recently seen a newfound competence and influence within its grasp. On the other hand, the fervent debate over political reform that began to break out in untold numbers of talk shows in late 2003, and the heady excitement that greeted the coverage of the Lebanese and Egyptian protests in early 2005, demonstrate that there is nothing inevitable about such a negativist turn.

Even if the power of a new international public sphere is growing, it is not at all clear that it is a *liberal* public sphere. The politics of the new Arab public sphere tend toward populism, the politics of identity, of authenticity, and of resistance. As frustration grows with American policies toward Iraq and Israel, as well as with the political and economic failures of Arab governments, open public argument might well lead to nonliberal conclusions. Furthermore, the growing influence of religious identity among Arabs has significant implications for the kind of public sphere that might be emerging. To the extent that the participants in public argument and the relevant audiences take religious rather than liberal values as their reference point, public argument and debate need not necessarily produce liberal outcomes. The prominence on al-Jazeera of the Egyptian moderate Islamist Yusuf al-Qaradawi, who has long advocated the centrality of dialogue to all aspects of religious and political life and has firmly opposed the textual absolutism characteristic of radicals such as Osama bin Laden, suggests an important intersection between the Arab public sphere and "moderate" Islamism (Lynch 2005).

Whether the Arab public sphere develops in a liberal direction or in a populist direction, consumed by questions of identity and authenticity, is one of the most pivotal questions shaping the Arab future. In the final chapter, I argue for an American public diplomacy that encourages, through dialogue and engagement, the emergence of a liberal Arab public sphere.

The book uses Arab attitudes, arguments, and policies toward Iraq from 1991 to 2004 to show how this public sphere has been transformed, how it matters politically, and how it approaches contentious political issues. I do not offer a detailed or comprehensive history of the Iraq issue, instead focusing tightly on questions of public opinion and the new Arab public sphere. This inevitably has led to some painful decisions about what to include and what to omit. Because of the tight focus of the book on the question of the impact and nature of the new Arab public, vital aspects of the Iraq issue are treated here in only a cursory fashion: the sanctions, the weapons inspections process, the international and American arguments over invading Iraq, the war on terror, the insurgency. I do not offer an "insider's" account of American or Arab decision making, or of al-Jazeera itself (Miles 2005). The book also does not offer a full treatment of the *news* coverage in the Arab media.

My focus is instead on Arab debates themselves, whether on the al-Jazeera talk shows or in the op-ed pages of the pan-Arab daily newspapers or in Internet chat rooms or inside social movements and political parties. While I have interviewed an enormous number of people involved in this issue, the vast majority of the book's evidence comes from published op-eds and transcripts of television programs. Far too much discussion of the Arab public ignores what that public actually says and does, or ascribes beliefs or motivations without adequate evidence. The methodological argument encoded in this book is that what people say in public matters more for shaping political identities and strategies than their private beliefs or internal deliberations.

Debates about whether Yusuf al-Qaradawi, say, "really" supports attacks on American civilians in Iraq even though he publicly declared his opposition strike me as irrelevant distractions: the public statements of an influential figure, delivered on a widely watched television station such as al-Jazeera, matter far more than do his private beliefs, even were it ever possible to truly know such private beliefs.

The book uses Iraq as a vehicle for showing the dramatic changes in the nature and quality of Arab public life. Chapter 2 delves into this new public sphere in depth, charting its evolution and the fierce debates about its significance and its quality. Chapter 3 focuses on the period from the end of the first Gulf War through 1997, during which Arabs grew increasingly mobilized over the sanctions on Iraq but lacked outlets to effectively express their anger. Chapter 4 examines the crucial period 1997–2003, including the American-British bombing of Iraq in December 1998 ("Desert Fox") that ended the United Nations weapons inspections, just as al-Jazeera emerged as a force in Arab politics. Chapter 5 examines the 2003 American-British invasion and occupation of Iraq, with a particular focus on the moments of uncertainty and open questioning after the fall of Baghdad that April. Finally, chapter 6 widens the lens to reconsider the prospects for the new Arab public, and its implications for American power, for democracy, and for the possibility for change in the region.

2

The Structural Transformation of
the Arab Public Sphere

Arab satellites have done probably for the Arab world more than any organized critical movement could have done, in opening up the public space, in giving Arab citizens a newly found opportunity to assert themselves.

—Saad Eddin Ibrahim (2004)

What does it mean to claim that a new Arab public sphere has emerged? The concept of the public sphere carries with it such theoretical baggage that many doubt whether the concept should be applied at all. Such dismissal is unwarranted, however. Arabs themselves invoke it, or something like it, to make sense of an emerging transnational public opinion critical of states and not reducible to their interests. What is most new about Arab politics since the late 1990s is the rapid emergence of a weak international public sphere that became the central focus of sustained, public, political argument for a vast Arab audience. As Lisa Wedeen (1998) might put it, the crucial political fact is that Arab political actors, from the most powerful states to the humblest civil society activists, *act as if* this new public matters.

The new Arab public should be understood in terms of the public arguments enacted by self-defined Arabs within a widely accessible new media. The new public sphere is not limited to television. Technology has helped the Arab press develop into a major forum for discussion and debate. Prior to Internet distribution, sensitive regimes could easily stop such newspapers at the border, and at any rate the newspapers were often too expensive for most people to read regularly. Dissemination on the Internet gives these newspapers far greater reach than ever before. Furthermore, the satellite stations regularly program roundups of the news and opinion published in the major Arabist newspapers, extending the reach of the press to those who lack the access or capabilities to read them on their own. Consumption of both press and television debate is often a communal affair, as cafes and salons pass around newspapers, compare the coverage of major events by al-Jazeera and CNN, and argue about what they see. Finally, the public for satellite stations and the pan-Arab press resides throughout Europe and the United States, in addition to the Middle East. Extensive diaspora networks can and do directly participate in the political debates of their homelands, a deterritorialization of the Arab public sphere the implications of which have yet to be fully appreciated (Roy 2004).

I begin this chapter by tracing the evolution of the Arab media, arguing that the emergence of a transnational public sphere was driven in part by domestic repression and in part by the existence of political entrepreneurs able to take advantage of the new media opportunities to invoke a shared identity. I then develop a public argument conception of the Arab public sphere. I draw on a large database of al-Jazeera talk shows to document what Arabs talked about in this new public sphere. Finally, I consider several key criticisms of the Arab public sphere, particularly concerns about its illiberal character and the ambivalent place occupied by Islamism.

Is There Really an Arab Public Sphere?

To the brilliant Lebanese journalist Hazem Saghiyeh, speaking of "Arab public opinion" makes no sense in the conventional meaning of the word.[1] Saghiyeh points out that "public opinion" usually refers to the opinion of citizens of a single country, which has tangible effects on that country's politics. In the Arab world, on the other hand, "the most important foundations in forming 'public opinion' in any Arab country continue to be foreign policy and religious identity and what most call national dignity." Public opinion expressed in the media tends to diverge quite sharply from real mass opinion: "most of society might take a hard and authoritarian position, but public opinion could take an extremely liberal and permissive position . . . because the dynamics of public opinion come from the city and from the most advanced and educated and professional and wealthiest sectors. . . . In the Arab world these sectors remain very small and limited." Public opinion rarely affects Arab rulers, who repress and control societies with abandon. In contrast to a public opinion working to "reduce the hand of the state," mass opinion tends to "instead struggle to incite the state to act more forcefully on religious or national issues." And, finally, mass Arab opinion tends to be highly stable and fixed, resistant to new information or to external influences: "if it is true that the Arab satellites today practice some kind of influence, then this influence hasn't changed much in reshaping broad mass sentiments or for improving them."

Such skepticism about the Arab media is deeply embedded. The pall that fell over Arab public life in the 1970s and 1980s, as oppressive states established hegemony over domestic media and Saudi Arabia used its vast oil wealth to seize a wide swath of the transnational media, left Arab intellectuals largely paralyzed. Critics ranging from Fouad Ajami to Edward Said, from the poets Nizar Qabbani and Adonis to the philosopher Mohammed Abed al-Jabiri, agreed on the pallid presence of Arab public intellectuals, their subservience to power, and their acceptance of self-censorship. One school of thought suggests that Islam lacks the distinction between public and private essential to the very concept of the public sphere. Yet another maintains that Arab and Islamic cultures are themselves fundamentally illiberal, beset by neopatrimonialism, tribalism, backwardness, and the legacies of Islam.

Despite this skepticism, the public sphere has been increasingly central to the analysis of Arab and Islamic politics. As democratic transitions stalled and civil society struggled to gain purchase against still-dominant Arab states, scholars cast about for ways to make sense of a revitalized public opinion disembodied from formal political institutions. When I was writing *State Interests and Public Spheres* in the mid-1990s, there was only a handful of precedents for conceptualizing the changes in Arab politics in terms of "public spheres" (Salvatore 1997). Today, dozens of articles and books focus on this theme (Anderson and Eickelman 1999; Schulze 2000). Similarly, international public spheres have received increasing attention from political scientists, particularly after Thomas Risse's (2000) influential article on communicative action in world politics (Bohman 2001; Samhat and

Payne 2003). Since 9/11, the potential for international public spheres to overcome the deadly spiral toward a clash of civilizations between Islam and the West has become a matter of urgent theoretical and real world concern (Lynch 2000a, 2005; Buck-Morss 2003).

In contrast to public sphere conceptions that revolve around particular institutions (the coffeehouse, television, civil society) or public opinion (as measured by opinion surveys), I define the public sphere in terms of active arguments before an audience about issues of shared concern. These dialogues require media that can bring arguments before a relevant audience, but media alone do not a public sphere make. Indeed, the mobilizational media characteristic of authoritarian Arab states can be seen as the antithesis of a public sphere, with a single voice driving out all dissent, questioning, and critical reason. Nor does argument alone make for a public sphere. Private arguments, carried out behind closed doors, lack the critical dimension of publicity. What makes a public sphere is the existence of routine, ongoing, unscripted arguments before an audience about issues relevant to many. A wide range of evidence suggests that, for Arabs, the most "attractive features of the new media options are that they are interactive and participatory. . . . Participation is crucial: television and radio shows that give room for the audience to call in, ask questions, voice their concerns, and vote for their favorite singer are popular" (Katulis 2004).

This public argument conception of the public sphere leads me to focus on talk shows and opinion essays rather than on news coverage. What makes the new Arab public "new" is the omnipresent political talk shows, which transform the satellite television stations into a genuinely unprecedented carrier of public argument. What makes it "Arab" is a shared collective identity through which speakers and listeners conceive of themselves as participating in a single, common political project. What makes it a "public sphere" is the existence of contentious debates, carried out by and before this self-defined public, oriented toward defining these shared interests.

It is not only the news coverage on al-Jazeera that unsettles the United States—it is also precisely the public sphere qualities embodied on the station. In a revealing interview with the *Washington Post*, the State Department's gifted envoy to "the Arab street," Christopher Ross, admitted to being "uncomfortable with the panel discussions and call-in talk shows that became a hallmark of al-Jazeera."[2] Ross preferred "situations in which he can remain 'in control.'" Ross described such situations as "short appearances in the context of news programs, where you are given the opportunity to present the U.S. point of view." Ross's discomfort perfectly captures the disjuncture between the American vision of public diplomacy and the ideal of a public sphere. What makes a public sphere a public sphere is precisely those aspects that dismay Ross: its unscripted character, its openness to multiple perspectives, its unpredictability . . . in short, that it is not possible to remain "in control."

Such a public sphere cannot be reduced simply to the more generic "public opinion," to the media, or to the infamous "Arab street" that might rise up in fury when sufficiently provoked. An arena of public argument outside the official channels of the state, the public sphere offers a zone of free and critical reason that might influence mass collective action but that cannot be reduced to it. The public sphere does not depend on the existence of democracy—and indeed the emergence of the Arab public sphere can be read as a direct response to the absence of democracy in almost every Arab country, which has led frustrated Arabs to seek out this new space for political argument and debate. Nor, finally, is the public sphere the same as "civil society," the more institutionalized network of social and civic organizations outside of the state.

While the new Arab public could not have emerged without the rise of new information and communications technologies, the new public sphere arose only because of what Arabs did with these new opportunities. The mere emergence of satellite television networks established the technical possibility of an Arab public sphere, simply by making it physically possible to create a space for direct and immediate communication and shared experience of the news. But it takes an orientation to public argument to make a public sphere. Only when al-Jazeera refocused the satellites away from entertainment and toward politics—more precisely, toward political argument about Arab issues defined by an Arab identity—did it become a public sphere. It is this emphasis on public argument about common issues, along with shared language and identity, that allows the new Arab public to transcend James Bohman's fear that transnational mass media are "unlikely to be locations for social criticism" or to be the foundations for a genuine transnational public sphere (1998: 195).

The image of multiple, crosscutting patchworks better captures the nature of the new Arab public than any singular conception of a unified spatial or temporal location: "messages and images in face to face conversations, newspapers, books, magazines, anonymous leaflets, video and audiocassettes, and satellite and regular television criss-cross, overlap, and build on one another. . . . When censored in one medium, such messages recur in another" (Eickelman 2001: 194). Movies and television shows serve as political metaphors and offer "safe" avenues by which to approach difficult and contentious topics (Armbrust 2000; Abu Lughod 1993). The distinction between elite and tabloid media, commonly employed in media analysis, does not hold in the Arab case: the Arab satellite stations, which stand accused of pandering to the masses through sensationalism, are also the premiere venue for elite political discourse. In one survey of Palestinian audiences, for example, al-Jazeera was most popular among those with the highest income (74 percent named it their preferred station, compared with 49 percent from the lowest income brackets) and the highest educated (76 percent of university graduates against 42 percent of illiterates).[3]

At the level of face-to-face interaction, many Arab countries have protected spaces of political debate and discussion that straddle the divide between public and private. In the *diwaniya* of Kuwait, for example, prominent personalities and ordinary citizens alike gather by invitation to hear political arguments and to discuss. Yemeni *qat chews* fill a similar social function (Wedeen, forthcoming). In Jordan tribal gatherings bring men together to discuss political issues, while political salons in the homes of prominent personalities fill a similar function for the elite. Coffeehouses once served as a vital spot for political argument in Egypt, with famous cafes hosting major intellectuals and political figures and popular cafes serving as communal sites to watch and discuss the satellite television news. In 2004, however, Abdullah al-Sanawi remarked that in contrast to those vibrant days, "I think that most of the government ministers would not dare sit in a public coffeehouse, or probably in any public place, and I think that a large number of the official intellectuals would not dare to sit in a coffeehouse and mix directly with the simple people."[4] In almost all Arab countries, mosques represent one of the most important of these protected spaces, while transnational Islamist networks offered a particularly important realm of information and argument. The new television stations create warm relationships among physically distant Arabs and greatly increase the emotional salience of political issues (Salvatore and Eickelman 2004: 20).

The near-universal exposure to this new public sphere is what gives it such a transformative impact. Throughout every Arab country, and extending through a widespread diaspora, Arab viewers consider themselves part of a single, common, ongoing political argument. A remarkable number of callers to al-Jazeera's talk shows live in Europe, as did nearly two-thirds of those who wrote letters to one Arab newspaper (Lynch 2003b). Because of its geographic and transnational expanse, this conversation highlights issues of shared rather than local concern. A collective narrative of the impotence and failure of the Arab regimes runs through and unites these core shared issues. Local issues are reframed—cast in terms of a wider grand narrative of Arab identity—so that a Jordanian clampdown on press freedoms, an Egyptian sweep against Muslim Brotherhood members, or a Syrian campaign to arrest political dissidents all cohere into a single narrative of the absence of Arab democracy. This core narrative insistently articulates the existence of an Arab people sharing a common story and a common identity.

Despite this common narrative, the Arab public sphere is deeply riven with intense disagreements, with discourse seemingly trending toward greater radicalism. Cass Sunstein's analysis (2003) of "enclave deliberation" offers a structural explanation for such polarization. Sunstein notes that in certain kinds of structural conditions, "members of a deliberating group predictably move toward a more extreme point in the direction indicated by the members' predeliberation tendencies." Sunstein argues that "it matters a great deal whether people consider themselves part of the same social group as the other members; a sense of shared identity will heighten the shift." Furthermore, polarization is more likely where there is a limited "argument pool," as well as when there are social and reputational pressures on speakers to present themselves as being in line with a shared consensus. And finally, "familiar and long-debated issues do not depolarize easily." Arab public spheres display all of these characteristics. Social and reputational pressures are strong, and Arabism provides an overwhelmingly salient shared identity. The issues are long-standing and highly polarized, and "polarization entrepreneurs" ensure a steady supply of extreme views. Enthusiasm for consensus, and fears of strengthening hostile external forces by revealing internal division, lead the Arabist public sphere to avoid difficult and contentious questions. What made the nascent Arab public sphere an enclave, then, was the unusually powerful set of shared assumptions and shared identity binding participants within the group.

From Voice of the Arabs to al-Jazeera

Before theorizing the new public, it may be useful to describe its evolution. This section lays out the historical development of the Arab public sphere (Rugh 2004a). Voice of the Arabs and al-Jazeera, each the defining media outlet of its era, embody two very different visions of an international public sphere.

Voice of the Arabs, Egypt's radio service in the 1950s and 1960s, was an instrument of a powerful state, used purely for strategic reasons and aimed primarily at mobilizing pressure from below on rival regimes. Radio broadcasting transformed the potential for Arab political action by bringing Arabist political speech (if not rational discourse) directly to the increasingly mobilized masses. This allowed pan-Arab movements to fundamentally challenge the legitimacy of relatively new Arab states. These radio wars featured little rational argument, and much invective and fierce rhetoric. It is this model that lingers in the minds of analysts obsessed with the "Arab street"—a model of emotional, angry rhetoric aimed at energizing dangerous mobs. But such speeches lost their credibility with the 1967 War, and despite many efforts nobody—certainly not Saddam Hussein—has successfully recaptured Nasser's mantle.

Al-Jazeera, by contrast, was hosted by Qatar, a small state with no aspirations to Arab leadership. Where the Arab radio wars of the 1950s suggest an international public sphere dominated by states, power, and strategic action, the satellite television of the late 1990s more resembled a public sphere of individuals engaged in open-ended arguments before an imagined (and real) audience of Arabs and Muslims spread across the globe. The new media of the 1990s involved two-way debate, as talk shows allowed viewers to call in questions and to vote in real-time opinion polls. The new media is commercial, driven more by market share than by ideology. The effect was to create a transnational media that defines issues as Arab ones which demand Arab solutions. Satellite stations such as al-Jazeera wield power very differently from Voice of the Arabs. Where the latter mobilized the masses through fiery speeches, al-Jazeera rose to prominence by giving voice to public opinion rather than directly attempting to mobilize or lead it.

The Dismal Years: The 1970s and 1980s

During the 1970s and 1980s, states struck back against the Nasserist radio wars by asserting near total state control over the media, to the point where little real public sphere remained, either within Arab states or at the transnational level. Arab states assumed overwhelming positions over individuals and society, with an overbearing state hand in the control of information. Censorship, both direct and indirect— via internalized "red lines" of self-censorship—closed down most public avenues of political debate. As for the press, as Faisal al-Qassem once asked, "are these newspapers . . . good for anything more than wrapping falafel sandwiches, with all due respect to the sandwiches?"[5] State-run television was a dreary affair, focusing on official business and completely closed to political opposition. The omnipresent secret police and intelligence services, along with the state's ability to control both freedom of movement abroad and employment, cast a chill over journalism: "a policeman on my chest, a scissor in my brain" (Anonymous 1987).

This repression led many intellectuals and media professionals to relocate to Europe, especially London. The Lebanese press, which had always been among the most free and most influential in the Arab world, similarly relocated in the 1980s because of the Israeli invasion and the subsequent horrors of civil war. But in this period newspapers published abroad could be easily stopped at the border, censored, or simply banned, and were at any rate too expensive for most Arabs to afford. Out of desperation, many Arabs turned to whatever foreign sources might be available, whether the BBC Arabic service, Radio Monte Carlo, the Voice of America, or even (in Jordan) Israeli Arabic-language television broadcasting.

In the 1970s and 1980s, Saudi Arabia used its dramatically increased oil wealth to establish a dominant position over much of the Arab press and electronic media (Rugh 2004a; Boyd 2001). It did so partly to exercise power, partly to defend against what it saw as a threat from external media, and partly to prevent reporting of sensitive internal developments such as the 1979 seizure of the Grand Mosque in Mecca. Saudi control led to what Abd al-Wahhab al-Affendi (1993) described as "an eclipse of reason" in the Arab world.

By the end of the 1980s, the Arab media was something of a waste-land. When Iraq invaded Kuwait, the Saudi media was able to suppress the news in its domestic media for several days, while Arab elites drew on CNN and the BBC for information about the crisis. By the early 1990s, the Arab public sphere seemed to have been conclusively down-graded by the combined impact of the Gulf War and the seemingly inexorable concentration of state power.

Domestic Liberalization and Retreat: The Early 1990s

In the 1990s tentative liberalization processes in a number of Arab states allowed limited debates about domestic issues, which turned attention inward. While avoiding real democratization, many of these experiments did expand public freedoms and conditionally liberate the print media.

Jordan in the early 1990s witnessed an explosion of newspapers (Lynch 1999). The weekly press pushed the boundaries of the "red lines" that governed Jordanian public discussion, fomenting a new kind of frank public discourse on sensitive matters such as Jordanian-Palestinian relations, the peace process with Israel, economic reforms, and official corruption. For a brief span of a few years, this domestic press emerged as a uniquely Jordanian public sphere, one focused on questions of Jordanian rather than Arab identity and interests. As the kingdom moved toward an unpopular peace treaty with Israel, however, the state began to crack down on the independent press. Through progressively more restrictive press laws, as well as prosecution and shutting down of numerous newspapers, the regime succeeded in choking off this nascent public sphere and reclaiming its dominant position in public life.

Similar stories can be told for other Arab countries. In Yemen, unification and liberalization in the early 1990s saw the publication of independent newspapers and the free circulation of information (Carapico 1998: chapter 6). Along with competing television stations and several daily newspapers, dozens of weekly tabloids sprung up that represented all political trends and focused a nationwide dialogue on political reform and change. As Sheila Carapico describes it, "the media constituted an arena for a 'war of declarations' and for competition to influence public opinion. Whereas in the past political rivalries were secretive, now they played out in front of television audiences more aware of political events than at any time in their history" (1998: 151–154). A national dialogue in the face of civil war attracted enormous public attention, with heavy media coverage and open political arguments before a highly attentive Yemeni public. With the civil war that broke out in 1994, and then the centralization of power under Ali Abdullah Saleh, this press—like its Jordanian counterpart—lost its energy and its centrality to political discourse. Since 2001 the Yemeni press has seen a steady encroachment by the state, with frequent crackdowns, harassment, and physical intimidation against journalists.[6]

Other countries saw similar, if less dramatic, openings. After the restoration of Kuwaiti sovereignty in 1991, the ruling family offered substantive concessions to public participation in politics. The combination of deep resentment of Arabs who supported Iraq in the Gulf War and a vibrant, contentious press drove a backlash against the Arab order as a whole, and even a real questioning of Kuwait's Arab identity. In Lebanon, the end of the civil war in 1989 and the return of electoral politics saw a rebirth of that country's proud press tradition, albeit one that remained in the shadow of the Syrian occupation and reflected widespread reluctance to touch sensitive communal issues which might respark civil war (Gonzalez-Quijano 2003). In Morocco, an independent press slowly emerged in the last years of King Hassan's reign, but suffered a general crackdown after King Mohammed VI ascended the throne in 1999 (Jamai 2005). Even Syria enjoyed a very brief "Damascus spring," with tentative moves toward political reform after the death of Hafez al-Assad, concentrated in private salons and discussions on the condition that they not enter the public sphere via the Syrian press, which remained tightly controlled throughout the 1990s (Azm 2000). While Saudi Arabia retained its fierce internal control over information, offering few concessions to its beleaguered reformists, Saudis had increasing access to the Internet and satellite television (Yamani 2000: 15–19 Wright 2004b).

The rollback of liberalization and tighter control over most national media in the mid-1990s helped create the market for al-Jazeera by displacing political argument into the transnational arena. Denied the opportunity to debate matters of public concern at home, Arabs turned to the new media. For example, al-Jazeera caused a sensation in Jordan with a program pitting regime critic Layth Shubaylat against a staunch regime loyalist. In the early 1990s Jordanians would not have needed to tune in to a Qatari television station to see such a spectacle, since they could have seen it in the Jordanian media. States seeking to more tightly control domestic political debate created the conditions for the rise of the independent political transnational media that by the late 1990s had definitively shattered their own control over information.

The Late 1990s: Al-Jazeera and the New Media

As recently as the first Gulf War, there were no Arab satellite broadcasts. By 1994, however, at least twenty different regional satellites had been launched, although their entertainment focus limited their political impact (Sakr 2001b). By the late 1990s the emergence of the satellite television stations and the increased availability of the European-based Arab press created the foundations for a public sphere relatively independent of states. This market-driven transnational broadcasting has facilitated a much stronger and more clearly articulated transnational public opinion.

The new media radically transformed the sense of distance among Arabs and Muslims, bringing them together in real time and in a common language alongside intense images and a shared political discourse. It has decisively broken the state's monopoly over information, even in repressive states such as Saudi Arabia and Syria (Ghadbian 2001). Ratiba Hadj-Moussa (2003) offers a telling description of the process in Algeria: "The national television network is so lacking in credibility that the only reliable sources of information about Algeria come from outside. . . . The advent of satellite television has created a circuit which begins in Algiers, goes back to Paris or London and back again to Algiers."

The emergence of the satellite television networks was necessary, but not sufficient, to create an Arab public sphere. It was the political arguments within those media that made the difference, not the media themselves. Long before al-Jazeera, Arabs could tune in to satellite television stations replete with Lebanese belly dancing and Egyptian television serials. It was not new media alone that created a new public sphere—it was al-Jazeera's prioritization of politics and its remarkable success in initiating a regionwide public discourse that quickly reached an incredibly widespread and diverse audience. In 1996 the satellite news station Orbit—a Saudi joint venture with the BBC—was abruptly shut down by its Saudi patrons after it aired a documentary that Saudi authorities deemed offensive. Veterans of this experience, many with long professional experience at the BBC, were therefore available when al-Jazeera was created in Qatar that same year.

Speaking to an explicitly transnational audience addressed as fellow Muslims and fellow Arabs, al-Jazeera quickly moved to the center of an emerging Arab public sphere (Miles 2005). Al-Jazeera revolutionized the Arab and Muslim media environment not by offering a regional news service, but by adopting an overtly political focus and a dramatic new style. Al-Jazeera has been accused by Arab writers of being everything from a CIA operation to a Mossad one, from a bin Laden outlet to a Saddam apologist, from an agent of Islamism to an agent of secularism. Al-Jazeera infuriated much of Arab public opinion by inviting Israeli speakers onto its programs, leading it to be regularly accused of being in the pay of the Mossad or of being an agent of "normalization."

Market surveys confirm the universal impression of the rapid rise of al-Jazeera.[7] In Jordanian surveys, those naming al-Jazeera as the most reliable source for Arab news grew from 4 percent in 1998 to 12 percent in 1999 and to 17 percent in 2000 (among those who owned a satellite dish, the numbers are more striking: in 1998 25 percent saw Jordan TV as most credible for Arab news and 24 percent al-Jazeera; in 1999 the numbers were 17 percent and 44 percent, and in 2000 they were 25 percent to 49.4 percent). Al-Jazeera's audience increased from 2.5 percent in 1998 to 5 percent in 1999 and to 8.2 percent in 2000; over the same period, Syrian television saw its audience shrink from 3.8 percent to 2.9 percent, while Israeli television went from 1.3 percent to nothing. Among those who owned a satellite dish, al-Jazeera's audience jumped from 18.9 percent to 42 percent in the same period. In 2003 Jordan's Center for Strategic Studies found that about 35 percent of Jordanians viewed al-Jazeera as the most trusted source for Arab and international news—beating Jordan TV in both areas—and that al-Jazeera was the second-most trusted source even for domestic news.[8] Palestinian surveys show similar findings: in September 1999, 51 percent of Palestinians named al-Jazeera as the most-watched satellite television station; 47 percent said the same in February 2000; and 58 percent in June 2004.[9]

Al-Jazeera's coverage of the December 1998 Desert Fox bombing campaign established the station as mandatory Arab viewing. Its coverage of the second Palestinian Intifada in 2000 galvanized Arab politics even more, with the repeatedly broadcast image of the death of young Mohammed al-Dura defining the shared Arab experience of the crisis and directly contributing to a resurgence of protest activity.[10] During the furious month of April 2002, as massive Arab street protests against the Israeli reoccupation of the West Bank rocked every Arab capital, al-Jazeera covered both events on the ground and the protests with equal vigor, bringing vivid images of the conflict into Arab homes, a direct experience without precedent.[11]

Al-Jazeera's monopoly position could not last, and within a few years rivals emerged to produce an intensely competitive and increasingly fragmented market. LBC formed an unusual partnership with the newspaper *al-Hayat* and upgraded the news side of its offerings. Abu Dhabi TV set out to capture the "moderate alternative" ground.

Almost every Arab country offered official satellite news stations, with Egypt particularly active in pushing its local product. Even the United States launched its own Arabic language satellite television station, al-Hurra, in February 2004. As Ibrahim al-Aris puts it, "If al-Jazeera had the media market to itself for a period before and after the Afghanistan war, now there are many stations. . . . The satellite media map is constantly renewing and al-Jazeera no longer has a monopoly even though it continues to enjoy a leading position."[12]

Perhaps the most intriguing, and most successful, of these challengers has been the Dubai-based al-Arabiya. In February 2003, with $300 million in startup money from Saudi Arabia, technologically advanced facilities taken over from MBC, and a veteran team of broadcasters, al-Arabiya set out to offer a more moderate (and, of course, more deferential to Saudi sensitivities) alternative to al-Jazeera. As its first managing director Salah al-Qallab revealingly put it, "We are not going to make problems for Arab countries."[13] Al-Arabiya's vision of the Arab media explicitly excluded the kind of open, free dialogue that made al-Jazeera a genuine public sphere: "all of al-Arabiya's interviews will be pre-recorded. . . . It seems clear that the station has no intention of opening such a wide margin for discussion and debate."[14] In other words, al-Arabiya's mission statement suggested an attempt to strip the satellite television stations of their public sphere qualities and return them to a more conventional news media.

During the Iraq war, nevertheless, al-Arabiya imitated al-Jazeera and won some success with a similarly nationalistic approach to the news. After the war, Saudi Arabia reigned in al-Arabiya, and appointed the pro-American former editor of *al-Sharq al-Awsat*, Abd al-Rahman al-Rashed, as its managing director (Shapiro 2005).[15] Al-Arabiya very self-consciously presented itself as the "moderate" alternative to al-Jazeera, with Rashed dismissing the station's critics as "those with a political agenda who were furious to have lost a platform as powerful as al-Arabiya," and describing his station's niche in these terms: "We attract liberal-minded people. Jazeera attracts fanatics."[16] Al-Arabiya set out to avoid using terms such as "martyrdom" or "resistance," instead adopting the "neutral" vocabulary preferred by American critics of the Arab media. In comparison with al-Jazeera, al-Arabiya played down the Palestine issue, while devoting a lot of time to covering Iraq, employing a more positive spin in line with American preferences. Given al-Jazeera's poor reputation with Iraqis, many of whom saw it as too sympathetic to Saddam's regime, al-Arabiya gained popularity inside Iraq relative to al-Jazeera. Al-Arabiya forged a close relationship with interim Prime Minister Iyad Allawi, who appeared frequently on the station for interviews and who ran a large number of campaign advertisements in January 2005. It ran into problems, even so: several of its correspondents were killed by American troops; the Iraqi Governing Council shut down its operations several times, just as it did al-Jazeera's; and in the fall of 2004 its Baghdad offices were decimated by a horrific car bomb.

Al-Arabiya talk shows tended to feature more Saudi and other Arab officials—foreign ministers, members of Parliament—and fewer independent and critical personalities than the al-Jazeera programs. Since al-Arabiya wanted to establish itself as the responsible alternative to al-Jazeera, it made sense to choose officials and pro-American voices over outspokenly critical figures. And Arab officials who feared and often loathed al-Jazeera as a threat made time for al-Arabiya to promote it as a safer version of satellite media. When President George W. Bush chose to grant interviews to the Arab media to contain the damage of the Abu Ghraib scandals, he chose al-Arabiya (along with the American station al-Hurra) as the outlet. The pressures of market competition can be vividly seen in the case of al-Arabiya, however. Over the summer of 2004, for example, despite an explicit commitment to avoid sensationalism, al-Arabiya broadcast numerous hostage videos, just as al-Jazeera had done; as managing director Abd al-Rahman al-Rashed explained, "there is only one condition for me to stop airing all these videotapes, which is that all TV stations in the region agree not to show them."[17]

Moving in the other direction, al-Manar Television offered a vision of Arab television as a fairly explicit propaganda machine. Run by Hezbollah in Lebanon, al-Manar relied on a steady diet of provocative, horrifying images layered in an impenetrable, univocal discourse of anti-American, anti-Israeli rhetoric (Jorisch 2004a). Al-Manar made no pretence either to objectivity or toward open dialogue, and indeed openly scorned the idea of objective journalism. In the summer of

2004 France moved to ban al-Manar for its anti-Semitic propaganda, while many accused it of inciting anti-Israeli violence. Al-Manar reached out to a niche audience, one looking for an explicitly anti-Israeli or anti-American perspective, rather than competing directly with mainstream satellite stations such as al-Jazeera and al-Arabiya. The Shia station did surprisingly well even in Sunni areas such as Jordan and Palestine, with its fiercely anti-Israel message, although this message did not seem to travel well beyond the Levant—a January 2005 market survey found al-Manar with less than 1 percent of the Greater Cairo audience. Its presence in the arena may have forced those stations toward a more radical position, however, for fear of losing market share.

A June 2004 survey by Zogby International found that despite new competition, al-Jazeera remained the most-watched Arab news source overall, with some regional and local variations: it ranked as the primary station for 62 percent of Jordanians, 54 percent of Moroccans, 44 percent of Lebanese, 44 percent of Saudis, and 46 percent in the UAE; and the secondary station for (on average) about 20 percent more in each country. Al-Arabiya was next, averaging about 7–8 percent in most countries (but 19 percent in the UAE), while LBC did well only in Lebanon (29 percent), and Abu Dhabi TV did well in Saudi Arabia (22 percent) and the UAE (17 percent). In other words, despite the repeated warnings of its impending loss of credibility or audience, al-Jazeera remained the market leader even as the market grew increasingly competitive. A September 2004 survey of Saudi television preferences found that 82 percent watched al-Jazeera regularly, followed by 75 percent who watched al-Arabiya, 33 percent the Saudi al-Ikhbariya, and then a number of stations clustered at the bottom with very small audiences.[18] In a late 2004 survey of the Greater Cairo area, 88.4 percent of households with satellite television watched al-Jazeera, followed by al-Arabiya (35.1 percent), Nile News (8.9 percent), CNN (6.6 percent), al-Hurra (4.6 percent), al-Ikhbariya (3.9 percent), BBC (3.1 percent), and al-Manar (each with 0.4 percent).[19] Also in late 2004, a survey in Jordan found 72 percent watched al-Jazeera and 54 percent al-Arabiya (only 1.5 percent watched the American station al-Hurra).[20] Al-Jazeera remained the standard-setter—and was the one station every Arab could assume that other Arabs had seen that day—but other stations offered a serious challenge.

A key development here is that choice in news sources has quickly acclimated Arab audiences to the expectation of disagreement. While there are certain programs that command loyal audiences—Faisal al-Qassem's "The Opposite Direction," or the Lebanese reality show "Superstar"—for news Arab viewers tend to switch rapidly between stations. Arabs watching news in cafes generally surf the satellite television offerings, comparing al-Jazeera to CNN, or al-Arabiya to Egyptian state television. Well-versed in the arts of deciphering political codes in the authoritarian media, these audiences now excel in comparing coverage and analysis and triangulating.

In the aggregate, amid the diverse media of the new Arab public sphere, virtually all positions, information, and ideas could be found. The new media has not noticeably changed the Arab state's desire to control information, but it has clearly eroded its ability to do so. Two examples from Egypt demonstrate this powerfully. In the summer of 2004 Mohammed Hassanein Haykal, the Arab world's most famous journalist, began to appear on the fledgling Egyptian satellite station Dream, with transcripts of his programs widely disseminated in the press. Haykal quickly ran afoul of the authorities by discussing critically the prospects of Gamal Mubarak succeeding his father as president, and was summarily banned from the Egyptian media. In response, Haykal signed a blockbuster deal to host a program on al-Jazeera, where his views immediately reached more Egyptians than on the domestic station (Lynch 2004c).[21] Similarly, the contrasting media coverage by the Egyptian state media and the satellite television stations of the 2004 terrorist attack at Taba could hardly be more stark. While al-Arabiya and al-Jazeera covered the explosions heavily, on Egyptian television "all the channels had the regular stuff going on—a play here, a video clip there—it was like this thing wasn't happening in Egypt. . . . It wasn't just the horrific images emerging from Taba that astounded them, but the seeming oblivion to those events being demonstrated by their local channels. On channel 1, a play continued without interruption. On channel 2, a video clip. Channel 3 was airing an interview, as was channel 4, and so on."[22]

Al-Jazeera as the Arab Fox News?

They're partisan in the same way that Fox TV are partisan and they portray themselves as a virtual Arab nation, always seeing things from the perspective of the suffering Arab people.

—Abdallah Schleifer[23]

It benefits al-Jazeera to play to Arab nationalism because that's their audience, just like Fox plays to American patriotism, for the exact same reason.

—Lt. Col. Josh Rushing, *Control Room*[24]

In the spring of 2004 a University of Maryland team released a report demonstrating that viewers of Fox News were far more likely than others to believe three demonstrably false things about Iraq: that weapons of mass destruction had been found, that ties to al-Qaeda had been demonstrated, and that most of international opinion had backed the war (Kull 2003). The nakedly partisan Fox approach to the war misled its viewers, according to this study, by reinforcing their prejudices while shielding them from contradictory information. The word choices of Fox news anchors reinforced the discourse preferences of the Bush administration. Fox talk shows were dominated by partisan Republicans, with opposing views represented either by ineffectual token liberals or else by extreme-looking leftists, thereby effacing the existence of a moderate, centrist opposition to the war. And as this approach gained it market share, competitors such as CNN and MS-NBC began imitating its style of coverage. In short, on first glance the profile of Fox News looks remarkably similar to that generally ascribed to al-Jazeera.

While useful as a starting point, the comparison of al-Jazeera to Fox News does not do justice to al-Jazeera, nor to the Arab public sphere as a whole. It does help to highlight some troubling but important developments, however. In news coverage, al-Jazeera and the rest of the Arab media resembled Fox not only in their patriotic rhetoric but also in their overwhelming focus on one side of the conflict to the exclusion of the other. Fox focused its coverage on the human experience of American soldiers—whether in combat or playing soccer with Iraqi children—while almost completely ignoring or demonizing the

Arab "terrorists." Al-Jazeera similarly focused on the human experience of Arabs and Iraqis during the war, while explicitly rejecting the American frame for the war. It is worth noting, as Yassir Abu Hilala points out, that "the correspondents of Fox News say that the army kills enemies and that the resistance is terrorists. . . . The Arab media do not call the occupiers in Iraq 'enemies' or 'terrorists.' "[25]

It is in the talk shows and in the conception of the public sphere where the comparison falls short but points to disturbing trends. Over the course of 2002–2003 it was possible to observe a "Fox-ification" of al-Jazeera, as an open, diverse, and free public sphere came to be increasingly dominated by hyperpartisan voices and emotional rhetoric. One hallmark of the Fox talk shows is that they tend to prefer extreme partisans rather than moderates, such that the far left is better represented than the mainstream of the Democratic Party. This creates a misleading sense of the actual distribution of opinions, and reinforces the belief of many of its viewers that the "other side" is more radical than it really is. The coarsening of rhetoric on al-Jazeera, as well as the growing trend toward entrenched positions and bitter accusations across partisan lines, follows this logic.

While American guests on al-Jazeera were plentiful, they more often came from the most conservative sectors of American politics—the Washington Institute for Near East Policy and the American Enterprise Institute were far better represented on al-Jazeera than was the Brookings Institution or the leftist Institute for Policy Studies. On the September 11, 2004, program to discuss the possibility of a "Dialogue of Civilizations," for example, Yusuf al-Qaradawi was pitted against not an American Muslim or an advocate of such a dialogue, but rather against the extremely hawkish "terror expert" Steven Emerson. This can partly be explained by the reality of a Republican-dominated Washington, making conservative views arguably more important for Arab viewers to understand, but it still tended to push argument toward extremes at the expense of a rational center.

Still, there are important differences. Where Fox positioned itself against a "mainstream media" that was characterized by norms of journalistic objectivity, al-Jazeera stood against a media tightly controlled by repressive Arab states. Where Fox began as an underdog, building a partisan audience while chipping away at a centrist mainstream media and at the same time closely cultivating ties with an ascendant Republican party, al-Jazeera established itself as a near-dominant market leader independent of the most powerful regimes and state forces and then faced competition from numerous new rivals.

Other New Media

Broadcasting and the Internet have revitalized the Arab press. Despite continuing high levels of illiteracy, the rapid expansion of mass education, combined with the traditionally high value placed on texts in Islamic culture, ensures that these globalizing processes encompass the print media as well (Eickelman 2000). As Abdallah Schleifer points out, "the first major impact of new satellite technologies upon Arab media was in the eighties, not the nineties, and it was the satellited daily newspaper, not television" (Schleifer 1998).

Newspapers such as *al-Hayat*, *al-Sharq al-Awsat*, and *al-Quds al-Arabi*, published in London and aimed at a pan-Arab audience, offered an early challenge to state control over information, and globalization has helped these newspapers to overcome their traditional difficulty in reaching an audience in the Middle East, which had resulted from their price and from the fact that governments could stop them at the border or censor their contents. These papers now circulate widely among elites, and most now post their content free online. What is more, satellite television news broadcasts routinely read from these newspapers, which allows them to reach a far wider audience. These papers therefore have a disproportionate impact among influential Arab elites, and "are a fundamental link between expatriate Arab communities . . . and the Arab world itself" (Alterman 2004: 230–231). In an earlier study, I found that 68 percent of the letters to the editor published in one newspaper in 2001 and 2002 came from Europe or the United States (Lynch 2003b: 65).

The circulation and influence of newspapers has declined in recent years, as satellite television has emerged as the crucial site of the public sphere. Abd al-Aziz al-Khamis, a Saudi editor, claims that the circulation of some papers and magazines has plummeted from hundreds of thousands to as low as 2,000, "not because they are forbidden or censored but because nobody will buy them."[26] And, as Ahmed Mansour notes, "the Arab press is living through a constant crisis because of the narrowing margins of freedom and expression. . . . Not a day passes without news of an arrest or trial of a journalist or stopping of a newspaper. . . . At a time of a global widening of media freedoms, many Arab states are issuing new laws and rules limiting the freedom of the press."[27]

At the micro-level, mobile phones and text messaging have played an important role in changing communication patterns and dissemination of information. For example, Jordanian activists arranging a demonstration against the sanctions on Iraq managed to circumvent close scrutiny by state security agencies by "blasting" the location of the protest over instant messaging only at the last minute. By the time the police reacted, the protestors had already been filmed by al-Jazeera and their message broadcast to a wide audience.[28]

Even before the explosion of satellite television dish ownership, videotapes of the most exciting and controversial al-Jazeera programs circulated freely to be played on already-ubiquitous VCRs. These mid-tech communications technologies pose real difficulties for regime control, given their centrality to business and their widespread integration into daily life (Eickelman 2001a). Early challenges to the legitimacy of the Saudi regime by Islamist dissidents such as Mohammad al-Masa'ri, for example, deployed information collected from local sources or from Western media, and then used fax machines, and later the Internet and email, to distribute information damning to the Saudi regime into the kingdom. The Ayatollah Khomeini famously used cassette sermons taped abroad to rally and mobilize Islamic protests against the Shah of Iran (Mohammadi and Mohammadi 1994). As discussed at the end of this chapter, cassette tapes of Islamist preachers circulate widely, creating a distinctive "a distinctive religious public" among a vast, transnational realm of pious Islamists (Hirschkind 2001).

The Internet has also emerged as an important site for the new public. While its impact is limited by state controls and by very low levels of access, it has still been increasingly relevant. Al-Jazeera's Web site, for example, has emerged as one of the single most popular sites on the Internet despite being in Arabic. Offering full transcripts of its talk shows, viewable news clips and audio, and a wide range of interactive features such as opinion surveys and chat rooms, aljazeera.net plays a crucial role in that station's overall impact. After its 2003 launch, al-Arabiya similarly put together a state-of-the-art Web site to compete with al-Jazeera at that level. That the American-run station al-Hurra did not create such a Web site contributed to its general failure to attract significant Arab interest or attention. Blogs (personal weblogs) began to make a political impact in 2004–2005, especially in countries such as Egypt (the Kefaya movement), Lebanon, Iraq, and Bahrain, even if their influence remained limited by language barriers to a very small numbers of users. Finally, Internet chat rooms, especially those associated with radical Islamism, have attracted increasing attention as an important source for information about attitudes in the jihadist community, and have also played a role in recruitment for those organizations (Wright 2004a).

Contrary to widespread expectations about the revolutionary impact of the Internet, Arab states have proven quite adept at developing new mechanisms of surveillance and control (Kalathil and Boas 2003). Arab governments have used techniques ranging from sophisticated censorship regimes to state-controlled Internet service providers and proxy servers to highly publicized crackdowns on Internet users to intimidate or prevent political uses of the Internet (Kalathil and Boas 2003; Burkhardt and Older 2003). The Middle East remains one of the regions of the world least connected to the Internet—one commonly cited statistic indicated only 2 million total Internet users in the Middle East out of a total population of more than 220 million—although the distribution patterns range widely. One less appreciated route by which the Internet has had an impact is that Arab journalists—both print and broadcast—now have much greater access to information (Rugh 2004a: 12–14). During their programs Arab television presenters routinely refer to materials gathered from the Internet, such as opinion polls and Western newspaper articles, giving wide audiences indirect access.[29]

Thinking Through the Arab Public Sphere

It is not enough to say that an Arab public sphere exists. What kind of public sphere is it? What kind of impact is it likely to have? What kinds of arguments dominate within it? Who are the participants? In chapter 1, I argued that the Arab public sphere represented a kind of enclave, a counterpublic largely hidden from the view of dominant publics until September 11 and the Iraq war brought it forcefully to the attention of Americans. While the Arab public sphere is unquestionably a *transnational* one, linking together Arabs across dozens of Arab and Muslim states as well as a vast international diaspora, it is not necessarily a *cosmopolitan* public sphere (Kohler 1998). Bounded by language and by the shared political concerns that defined its participants as Arab, this transnational public sphere encouraged a politics of identity and of resistance at odds with the normative expectations of the advocates of cosmopolitan democracy.

Claims for the radicalizing impact of this new media in the Arab context must be set aside conventional arguments that globalizing television has the reverse, depoliticizing effect, as a global, market driven corporate media induces passivity and consumerist values in its audiences (Bennett 2004). A long-standing critique of the mass media is that it tends to demobilize societies, to discourage political action in favor of the passive consumption of political information (Gamson 2001). The new Arab media, by contrast, takes an active role in attempting to mobilize mass publics to become politically involved. One key difference between the Arab transnational media and generically globalizing media is the preexisting collective identity and shared political interests across Arab state borders. Where a globalized media might "exclude much of local politics, citizen activism, public policy analysis, and deliberation," the new Arab satellite stations for the first time included exactly those things—with core Arab concerns such as Palestine and Iraq standing alongside demands for democratic reform as "local issues" (Bennett 2004: 126).

The impact of this new media within the Arab world has arguably been unique because of a conjunction of factors. In particular, the preexisting transnational political community made it conceivable that a politically oriented transnational new media would find a ready audience. This audience was particularly primed by the relative closure and stagnation of domestic publics, and the near absence of meaningful domestic democratic politics. Arab audiences have become rapidly acclimated to having a genuine choice of engaging, independent media and have little to no interest in stodgy, politically controlled state broadcasting.

What the new media actually amounts to remains deeply contested. For example, al-Jazeera host Ghassan bin Jadu argues that "the satellites feel the pulse of public opinion, and . . . are able to contradict what has been asserted in the Arab media for decades."[30] But Kawther al-Bashrawi retorts that "this platform for free expression doesn't express the truth of what happens on the Arab street or what happens in the heart of our society. . . . The masses are beginning to tire of media slogans."[31] Shaker Nabulsi, by contrast, accepts that the Arab media does roughly convey the sense of the Arab street, but takes this as grounds to fiercely denounce both. In this section, I attempt to get a handle on these violent political debates by laying out some of the core theoretical issues raised by an international public sphere.

A "Weak" International Public Sphere

We are talking here about a news station, not about a political party or a national liberation movement. Why do we burden al-Jazeera with the functions of the failed movements and failed political parties?
—Mahmoud Shimam, July 2004[32]

While the new Arab public sphere has had strong effects at the level of mass attitudes and elite opinion, its structural position is weak. It has succeeded at harnessing the attention and participation of a striking portion of the Arab world, but it remains detached from legitimate policy avenues and unable to translate its consensus into political outcomes. Drawing on the wider literature on international public spheres, I would describe the Arab situation as a *weak international public sphere*.

International public spheres are generically problematic because they are severed from the state (Bohman 2001). In Habermas's ideal type (1996), the public sphere acts as a conduit to the democratic state, which in turn can act effectively on the ideas arrived at through free public reason. But the international public sphere has no such direct target, no means for translating opinion into policy, rendering it what

Nancy Fraser (1992) has called a "weak public" (Nanz and Steffek 2004). But "weak" should not be taken to mean that its political significance is minimal—only that it lacks these institutionalized mechanisms for affecting policy: a weak public "has moral influence but no legally regulated access to political or administrative power.... [But] the communicative power of a weak public can have profound political impact" (Brunkhorst 2002: 677).

The Arab public sphere can mobilize public outrage, pressure leaders to act through ridicule or exposure, shape the strategic incentives for rational politicians, and even incite street protests. But it cannot, in and of itself, act. It cannot pass laws, declare war, call elections, sever diplomatic relations, or lower trade barriers. This structural weakness, combined with its manifest power to shape public opinion, defines the realm of its political possibility. As Khaled Haroub argues, the new public gives Arabs a chance to talk about the reality of the problems of the Arab world, but no opportunity to offer any solutions.[33] Hence, the Arab media can be seen as a catalyst for change, but it would probably be an exaggeration to cast them in the lead role as the primary driving force for reform. Even the most open and frank and vigorous discussions on the satellite television talk shows, he concludes, can too easily remain just remain words in the air.

Put bluntly, if Arabs cannot act on their opinions, then do those opinions matter? Will the new public sphere create, as Yusuf Nur Awadh fears, "a culture of talk instead of a culture of action"?[34] or perhaps even reduce the prospects of effective political action, by allowing people a "safe" outlet for their frustrations and diverting their energies away from concrete political mobilization? For Arabs, the absence of democratic states makes even more urgent the question of who is listening to these public arguments. In crucial ways, the Arab public sphere is self-referential, constituting a new Arab identity explicitly independent of and often critical of Arab states and the official Arab order. To what extent can a satellite television station actually claim to represent Arab public opinion? Munir Shafiq argues that "the power of al-Jazeera comes from its programs and some of its participants, who give the people the chance to speak their minds freely on the air.... It is public opinion that shapes al-Jazeera and not the opposite."[35] Rather than directly producing outcomes, the new media has become the primary location for Arabs to work out their identity and their interests through public argument and debate. As it has risen to prominence and it has become a core ingredient of the shared social knowledge of all politically aware Arabs—it is not the fact that everyone watches al-Jazeera, but rather that everyone knows that everyone else watches it, that shapes its strategic centrality.

Self-Conception as a Public

A certain narcissism defines the new Arab public, which is relentlessly obsessed with "Arab" issues and with its own importance. This self-obsession, ironically, may be one of the things that most identifies it as a public. Michael Warner writes that publics "exist by virtue of being addressed" (2003: 67). For Jim Bohman, "a public sphere requires not only a social space for communication to an indefinite audience but also that diverse members of a society interact in distinctive ways and thereby come to regard themselves as a public" (Bohman 1999: 186). By that standard, the question of the existence of an Arab public sphere answers itself. There is simply no doubt about the abundance of voices that address an Arab public *as* an Arab public, creating the public sphere through this act of address. When Arabs appear on al-Jazeera, they understand themselves to be speaking as Arabs, to Arabs, and about Arab issues. What makes the Arab public a "public," then, is that self-identified Arabs routinely and frequently address and invoke it as such, via media that reach the prospective members of the public, about matters collectively defined as of common interest.

There is a remarkable amount of reflexive, self-conscious discussion within the Arab public sphere about itself. Al-Jazeera regularly airs programs devoted to questioning its own importance, its own behavior, its own mistakes. On April 20, 1999, for example, Faisal al-Qassem devoted his program to the Moroccan government's decision to ban his program. On May 23, 2000, Qassem's program considered "Questions about al-Jazeera," and on October 31, 2000, he inquired into "The Arab media and its role in the Intifada" (a question taken up again by Ghassan bin Jadu on April 27, 2002). In January 2002, a two-part special explored "the future of the Arab media." On June 30, 2001,

Ghassan bin Jadu's program focused on "freedom of expression in the Arab media." Bin Jadu, in a December 2, 2003, program about the political impact of the satellite television stations, modestly concluded that "the satellites play a large and influential role in the arena of Arab society."[36] An April 2005 program explored "the Arab media and the question of Iraq."[37] A February 2004 episode of *The Opposite Direction* even took on the politically loaded allegations of Iraqi "oil coupons" being used to buy support in the Arab media, including al-Jazeera.[38] And the explosive question of the Arab media's relationship to al-Qaeda, as well as criticism of its coverage of the wars in Afghanistan and Iraq, received the attention of multiple programs.

Counterpublics and Hidden Transcripts

A counterpublic maintains at some level, conscious or not, an awareness of its subordinate status. The cultural horizon against which it marks itself off is not just a general or wider public but a dominant one. And the conflict extends not just to ideas or policy questions but to the speech genres and modes of address that constitute the public.

—Michael Warner (2003: 119)

The Arab public sphere has long identified itself as a subordinate, dominated counterpublic, struggling against Western hegemony and tenaciously resisting pressure to conform from all sides. It has embraced this subordinated self-concept even more firmly in the face of the increasing attacks by the United States and Arab governments after 9/11. This drives a stubborn assertion of a distinctive Arab identity and discourse, and a refusal to "toe the line." Frustration and resentment at the political and economic stagnation of the region, at Western domination, and at Israeli treatment of the Palestinians permeates the public arena. Arabs define their identity in part against this sense of subordination and exclusion from a globalizing and universalizing Western public.

American policymakers generally failed to appreciate the significance of Arab public opinion or to engage with it seriously, and when they did take it into account it was only out of fear of overly provoking the so-called Arab street. This meant that from 1998 to 2001, the new Arab public sphere—for all of its dramatic internal publicity—produced what James Scott (1986) has called a "hidden transcript." The Arabs arguing about sanctions on Iraq or about the Palestinian Intifada did so knowing that Americans—the powerful—would largely not be listening, nor would they be participating.

The Arab public emerged as a counterpublic, self-consciously and intentionally challenging the dominant narrative and terms of discourse within American and global media. The Arab media consciously rejected a Western standpoint, and took upon itself the mandate of building Arab identity and political consciousness. More than one Arab journalist explained that they proudly took their Arab identity as a starting point, but that this in no way compromised their professionalism. And, they pointed out, American journalists who wore American flags on their lapels while reporting the war in Iraq were hardly in a position to criticize. Al-Jazeera prided itself on breaking the Western monopoly on news coverage, as well as on breaking the hegemony of state-dominated media in the region. Its reporting did begin from an Arab and Islamic worldview, covering the issues that mattered to Arabs and Muslims in a language that spoke to—and over time shaped and reinforced—their norms and beliefs. The impact of the new media has arguably been most deeply felt in the areas of identity, a phenomenon of some concern to those hopeful that it might instead promote liberal notions of democracy.

The relationship between a subordinate Arab public sphere and an American-dominated international public sphere suggests an analysis in terms of domination and resistance rather than dialogue. The conflicting demands of these multiple publics—the need to appear pro-American on CNN and Arabist on al-Jazeera—contributes greatly to the profound hypocrisy that has been so devastating to public discourse and legitimacy in Arab politics. Dependence on American power did not eliminate the Arabist discourse, but rather drove it underground and separated it forcefully from political practice. This generated a rich Arabist hidden transcript, an alternative, coherent, widely shared interpretation of political structures and relations that could not be openly aired or translated into practice because of the realities of weakness and subordination.

While the public transcript defines the mainstream of acceptable political debate among the elite, among themselves the subordinated talk about issues in very different ways. These hidden transcripts constitute entirely different understandings of power relations, moral values, and political interests. Much of what are seen as "conspiracy theories" fit within this general type of hidden transcript, thriving within a perspective of powerlessness combined with radical mistrust of official voices. It should not be surprising when Arab speakers aim for precisely the areas most likely to outrage the powerful—whether anti-Semitic slanders, assaults on Western ideals of democracy, or dramatic accusations about murdered Iraqi babies.

The transcript was not hidden from Arabs, obviously—indeed, the remarkable impact of the new Arab public sphere rested upon its bringing previously private political debates into the glaring light of publicity. What kept it hidden was that the dominant power, the United States, largely ignored this transcript prior to September 11, which allowed Arabs to carry on their public arguments largely without concern for American views or objections. One consequence of September 11 has been an end to this insulation. Hearing does not mean comprehension, however. When Americans heard Osama bin Laden for the first time, most found his rhetoric literally incomprehensible—laden with symbolism, history, assumptions, and references that resonated within Islamic public spheres but were totally alien to the American public. Those first Western sightings of the Arab public sphere produced breathless reports on "anti-Americanism," seemingly irrational "conspiracy theories," and "cultural hostility." Statements and political rhetoric that made perfect sense in one public sphere, tapping into well-established motifs and languages, seemed literally incomprehensible in others. Arabs could not comprehend how Americans could see themselves as innocents in the Middle East; Americans could not fathom why some Arabs considered the United States a legitimate target.

When Arabs heard American arguments for invading Iraq, they could not help but interpret them through a powerful narrative of Iraqi suffering. As competing narratives about Iraq consolidated, this problem of unintended exposure tended to exacerbate misunderstanding and conflict. Incompatible frames of reference render action within one discourse literally incomprehensible to the other. Words that resonated with an American public conditioned to hate and fear Saddam Hussein grated upon an Arab public that had for half a decade been more focused on Iraqi suffering and American unilateralism. The atrocities of September 11 can be seen as the violent eruption of this hidden transcript: not in the sense that al-Qaeda spoke for mainstream public opinion, but that bin Laden's self-presentation deliberately invoked the core themes of that public opinion in a bid to win Arab and Muslim popular support.

The October 2000 "airplanes challenge" to the Iraq sanctions offers another, less traumatic, example of an eruption of the Arab hidden transcript into the public realm. Since 1991 there had been almost universal adherence to a ban on civilian air travel to Baghdad. After an initial Russian and French probe had revealed the lack of international support for enforcing the flight ban, Jordan became the first Arab state to send in a flight. In the euphoric atmosphere that followed, virtually all Arabs celebrated, in a raw outpouring of joy, this open defiance of the sanctions regime. This emotion should not conceal the strategic dynamics of this episode, the cascade it set in effect, or its relation to the high politics of the Security Council. Still, it was *both* the act and the highly public celebration of the act that established its political importance. The airplanes challenge represented a "public refusal, in the teeth of power, to produce the words, gestures, and other signs of normative compliance. . . . When a practical failure to comply is joined with a pointed, public refusal it constitutes a throwing down of the gauntlet, a symbolic declaration of war" (Scott 1986: 203). Sending a civilian flight to Baghdad in open defiance of the United States, and escaping punishment, offered a rare sense of power, of liberation, of joy. One of the key dynamics this book sets out to capture is this symbolic battle, the interaction between strategy and rhetoric, between legitimacy and power. And it is in the hidden transcript, the coherent, vivid worldview constructed in these subordinate public spheres, where this alternative legitimacy is publicly constructed and measured.

Greater attention to the subordinate public by the powerful, as with the American discovery of the Arab media after 9/11, could be positive or negative. Following Habermas, I would argue that such a direct engagement and mutual awareness is absolutely necessary to reconcile Arab and American worldviews, and thus to make rational dialogue possible (Lynch 2002a, 2005). Greater interaction could also drive greater clash and conflict, of course, particularly when the powerful shows little interest in understanding the arguments of the weak. Either way, there is no question that from September 11, 2001, to the present the two public spheres have intersected and interacted in ways which they never had before. Surveillance, engagement, monitoring, pressure, and some tentative steps to dialogue directly challenged the Arab public sphere's enclosed nature. This generated even greater resistance among Arabs accustomed to arguing among themselves—anger, resentment at the intrusion on this enclave of Arabist argument. But it also empowered voices who had been either disenchanted with the conformities of the Arabist public sphere—the pro-American liberals, the secularists—as well as the losers in the Arabist debate, such as Kuwaitis and the Iraqi opposition.

Civility and the Quality of Public Discourse

Even those who admit the political significance of the new Arab media often object that the content and quality of Arab political discourse fall far short of Habermas's ideal of rational discourse. Arab critics have relentlessly attacked the rhetorical style of Arab political discourse. Mohammed Abed al-Jabiri's *Arab Political Discourse* and *The Formation of Arab Reason*, like Burhan Ghalyoun's *Assassination of the Mind* and other critical works, suggest the evolution over centuries of a deeply constitutive mentality that prejudices Arabs against rational-critical discourse. Arab thinkers, particularly those in exile through the 1980s, were brutal in their own dissection of Arab political discourse. Fouad Ajami's *The Arab Predicament* (1991) and *Dream Palace of the Arabs* (1999) dissected the pathologies of Arab political discourse, while Kanan Makiya's *Cruelty and Silence* (1995) bitterly traced the failures of Arab intellectuals to respond to Iraqi tyranny. Edward Said, from the opposite side of the political spectrum, routinely denounced the cowardice and opportunism of Arab intellectuals and the poverty of Arab discourse. And Asad Abu Khalil witheringly observes that "opinion in my country is bought and sold . . . [or] is for rent. . . . There is a sickness which ravages the body of the Arab press and Arab media."[39]

Such Arab critics, no less than their Western counterparts, bemoan the deficiencies of Arab political discourse, with its confrontational clashes of rigid ideologies and avoidance of self-criticism. The corrosive impact of decades of state pressures, censorship, and self-censorship should not be dismissed, but such caution should not deny to new generations the potential to fight against and transcend these legacies.

Americans most often object to the content and political orientations of Arab public discourse, along with the graphic and allegedly biased presentation of news. A particularly potent criticism focuses on the anti-Semitic content of the media, a concern amply supported by examples of hateful and stereotypically anti-Semitic images and arguments.[40] That such offensive imagery and rhetoric can be found throughout the Arab media is undeniable. But it is quite striking that such anti-Semitic discourse appeared far more frequently within the government-controlled media of Saudi Arabia and Egypt and in the tabloid press than in the elite Arab public sphere, however. Of the 976 al-Jazeera talk shows in my primary database, for example, there are only a handful that sound explicitly anti-Semitic themes: a February 3, 1999, *No Limits* episode on "World Zionism"; a September 13, 2000, *No Limits* program discussing David Irving's views on the truth of the Holocaust; an October 10, 2000, episode of *The Opposite Direction* devoted to similarities between Nazis and Zionists; a March 19, 2002, *No Limits* focused on the Protocols of the Elders of Zion. These were the exception rather than the rule, however. In the fall of 2002, Western and Israeli charges of anti-Semitism in the Arab media over the airing of a television serial based on the Protocols of the Elders of Zion on Egyptian television sparked serious discussion on al-Jazeera.[41]

In the quest for authenticity and identity, argue some Arab critics, the Arab public sphere valorizes authoritarian modes of discourse, celebrating the power of the state or the glories of the past. Progressive Arab critics fear that unleashing the Arab public will actually push, then, to more conservative political outcomes under the pressures of the tyrannies of the mob. Barry Rubin's dismissal of al-Jazeera as "critical of the incumbent dictators, but [wanting] to replace them with even more extreme dictatorial regimes" is unfair and simplistic, but does capture some of these fears (Rubin 2002: 259). The affinity between right-wing neopopulism and the mass media has been frequently noted (Calhoun 1988). By appealing directly to the masses in the name of a shared identity, and by attacking existing political systems as corrupt and useless, the new Arab media might structurally empower these populist forces rather than more liberal ones. Hazem Saghiyeh (2004) fears that "whereas newspapers were born, a century ago, as part of a wider project to modernise the Arabs, satellite television stations fundamentally seek to defend them, reinforce their prejudices, and tell them that they are right whatever they do."

The quality of debate on the talk shows reinforces these concerns (Fandy 2000: 387–389). The Kuwaiti critic Ahmed al-Rubai argues that "the rivalry between the Arab satellites leads to extremism. . . . Whether in the issue of sex or in the issue of pop songs, or in dialogues, there is no meaning to it and no goal other than sensationalism."[42] Al-Jazeera host Mohammed Krishan admits that "the long absence of dialogue makes it more conflictual at first. . . . Over time I think that we will be able to raise the traditions of dialogue."[43] Some Arabs attacked the new media for intensifying Arab conflicts. As the Egyptian analyst Mohammed Bakri argued in response to al-Jazeera's coverage of the Palestinian uprising, "al-Jazeera is playing a role with Arab contradictions that is not in the interest of a common Arab goal. . . . To the contrary, the station has raised doubts about Egyptian nationalism, accuses some of treason. . . . It allows Israelis into our house. . . . This serves Israel's goals. Israel wants to break the psychological wall."[44] Naif Karim, chair of the governing council of al-Manar, says: "There are very few stations that really deal with the issues of the Arab citizen and the Arab street and try to exert a positive influence far from intensifying the internal predicament of the Arab world and inflaming [its] internal problems."[45] Even al-Jazeera's defenders have worried of a development away from what might be called the CNN effect—immediate, objective news coverage of regional and world events—into something more like a "Fox effect"—politically partisan coverage, loud voices, and a preference for opinion over news—the spread of which may prove detrimental to critical public reason (see chapter 6).

Jon Alterman suggests that as the years moved on, the tone of the al-Jazeera arguments grew coarser, angrier, and more confrontational and began to reinforce rather than to break down old ways of thinking: "Instead of a voice for change and political courage, the TV stations and newspapers too often play to the galleries, legitimizing harebrained ideas and coarsening public debate."[46] Discourse became more defensive, more about resistance than about hopes for progressive change. While the same topics often reappeared—human rights, reform demands, democracy—the tone of the arguments was more bitter, more frustrated, and uglier. The United States increasingly became a central topic of debate, with programs such as "American plans for hegemony over the world" (*No Limits*, February 13, 2002), "America: What for it and what against it?" (*Opposite Direction*, July 15, 2003), "possibilities for resisting America" (*Opposite Direction*, September 2, 2003), and—most bluntly—"The American enemy" (*Opposite Direction*, June 12, 2001). At the same time, al-Jazeera covered American politics extensively, especially during the 2004 election campaign, and aired large numbers of speeches and press conferences by American officials.

Arab states often leveled accusations of a lack of professionalism on the part of al-Jazeera. This accusation must be read in the context of the norms of Arab journalism, and within the context of the determination of Arab states to maintain control over the public realm. Precisely because the satellite stations insisted on pushing the boundaries of debate, they inevitably violated the "red lines" that typically governed public discourse in Arab countries. Professionalism too often was a code word for political compliance. The Arab Broadcasting Union, for example, refused al-Jazeera's application while happily accrediting television stations that broadcast little but near pornography. Thus there did exist both true unprofessionalism and attempts by states to dismiss as unprofessionalism real attempts to push the boundaries of acceptable public discourse. As Wahid Abd al-Majid put it, many of al-Jazeera's problems came not from its free-spirited arguments but simply from sloppy or biased journalism—a charge al-Jazeera's journalists themselves fiercely reject (Miles 2005).[47] Mohammed al-Rumayhi, a fierce Kuwaiti critic of Saddam Hussein, dismissed Arab coverage of the 2003 Iraq war as being "closer to 'desire' than to 'reality.'"[48]

The Arab states have often viewed this new media as a threat. Almost every state has harassed or shut down the bureaus of independent satellite stations, banned circulation of independent newspapers, or arrested independent journalists. Even relatively liberal Lebanon in January 1997 introduced laws featuring prior censorship of news programmes and authorizing the blocking of "the transmission of any news or political item affecting state security," while Jordan issued a series of ever more restrictive media laws in the late 1990s (Sreberny 2001; Lucas 2003). When pro-Iraqi advocates managed to organize a rally outside the Iraqi embassy in Jordan, for example, the al-Jazeera cameraman was the first target of Jordanian security forces—the Jordanian government did not want to project an image of instability—or a pro-Iraqi image—or to attract undue attention to its repression of the rally (Schwedler 2003). In October 2002 the Gulf Cooperation Council passed a resolution boycotting al-Jazeera for "insulting" the Gulf. As Abd al-Aziz al-Khamis, a Saudi journalist, explained, "they are really afraid of [the satellites] . . . [because] they do not want real dialogue in Gulf societies. . . . Some of them want to stop free media in the Arab world from broadcasting controversy and dialogue. . . . They want no controversy and no dialogue and no discussion of events."[49]

Material Foundations

> The greater scandal will be in the oil coupons program and the names of those who benefited from it. . . . Iraqi and Arab citizens must know the motivations of those party leaders who went on satellite television defending the tyrant, and of those delegations that went to Baghdad in the name of solidarity with the Iraqi people and against the blockade.
>
> —Ahmed al-Rubai[50]

For many observers, the Arab media's biases in the Iraqi issue can be explained simply: "Scores of journalists throughout the Arab world and Europe were on Saddam Hussein's payroll" (Hayes 2004). This position was reinforced when Ahmed Chalabi's INC produced documents that allegedly showed vast payments from Saddam Hussein to Arab politicians and journalists over the past decade (Miles 2005). One attack against al-Jazeera involved documents alleging that station director Mohammed Jassem al-Ali had been on the Iraqi payroll and lead to his removal from his position in May 2003 (without admission of guilt).[51] An Iraqi newspaper, *al-Mada*, ran documents claiming proof that billions of dollars in lucrative oil vouchers had been distributed to a wide range of people across the Arab world, including journalists and politicians, with the Saudi-owned newspaper *al-Sharq al-Awsat* taking a particularly hard line against the Qatar-based station. Others attempted to prove, rather less convincingly, that the popular talk show host Faisal al-Qassem had relations with the Iraqi regime. In December 2004 the American satellite station al-Hurra broadcast a videotape allegedly showing al-Jazeera officials meeting with Uday Hussein.[52] But even those tapes were inconclusive at best: an obsequious meeting between al-Ali and Uday Hussein, which proved only that al-Jazeera hoped for access to cover events inside of Iraq; a similarly fawning encounter with a Syrian journalist who had no association with al-Jazeera; and an oblique reference to Iraqi approval of the hiring of Ahmed Mansour, a very popular and effective interviewer who would have been a desirable hire for almost any television station.[53] But the transparently political motivations behind these revelations made them difficult to evaluate. For the Iraqi opposition, in particular, these allegations—and the INC search for incriminating documents in the Iraqi archives after the war—were a crucial part of an ongoing campaign against the Arab media that will be described in detail in later chapters.[54]

There is little doubt Saddam's regime used financial inducements to influence Arab media coverage over the years, such as in alleged vast payments to Jordanian journalists.[55] At the same time, the influence of material foundations on the Arab public sphere go well beyond alleged Iraqi payments. By far the largest owner and financier of Arab print and broadcast media has always been Saudi Arabia, while other wealthy Gulf states such as Kuwait and Qatar have been widely active. Saudi ownership of the print and broadcast media (including al-Arabiya and MBC) is overwhelming, while the centrality of the Saudi market for most Arab advertisers gives it even greater indirect influence over media content. The Saudi owners of al-Arabiya replaced its management in early 2004 despite its success in competing with al-Jazeera, putting in a more pro-American editorial team even at the risk of losing market share. *Al-Hayat* and *al-Sharq al-Awsat* are owned by Saudi princes, while most Arab satellite television stations are owned by governments. Prominent independent commentators were often offered lucrative columns in Saudi-owned publications as a way of influencing their positions. In January 2005 a London court heard evidence that *al-Zaman*, a major Iraqi opposition newspaper published by Saad Baz-zaz, had begun with major Saudi financial support.[56]

Patronage clearly affected the content of particular media outlets. While their editorial lines and approaches differed dramatically from the traditional Arab media, none of the major stations was completely independent of state support. Al-Jazeera remains dependent on Qatari finances, as major advertisers steer clear for fear of offending Saudi or other Gulf markets. Saudi-owned publications and media consistently avoided touching on sensitive domestic topics in Saudi Arabia, just as al-Jazeera avoided dealing with internal Qatari politics. Even the few "independent" outlets, such as London's Arabist *al-Quds al-Arabi*, raise other suspicions.[57] Still, the diversity of the emerging media market mitigated against this problem. By watching and reading a variety of sources, as many participants did in the new Arab public, a generally rounded picture could be found.

Public Opinion Polls?

After the launch of the American Arabic-language satellite station al-Hurra, station director Muwafac Harb said that the reaction of Arab audiences would not be known until systematic opinion surveys had been conducted: "We go for scientific research. If [Egyptian commentator] Mustafa Bakri writes a piece, that is not a reaction."[58] This preference for public opinion surveys over public rhetoric is a common, and powerful, alternative conception of public opinion.

For many analysts, the absence of public opinion polls makes it pointless even to discuss Arab public opinion. From this perspective, the media—controlled by states and dominated by a compromised, unrepresentative intelligentsia—offers a distorted and controlled image of Arab opinion. State censorship and omnipresent security services intimidate independent voices. Where public opinion polling does exist, real questions arise as to the reliability and significance of its findings. Do questions posed to Iraqis in the aftermath of Saddam's regime and the American war genuinely capture authentic preferences? Are respondents offering "authentic" views or those they want their American interviewers to hear?

Public opinion polling has become far more common in recent years, however. Highly publicized cross-national polls in the Arab world by Zogby International, the Pew Foundation, and the Gallup Organization have shattered this conventional wisdom and have offered invaluable snapshots of mass attitudes (Tessler 2003). The Center for Strategic Studies at the University of Jordan established a public opinion unit in the early 1990s that runs both topical polls and an annual "Democracy in Jordan" survey. Jordanian governments had begun using private opinion surveys as early as 1989, when then–Prime Minister Sharif Zayd bin Shakir wanted to know how the kingdom's first elections would turn out. According to Mustafa Hamarneh, Abd al-Karim Kabariti's government (1996–1997) extensively polled Jordanian opinion, using private polls to help shape foreign policy, economic policy, electoral maps, and even local initiatives.[59] The al-Ahram Center in Cairo began public opinion polling in Egypt in 1998.[60] Iraq, under American administration, has been heavily surveyed, with polls carried out by the CPA, international agencies, and local Iraqi research centers. In the spring of 2004 the Saudi regime released a poll conducted the previous fall that demonstrated the growing popular appeal of al-Qaeda in the kingdom along with wide support for a change in policy. The poll was far more striking for the admission that the Saudi government carried out such surveys than for its findings.[61]

When published, these polls have often set off important public debates about sensitive issues, such as when a joint Jordanian-Palestinian poll explored the question of relations between the two groups. Mustafa Hamarneh, director of Jordan's Center for Strategic Studies, for example, was dismissed from his position after a survey found dramatically higher levels of unemployment than claimed by the government.[62] Another poll by the center showing that hardly anyone read many prominent columnists infuriated the humiliated pundits. Khalil Shikaki, director of the Palestinian Center for Research and Studies in Nablus, was harassed by an angry mob after publishing a poll that showed wider willingness to accept a compromise on the right of return than most had asserted (Umansky 2004). Tharya al-Shahri argues that many Arab journalists dislike public opinion surveys in the Arab context because they see them as easily manipulated and lacking objectivity, while states fear that they will undermine their legitimacy.

But, al-Shahri notes, opinion surveys do have the virtue of "empowering those who fear to speak out . . . [and thus] breaking the ability of extremists to claim that they represent the majority."[63]

Even in more propitious conditions, critics have identified systematic distortions introduced by public opinion polling (Bourdieu 1979; Herbst 1993; Lewis 2001). Such polls privilege the relatively uninformed—and often lightly held—opinions of a mass of people, while downplaying the opinions of motivated and better-informed activists. From this perspective, the absence of public opinion surveys might carry the unintended but real benefit of empowering the more engaged and politically motivated members of society over their more apathetic counterparts. I make a somewhat different argument in this book. To a remarkable extent, public opinion polls in the Arab world have tracked the public discourse in the new media. Rather than undermining the public sphere, or undermining its representative claims, public opinion surveys have powerfully reinforced the public sphere's influence. The findings of the Pew Global Attitudes survey of 2003 offered nothing new with respect to the fundamental trajectory of growing public hostility to the United States reported by area specialists. But only when the Pew survey put numbers on these trends was it taken seriously by the mainstream media, foreign policy think tanks, and the American government.

As I argue below, the convergence of the new media and mass attitudes is partly explained by the impact of news coverage and the widely viewed talk shows. But on a deeper level, the new public sphere has had an enormous effect in shaping the underlying narrative structuring how the Arab public understands events: the context, the stakes, the storyline, and their own identity.

Public Spheres and Political Strategies

Debates over Iraq or the war on terror often invoked a fear of—mixed with a contemptuous but wary dismissal of—the so-called Arab street (Lynch 2003b; Bayat 2003). In crude forms, these arguments revolved around whether the Arab masses would rise up in furious anger over a particular action and threaten friendly regimes; in more sophisticated forms, they asked whether rising anger and frustration would increase receptivity to radical appeals such as bin Laden's, which might provoke future terrorism. In both cases, the only "value" of Arab opinion lay in its potential for violence. Because Arab leaders can generally ignore or repress public dissent, many assume that Arab public opinion does not matter. But, as Shibley Telhami has pointed out, "Arab leaders act as though Arab public opinion matters" (1993: 439).

Realists remain justifiably skeptical: Arab states remain dominant and no regimes have been overthrown, and Arab governments have resisted popular pressure to act against Israel or to oppose the American invasion of Iraq. While the new public might have some relevance for domestic political struggles, the impact on major foreign policy issues seems more dubious. Burhan Ghalyoun argues that "there are no regimes today which pay attention to public opinion"; today's regimes, he argues, are "willing to engage in dialogues with the United States, with Europe, even with Israel—with anyone except with their own people."[64]

How, then, does public opinion matter? I suggest three ways in which the new Arab public sphere affects international politics: by changing the strategic calculations of rational politicians, by shaping worldviews, and by transforming identities. The bottom line is that while no Arab regime was forced to change its position toward Iraq by a mobilized public, every Arab regime formulated its policies within a set of assumptions, ideas, and beliefs that were conclusively shaped by the new public sphere. Even those who doubt the direct influence of Arab opinion on state policies tacitly admit its longer-term constitutive power. Concern over anti-Semitic and anti-American rhetoric in the Egyptian media, for example, only makes sense given the belief that such language poisons the background beliefs held by Egyptians, and that ultimately this matters. The Bush administration has argued with escalating regularity that anti-American Arab television has spurred violence, terrorism, and anti-Americanism in the region. But if it can matter in this pernicious way, then it must also potentially matter in other, more positive ways.

The emergence of the new Arab public sphere empowered a new kind of Arabism, one far more concrete and grounded in directly felt shared identity and interests than in the past. The new Arab public set the agenda for public debate across Arab countries, an agenda dominated by issues defined as core shared Arab concerns: Palestine, Iraq, and political reform. All Arabs—leaders and ordinary citizens alike—were forced to adapt to this agenda. The limitations of state responsiveness to the public sphere continued to frustrate critics such as Ragheda Dergham: "Most Arab leaders have picked up elements of this consensus and started playing with them to serve ulterior objectives. . . . The initiatives they come up with should not be designed merely to contain public feelings but to reflect them."[65] Still, it seems accurate to say that "Arabs have increasingly engaged in . . . discussions throughout the region that have served to shape government opinion instead of merely being shaped by it."[66]

My argument assumes that Arab regimes are strategic, rational, and not particularly motivated by Arabist convictions or ideals. They do, however, wish to win in a game whose stakes, rules, and meanings are increasingly driven by the new public sphere. As the transnational media gained prominence in the ways described above, these public debates increasingly established the background, "taken-for-granted" conventional wisdom of politics. Even the most self-interested, power-seeking Arab leader must engage with these broadly defined Arab interests in order to generate power. Arab states typically attempt to assert Arab leadership through demonstrations of effective support for popular causes. Opposition figures also often attempt to compensate for their lack of conventional political opportunities by leveraging this consensus. Seeking power therefore requires careful attention to trends in Arab opinion. When the perceived Arab public consensus shifts, rational leaders who wish to be politically successful must respond. If it were true that Arab states alone shape the content of this public consensus, then Arab public spheres might be dismissed as irrelevant, but the Iraq case demonstrates clearly that the Arab consensus develops independently of the preferences of states.

States competed to position themselves relative to this consensus, regardless of their "real" preferences, for both principled and pragmatic reasons. They did so not only because of a fear of an explosion of "the street"—they did so because this was the best way to "win" in Arab politics: by successfully defining self-interest in terms of Arab identity and collective interests. Their rhetoric, in turn, shaped the expected political payoffs of different concrete policy choices.

The public sphere therefore established expectations about the normative payoffs within which strategic actors maneuvered. In the case of Iraq, this meant adapting to a powerful public consensus on the need to alleviate the suffering of the Iraqi people. As documented in chapters 3 and 4, a flood of newspaper articles, television broadcasts, consciousness-raising campaigns, documentary films, and personal encounters with Iraqis shaped the perceptions of most Arabs. Beginning in January 1999, for example, the United States and United Kingdom maintained a steady bombing campaign against Iraq, to put pressure on the Iraqi military while remaining below the threshold of media attention. In the Western media, this strategy almost completely succeeded, as even attentive followers of the American media had little idea of the extent of this ongoing military action. In the Arab public sphere, however, this bombing campaign was a daily front page story, highlighted on al-Jazeera newscasts and featured in daily political discourse, generating the inescapable sense of ongoing American aggression against Iraq.

It is not the impact of a single story or a single event, but rather the impact of a constant stream of converging information from multiple sources that builds the conventional wisdom of society. Televised images of starving Iraqi children influenced Arab audiences, just as images of Kosovar refugees or starving Ethiopians galvanized Americans. Once the humanitarian crisis was introduced into the public sphere, the politics of the Iraq sanctions became a framing contest, a public argument to establish the conventional wisdom about the reality of the humanitarian problem in Iraq, the attribution of blame for that problem, and the appropriate response.

The key point here is that these public arguments have a constitutive impact *even if* leaders engage with them only strategically. The public consensus shaped expectations about what kinds of arguments would be positively received, and about what other actors were likely to do. This argument rests on a theoretical proposition drawn from social psychology literature: actors at least in part form their preferences and their expectations by surveying the cues in the discursive environment about how many others support a position, the costs of supporting that position, and the identity of those supporting each position (Schuessler 2000). Rhetoric serves as an indicator of how actors *expect* to be rewarded (or punished) for particular positions. The response of other actors provides information about how accurately actors have judged this background consensus, providing crucial information for all actors in evaluating this social environment. By speaking out against the sanctions the UAE, for example, came to be viewed as brave and authentically Arab, while the Arabist public increasingly vilified Kuwait as selfish and vindictive; all others learned from this experience. These cues about the social environment—the perception of consensus—then shapes the subsequent strategies of all actors, creating an ongoing recursive process of self-fulfilling dynamics. Siding with the perceived consensus offers "an enhanced public image in the eyes of others, who will be led to think better of them because of their publicly declared affiliation" (Mutz 1998: 209). In other words, Arabs in part came to oppose the sanctions because the signals in the media suggested that this is what *all* "good Arabs" believed.

Confusion about the strategic logic of public rhetoric abounds. For example, American leaders consistently argued that Arab leaders oppose their policies towards Iraq in public but are much more accommodating in private. Arab states faced with strong public pressure to support Iraq and strong private American pressure to support containment used "two voices," as they were "forced to resort to misrepresenting their private and public views."[67] The assumption that the privately expressed preference is more authentic than the public, and therefore will serve as a more reliable guide to behavior, is almost certainly wrong. If actors formulate their policies with an eye toward their beliefs about the beliefs of others, then they are more likely to follow their public than their private preferences absent some change in the public consensus. When Gerhard Schroeder rescued his 2002 reelection campaign by taking a strong position against war with Iraq, it told us little about Schroeder's private preferences, but quite a bit about how he perceives German public opinion on the subject. Given their consistent need to read public opinion to seek political advantage, then, what leaders say in public may be a more reliable guide to how they will act than what they say in private. This is the mistake made by U.S. Vice President Dick Cheney in March 2002, when he expected that Arab leaders would live up to the private opinions against Iraq rather than their public statements. Instead, he was met with a universal public rejection of the American position, as each Arab leader asserted in the clearest possible terms that they did in fact mean what they said.

The Arab Street?

The Arab street is dead. . . . It raised the banner of every lost or failed cause. It supported the dictatorship at home. . . . It was run by the authority's remote control. . . . It called for freedom but did not stand up for it when it was slaughtered right before its eyes. . . . We heard much talk but no action. . . . One million Americans, a million Britons, and other millions demonstrated against the war on Iraq. The Arab street still slept. How would it move when it is dead?

—Jihad al-Khazen, *al-Hayat*, December 27, 2004

Faced with the refusal of Arab states to take more than symbolic measures in support of the Palestinians even in the face of unprecedented popular mobilization in the spring of 2002, many Arab pundits joined American conservatives in declaring—yet again—the "death of the Arab street." On the other hand, the massive rallies that swept through the Arab world in April 2002 unleashed an outburst of exuberance about its revival that raised unrealistic expectations. Neither the dismissal nor the exuberance captures the complex role played by the "Arab street" in the politics of Arab public opinion. Protests played an important role in forcing the new Arab public onto the agenda of Arab states and of the West— whether massive protests at Cairo University against the invasion of Iraq, quietly intense protests against Hosni Mubarak's standing for a fifth term as president, marches of hundreds of thousands of Moroccans to protest the sanctions, tense standoffs between police and marchers intent on reaching the Israeli embassy in Amman, or wildcat protests against the sanctions in front of the Iraqi embassy in downtown Amman.

As with popular politics throughout the world, the Arab street needs to be placed within a wider conception of the Arab public's political role (Nabulsi 2003; Chatterjee 2004). The "street" is often invoked by actors on all sides: by regimes looking for an excuse not to act, and by opposition figures looking for a credible source of influence. Arab leaders thus invoked their fear of the street instrumentally:

"In private discussions with US government officials in late 1997 and early 1998, regional leaders frequently cited public opinion concerns to explain their reluctance publicly to support the use of force against Iraq, regardless of their distaste for Saddam Husayn" (Alterman 1999). Opposition politicians with a credible reputation for representing the street similarly can influence leaders by threatening popular uprisings. For example, Layth Shubaylat, a popular Islamist opposition figure in Jordan, warned that "anyone who contemplates Jordan taking part in a military offensive against Iraq should take into account the Jordanian peoples' reaction"—again, a warning of a threshold that will provoke violent popular reaction.[68] This is not so much a public sphere as an attempt to leverage the public sphere against state power.

Purposive, strategic protest behavior cannot be reduced to mindless rage or crude responses to state provocations. The new Arab public has dramatically changed the strategies and the potency of action on the "Arab street," shifting the target of protests and their reach, while allowing each protest—no matter how small or swiftly contained at the local level—to fit in to a wider Arab narrative of contentious politics (Tarrow, Tilly, and McAdam 2002).

Most invocations of the "Arab street" have a Nasserist model in mind, one in which mass riots can be summoned through incendiary political rhetoric. Arab public discourse has internalized the idea of the "Arab street," using it within its own argumentation as frequently as do Western observers. Enthusiasm for the Arab street dates both to the anticolonial struggles of the first half of the century and, even more, to the rowdy street politics of the Nasser era. Mustafa al-Fiqi claims grandly that "the street is in every country the true expression of public opinion."[69] Despite all its setbacks and shortcomings, he argues, the Arab street remains strong and influential—the force behind the (first) Intifada and the expression of anger over the sanctions on Iraq and the real power that expelled Israel from south Lebanon—and, empowered by technological changes sweeping the world, the "street" is growing even stronger despite constant affirmations of its death.

Baghat Korany similarly defends the use of the "street" concept for making sense of what people really think: "Subway conversations, letters to the editor, popular radio and television programs, repeated discussions with the oft-cited taxi driver. . . . [The street] is a rough barometer of spontaneous mass reaction in both democracies and non-democracies, especially in times of crisis."[70] Ibrahim Hamidi, by contrast, despairs that "there is no Arab street that is capable of expressing itself freely and able to influence government policy in any meaningful way."[71] But these should be analytically distinct: the failure of the "street" to affect policy says nothing of the actual existence of a "street" as an important location for public opinion (Bayat 2003).

The dominant model of the Arab street is as a threshold constraint, in which certain acts that violate public opinion on the Arab street can trigger violence. Arab leaders need to take into account the likely reaction of an inarticulate mass public when formulating their otherwise rational or strategic policies. The street rarely acts, but when it does the resulting riots can be devastating and can undermine regime legitimacy for a long time. This threshold model is adopted even by those who sympathize with Arab public opinion: "The massive waves of protests on the streets of the Arab world shows how wrong the Americans were to treat Arab public opinion with such contempt and disdain. The Arab public has served notice that there are indeed 'red lines' which the US mediators thought did not exist, or that they could ignore."[72] When the *New York Times* took notice of Arab public opinion in the context of war in Afghanistan, it naturally fell back on the threshold model: "The street, once all but powerless, has become a real force, exposed to more sources of information that repressive governments do not control, harder to rein in once inflamed, and more susceptible to radical Islam."[73] When analysts posit that "Arab public opinion . . . serves as a real constraint on Arab cooperation in schemes for the violent removal of Saddam Hussein," this model can be seen: though these leaders allegedly want Saddam gone, they see public support for his removal as a threshold likely to trigger the street and therefore forgo this policy.[74]

Regardless of the reality of such a threshold, it becomes politically real when Arab leaders adjust their behavior based on their anticipation of such a reaction. During times of crisis, Arab governments demonstrated their own conception of public opinion as a street that needed to be contained. Some even complained about the absence of demonstrators at times when they hoped to persuade the United States to ease its demands for public endorsements of its policies.

I argue in chapter 4 that the "Arab street" returned to life in 1998 with the protests against an American attack on Iraq in February and then against Operation Desert Fox in December. When those protests broke out, news coverage emphasized violence, and mobs—all indicative of this conception of a mindless, reactive, violent, irrational public opinion. Crucially, the Iraq protests did not come out of the blue, as an unpredictable reaction to a direct stimulus. They came after years of intense public arguments and a series of highly tense crises covered heavily by the emerging new Arab media. Within that public sphere, there was much discussion of the role the Arab street should and could play, as well as of the fecklessness of Arab leaders. As the crises came to a head, a sizable portion of the Arab public had already been closely following these public debates and the escalating events. When Arabs poured out into the streets they did so not spontaneously or irrationally, but with a consciousness of playing their role in the political drama playing out on television screens in unprecedented ways.

What Arabs Talk About

In October 2002 Kanan Makiya complained that "the spectrum unfortunately of what it is possible to talk about in Arab politics these days runs from Palestine at one end to Palestine at the other with no room for the plight of the people of Iraq."[75] Nothing could have been further from the truth. In this section I offer an overview of the contents of al-Jazeera talk shows as a useful proxy for "Arab political conversation." Al-Jazeera is far from the sole component of the new Arab public sphere, but it has been the most influential and the most widely viewed. Its talk shows often set the agenda for local arguments and debates, as well as reflecting the issues considered important among the Arab intellectual elite. And its talk shows have been far more free, controversial, live, and uncensored than those of most of its competitors.

The analysis draws on a set of 976 episodes of the five most important general interest talk shows appearing on al-Jazeera between January 1999 and June 2004.[76] In later chapters I present more textured descriptions of many of these programs, to get beyond the numbers, including chapter 5's discussion of the live call-in shows on al-Jazeera after the fall of Baghdad, an open and uncensored public discussion arguably representing the purest public sphere in Arab history.

Before content is examined, the names of the talk shows themselves offer interesting insights into the varied meanings and aspirations of the new public. Al-Jazeera's tagline—played between segments and repeated endlessly—is, famously, "The opinion . . . and the other opinion" (*Al-Rai . . . Wa al-Rai al-Akhr*). This slogan is less progressive than it might at first glance appear. "The Opinion and the Other Opinion" suggests the existence only of two competing, oppositional opinions, while also—crucially—suggesting that al-Jazeera's oppositional "other opinion" represents the voice of the people against that of power. Six major al-Jazeera talk shows suggest alternative metaphors for what al-Jazeera does—or might—stand for.

The first discussed here, Sami Haddad's *More Than One Opinion* [Akthar Min Rai], resembles the station's tagline, but with one crucial difference: rather than indicating an opposition between two discreet views, the phrase "more than one opinion" suggests a multiplicity of overlapping, contradictory, and potentially reconcilable opinions. But although it suggests an Arab public defined by pluralism of views, it says nothing about how those views might be reconciled. One might be imposed by force, another might be shunned, a third might be shouted down, a fourth might be excluded from the debate. Nothing about rational critical debate can be inferred from the existence of more than one opinion.

The second major program, *No Limits* [Bila Hadud], conveys the determination of the new media to push red lines and shatter taboos. During the period under study Ahmed Mansour's program focused more intensely on Palestine than did the other programs, and was far more open to anti-Zionist or even anti-Semitic guests and discussions. Such a transgressive mission can push in different directions, however. In the early days of the new Arab public, stultifying government control ensured a plethora of red lines preventing discussion of vital issues facing the Arab world: democracy, human rights, accountability, corruption, women's rights, and so forth. But as those taboos were broken and political dialogue normalized, the transgressive mandate of *No Limits* could easily tip over into sensationalism. The pursuit of graphic war footage, for example—what Mamoun Fandy has called a "political pornography"—reflects this transgressive urge.

The third major talk show is Faisal al-Qassem's *The Opposite Direction* [Al-Itijah al-Mu'aks], whose title suggests an orientation toward contrarianism, toward controversy for its own sake.[77] *The Opposite Direction* sought out polarized views, reveling in pitting opponents against one another and urging them toward confrontation with little effort to seek reconciliation or common ground. Qassem's style generated enormous controversy and resentment among those with whom he disagreed, or who felt mistreated in the course of the arguments. Tellingly, this program is far and away the most popular—and controversial—political program, not only for al-Jazeera but for the entire new Arab public (matched only by the Lebanese reality show Superstar). That contrarianism, rather than open dialogue, might mark the spirit of the new Arab public hints at the priority of political controversy over a commitment to democratic process.

Two other major talk shows, *Open Dialogue* [Hiwar Maftuh] and *al-Jazeera's Platform* [Minbar al-Jazeera], go beyond the existence of multiple opinions to define a process for their interaction. The phrase "open dialogue" suggests a Habermasian commitment to the public sphere, to open and free debate among all these multiple positions. The format of *Open Dialogue*, interestingly, differs from that of the other four major programs: Ghassan bin Jadu brings a panel of a dozen ordinary Arabs into the studio along with his guests, and gives them the chance to pose questions and participate in the conversations. Jumana al-Namour introduced the first episode of her program *Minbar al-Jazeera* on June 27, 2002, as "an open arena for dialogue," which "we hope will offer a window to all who hope to hear the interventions and opinions of all the followers of al-Jazeera, including the Arab elite, which loves to express its positions on Arab issues."[78] These programs offer a vision more closely aligned with that of the public sphere. Each began broadcasting in mid-2002, suggesting a shift in that direction. And they also tended to focus disproportionately on Iraq: during the month of April 2003, at the height of the war, virtually all of the other talk shows stopped broadcasting, while *Minbar al-Jazeera* went out nightly to discuss the most recent developments in the war—usually focusing on viewer calls rather than on in-studio experts.

Another major al-Jazeera talk show is very different from the first five: *Sharia and Life* [Sharia wa Hayat]. Where the first five programs explicitly address a universal Arab public defined by their shared identity and shared commitment to a set of common political issues, *Sharia and Life* explicitly addresses those Muslims who wish to make Islam central to their lives. While *Sharia and Life* often touches on political issues, it also spends considerable time dealing with social and religious aspects of Islam—religious interpretation, gender, education. The dominant figure on the program, Yusuf al-Qaradawi, has long represented a moderate strand of Islamism from within the Muslim Brotherhood tradition (see below). Qaradawi's immense popularity again suggests conflicting interpretations: on the one hand, it reinforces the creeping intrusion of Islamism into all aspects of Arab life; on the other, Qaradawi has for decades stood strongly against extremism and intolerance such as bin Laden's.

What Gets Discussed?

What gets discussed on these talk shows? They focus overwhelmingly on Arab concerns, and if extended to "Arab-Islamic" this focus becomes almost universal. Out of the 976 talk shows, only a tiny number deal with non-Arab/Islamic issues, and even those issues are often approached from an Arab perspective. Many of that small set deal with scientific or medical developments such as cloning (surprisingly topical, with at least four programs)—but the debates often invoke Islamic views or concerns about Western imperialism. Some attention is given to American or European elections, although even there the conversation often turns quickly to how the outcome will affect Arab concerns. As Egyptian analyst Magdi Khalil noted, "the Arab street is cut off from the international street in its concerns and its goals—globalization, the environment, human rights, unemployment, women's rights, freedom of religion, right to development."[79]

Of the "Arab" issues, three dominate. The first two are unsurprising: Palestine and Iraq. Palestine is central to Arab conceptions of identity and interests, and Palestinian issues have always been primary to Arab public discourse. This only increased after the outbreak of the Palestinian uprising in September 2000. As table 2.1 below shows, Palestinian issues went from 24.6 percent of programming in 1999 to over a third of all programming in 2001 and 2002. Iraq was the second most prevalent issue. From 1999 to 2001, this was a distant second—but clearly stood above any other conflict or single issue. In line with the American mobilization and then invasion of Iraq, it shot to the top of the list of Arab issues of conversation (44 percent in 2003)—but was not, even then, the single or exclusive topic of debate.

The third primary axis of argument in these talk shows is the question of reform. Almost every election in the Arab or Muslim received considerable attention. The intense focus on Iraq in 2003 crowded out discussion of a number of elections, however, cutting against the idea that the invasion would trigger more democratic discussion in the region. Among the elections ignored in 2003 were Syria's March Parliamentary elections, Yemen's in April, Jordan's in July, and Oman's in October. Referenda, the Charter Movement in Bahrain, the closing of the Egyptian Labour Party and the Turkish Fadila Party—all were deemed worthy of public discussion on one of the five major talk shows. Qatar's decision to postpone Parliamentary elections in 2001 did not receive coverage, however, strengthening the argument of those critics who saw al-Jazeera as a tool of Qatari foreign policy. Beyond specific elections, broad questions about "democracy and the Arab world," "the Islamist movement and democracy" (*Open Dialogue*, July 28, 2001), and "the accountability of rulers" (*The Opposite Direction*, July 3, 2001)

TABLE 2.1. Number of al-Jazeera Talk Shows Devoted to Palestine and Iraq, 1999–2003

	Palestine		Iraq	
	Number	Percentage	Number	Percentage
1999	33	24.6	13	9.7
2000	39	27.6	14	9.9
2001	56	34.4	14	8.6
2002	66	34.6	33	17.3
2003	31	13.1	104	44.1
Total	225	26	178	20.6

were routinely posed before and after the American invasion of Iraq. As early as August 2001 *No Limits* was debating the implications of "Western support for democratic reform in Syria."

Talk shows routinely took on the most basic foundations of the Arab status quo, challenging audiences to question even the most sensitive red lines. As Bashir al-Nafii put it, the focus was "not only the issue of war or peace with Israel, but how that confrontation reveals the wider deficiencies of the existing Arab order."[80] The March 5, 1999, *The Opposite Direction* asked whether this generation of Arabs might succeed at democracy where their fathers had failed. The May 10, 1999, *More Than One Opinion* looked frankly at the Israeli elections. The August 31, 1999, *The Opposite Direction* asked how the perennial states of emergency in the Arab states could possibly be justified. The June 27, 2000, *The Opposite Direction* asked about the

TABLE 2.2. Elections Discussed on al-Jazeera Talk Shows, 1999–2004

Israel	January 1999
Algeria	January 1999
Israel	May 1999
Kuwait	June 1999
Tunisia	October 1999
Iran	November 1999
Iran	February 2000
Egypt	July 2000
Lebanon	August 2000
United States	November 2000
Lebanon	November 2000
Israel	February 2001
Iran	May 2001
France	May 2002
Algeria	May 2002
Morocco	October 2002
Bahrain	October 2002
Israel	January 2003
Kuwait	July 2003
Mauritania	November 2003
Iran	February 2004

commitments of the "new Arab wealthy." The July 19, 2000, *No Limits* asked about the state of women's rights in the Arab world. The January 1, 2001, *The Opposite Direction* asked whether the Palestinian Intifada was "a waste of time." The March 27, 2001, *The Opposite Direction* looked critically at the Taliban's destruction of the great Buddha statues. The June 11, 2002, *The Opposite Direction* mocked the 99.99 percent electoral victories of Arab presidents. The July 11, 2002, *Minbar al-Jazeera* took on the spread of AIDS in the Arab world. And, most cruelly, the March 7, 2003, *The Opposite Direction* asked, "why have Arabs become the joke of the world?"

Few countries escaped the scrutiny of al-Jazeera's talk shows, although some were covered more heavily than others. Many responded with considerable hostility to these unusually frank and open discussions, considering their airing to be an aggressive act. Morocco received considerable attention, in part because of interest in the ongoing Western Sahara conflict—and responded as early as April 1999 by shutting down al-Jazeera's operations in the country. Egypt deported Faisal al-Qassem's brother, a popular singer. Algeria—with its elections, mass violence, and Berber conflict—was the topic of no less than twenty shows; in July 2004 President Bouteflika finally responded to attention deemed unwelcome by shutting down al-Jazeera's Algerian offices, and in one remarkable instance cutting power to the city of Algiers to prevent citizens from watching a particularly inflammatory program. Jordan shut down al-Jazeera after a guest talked about King Hussein's long-standing ties to the United States and made several uncomplimentary remarks about the late monarch.[81] Lebanon and the Sudan received a surprising amount of attention, again likely because of their turbulent political situations. Qatar received little attention, as al-Jazeera's critics often noted, but other small Gulf states such as the UAE and Bahrain received little more. Kuwait banned the station for a month in 1999 for comments critical of the emir by a caller, and closed the al-Jazeera offices in November 2002 for being "not objective."[82] Israel attacked al-Jazeera in June 2002 for "spreading hatred." Bahrain criticized al-Jazeera in May 2002 for "insulting Bahrain and the Bahraini people." The Palestinian Authority closed al-Jazeera's offices in March 2001 in protest over its coverage. As one witty person suggested at one point, al-

Jazeera risked becoming the first Arab station to not have offices in any Arab country!

Islamist Publics

Contrary to reckless allegations about al-Jazeera's being some kind of "Jihad TV" or "on-line madrassa," the new Arab public sphere, given its ever-greater centrality to Arab public life, actually under-represents Islamism. The beautiful, unveiled anchorwomen of al-Jazeera—to say nothing of the steamy music video clips of Nancy Ajram, Haifa Wehbe, and others that dominated the popular entertainment satellite channels—profoundly challenged Islamist notions of gender and correct behavior (Mernissi 2004). While a thorough examination of Islamist public spheres is outside the scope of this book, it is important to recognize the parallel existence of Islamist publics that are often quite distinct from—even insulated from—the mainstream. These Islamist publics had their own publications, including mass circulation pamphlets, magazines, and newspapers. As Jon Anderson puts it, "ideas and issues circulated in intellectuals' books a generation ago are now found in popular chapbooks and on street corner newsstands" (Anderson 2003). They also relied on the dissemination of cassette sermons, by which popular preachers could reach large audiences. Islamists have not generally focused on television, with the recent exception of Hezbollah's al-Manar, preferring to cultivate their own alternative media zones. But Islamism has developed its own counterpublic, an increasingly pervasive parallel sector with its own language, its own terms of reference, and its own priorities.

As Charles Hirschkind (2001) argues, this Islamist counterpublic has pioneered its own media forms, including very cheap pamphlet books and cassette sermons. This Islamist public sphere has shifted from a national to a transnational focus over the last two decades, with matters of shared concern to Islamists—from Palestine to Chechnya—becoming central to local political discourses. At another level, information technology has scaled up the Islamic *umma* (community), facilitating mediated dialogues over the Internet on issues ranging from correct Islamic practice to the validity of Osama bin Laden's invocation of jihad (Mandaville 2001; Bunt 2003). These electronic networks, as with cassette sermons, have transformed the relationship between diasporas and homelands, giving substance to the abstract concept of an Islamic community (Roy 2004). This new media "opened up new spaces of religious contestation where traditional sources of authority could be challenged by a wider public," while at the same time driving a kind of "media Islam" or "soundbite Islam" open to political mobilization (Mandaville 2001: 70).

Iraq—or more specifically, the suffering of the Iraqi people under sanctions—was a key part of this new Islamist counterpublic. This did not derive from any sympathy for Saddam Hussein's regime. Islamists always had a tense and confrontational relationship with his Baathist regime because it was explicitly hostile to Islam, especially as Iraqi rhetoric cast its war with Iraq as one of defending secular Arabism from the threat of Iranian Islamic fundamentalism. The Muslim Brotherhood, which thrived in almost every Arab state, was ruthlessly repressed in Iraq. But Iraq nevertheless played a pivotal role in the parallel development of Islamist movements in this time period. The ongoing sanctions on Iraq provided a crucial unifying theme, as Islamists and Arabists could agree on condemnation of the unjustified misery of the Iraqi people.

After the Gulf War, Islamist movements focused their attention on the misery of the Iraqi people, without strongly supporting the government of Saddam Hussein. Reports on the suffering of Iraqi children and civilians became a regular feature of the Islamist newspapers, Web sites, and sermon cassettes circulated throughout the Arab world. As demonstrated by Osama bin Laden's inclusion of the Iraq sanctions on his list of major complaints against the United States, Islamist parties raised the suffering of the Iraqi people into a touchstone issue for demonstrating Islamic credibility, using transnational and domestic networks to spread information and to mobilize in support of the Iraqi people. Iraq became a staple in the Islamist mosques, with innumerable collections of charitable contributions, books, and clothes for the suffering fellow-Muslim people. A more perfect vehicle could scarcely be devised: the suffering of an Arab-Muslim people inflicted with the cooperation of repressive Arab rulers in the interests of the United States and Israel. While this took place outside the mainstream Arab public sphere, it intersected at key points and in ways of clear importance to the wider questions at hand.

Even as Islamist movements have been thwarted in their bids for political power—either through violent means or through electoral participation—they have gained increasing influence over the content and style of public discourse throughout the Middle East. On the one hand, Islamists have developed their own virtually autonomous counterpublics, based in mosques and cassette sermons and an astonishing amount of cheaply priced and widely disseminated pamphlet literature. On the other hand, Islamists have assumed an increasingly hegemonic role over permissible public argument and speech.

The Egyptian case offers perhaps the most striking—and widely noted—example of this Islamist war of position. The Egyptian government ceded a great deal of control over media content to the Islamic conservatives at al-Azhar University. Over the course of the 1990s, a conservative Islamic discourse permeated the official Egyptian media, casting something of a pall over cinema and television productions. The assassination of the secular critic Farag Fuda in 1992 seemed to show an even darker threat behind the Islamist intolerance of critical discourse. The Egyptian state's antiterrorist offensive in the 1990s placed even tighter boundaries on acceptable public discourse, ostensibly in response to the Islamists but often simply to protect an increasingly intolerant and unpopular regime. Islamists launched cultural offensives against novels by, among others, feminist Nawal al-Saadawi (*Fall of the Idol*), Naguib Mahfouz (*Geblawi's Children*), Haydar Haydar (*A Banquet for Seaweed*), and Ahmed al-Shahawi (*Wasaya fi Ashiq al-Nisa*). In 2004 the Egyptian government greatly expanded al-Azhar's power to censor and ban publications.

The problems were not limited to Egypt. In Jordan, which prides itself on being pro-Western and tolerant, three journalists from a weekly newspaper were arrested in January 2003 for an article deemed insulting to Islam.[83] Muslim Brotherhood campaigns against poets Ibrahim Nasrallah and Musa al-Hawamdeh for demeaning Islam led to the latter's conviction. Yemeni Islamists campaigned against Muhammad Abd al-Mawla's novel *Sanaa: An Open City*, with Shaykh Abd al-Majid al-Zindani of the Islah party denouncing journalists and defenders of the novel as "apostates."[84] Kuwaiti Islamists forced some 300 books to be banned from the November 2000 annual book fair, as well as the cancellation of a concert by a popular Lebanese singer, and in 2004 forced an already conservative minister of information to resign over "scandalous" appearances by popular Arab singers. Bahraini Islamists sparked a political crisis over the filming of an Arabic version of "Big Brother" for the LBC satellite television station.

Too many Islamists have turned their project into a means to close down public debate and discourse. Arab and Islamic public spheres have witnessed a powerful wave of Islamist efforts to impose censorship of the media, to tightly control the bounds of legitimate public discourse, and to threaten, prosecute, or even kill those found to have "offended Islam."

While Islamist discourse has become increasingly dominant in national publics, it has been suprisingly less central to the new Arab public. Islamist voices are regularly heard, but outside their own media outlets they do not occupy a hegemonic position. Yusuf al-Qaradawi's hugely popular program on al-Jazeera advances an Islamist understanding of all aspects of life, but it occupies a singularly anti-bin Laden position within the realm of intra-Islamist argument. Al-Arabiya promotes a range of "moderate" Muslim voices and routinely criticizes radical Islam. The same can be said of the major pan-Arab newspapers. Al-Sharq al-Awsat features a number of fierce critics of radical Islamism, while al-Quds al-Arabi's most prominent Islamist writer, Abd al-Wahhab al-Affendi, is a moderate Islamist who has also been fiercely critical of bin Laden.

While sometimes serving al-Qaeda's media strategy, al-Jazeera and the new Arab public sphere are in fact a powerful rival to the radical Islamist project. Al-Qaeda and other radical Islamists use the media effectively to transmit propaganda, and benefit from the rising anger and outrage generated by televised wars and images of Arab suffering. Al-Qaeda sent tapes to al-Jazeera and al-Arabiya because they provided access to a wide audience, and those stations generally aired them, for their news value and as a way of attracting audiences. But few radical Islamists participate in the talk shows on these stations, and few of the hosts sympathized with their agenda. Al-Jazeera and the new Arab public exemplified a commitment to public dialogue and reason, an insistence on opening all issues to contentious debate that was deeply at odds with the radical Islamist agenda of propagating a single, unquestionable truth. For example, when al-Jazeera broadcast an exclusive video from al-Qaeda second in command Ayman al-Zawahiri in May 2005, it presented it in the form of a dialogue, with liberals and moderate Islamists invited to respond point by point to Zawahiri's arguments.

Qaradawi, the most prominent Islamist face of al-Jazeera, was an avowed moderate committed to public dialogue and openly antagonistic toward bin Laden (Baker 2003; Lynch 2005). Qaradawi drew on a powerful but often neglected critical strand of Islamist thought that takes dialogue as a foundational point for its social theory and practice. These "New Islamist" thinkers hold up a counterfactual ideal of *hiwar*—dialogue—as a preliminary move toward overcoming these pervasive failings of Arab public reason. Many of the problems of the Islamic world, according to Abd al-Wahhab al-Affendi (2002), can be explained by the fact that Islam's normative commitment to public reason has too often been subordinated to politics and the imperatives of power. Indeed, the distinctions drawn by New Islamists such as Tariq al-Bishri between *hiwar* and other forms of exchange such as *jadal* [argument] and *sira'a fikri* [intellectual combat] echo Habermas's distinction between communicative and strategic action (Baker 2003: 43). These Islamists have criticized the closed, intolerant neofundamentalist Islamism associated with bin Laden's network.

Qaradawi has long been an outspoken advocate of dialogue: "Islam is a religion of dialogue, and the Quran is at its base a book of dialogue."[85] He asserts that "all Muslims believe in dialogue, because we are commanded to do so by the Shari'a, and the Quran is full of dialogues between the prophets of God and their communities, and between God and his slaves, and even between God and the Devil."[86] He takes to task those "extremists [who] pretend that there are no points of agreement between us and the Jews and Christians." Indeed for Qaradawi, the first indication of extremism is "bigotry and intolerance, which make a person obstinately devoted to his own opinions and prejudices. . . . Such a person does not allow any opportunity for dialogue with others. . . . [This] attitude contradicts the consensus of the Islamic community, that what every person says can be totally or partly accepted or rejected" (Qaradawi 1981/2002: 199).

But for all his commitment to dialogue, Qaradawi remains intensely focused on the ways in which Islamic openness might be exploited by a West that "seeks to destroy Arab and Islamic civilization" and to keep the Islamic world living in fear of its power.[87] Qaradawi may be a democrat but he is not a liberal. His fundamental orientations are to the social Islam of the Muslim Brotherhood and toward spreading a conservative Islamic way of life and way of thinking. While his orientation toward dialogue makes him a powerful proponent of a public sphere, this should not be misread as a commitment to liberal outcomes. For many critics, his pervasive influence on al-Jazeera suggests a wrong turn taken by the new Arab public: a turn away from liberalism and to something more populist, more conservative, more consumed by questions of authenticity and identity.[88]

3

The Iraqi Challenge and the Old Arab Public

In the aftermath of the first Gulf War, Arabs grappled with a set of profound interlocking questions. How could the Arab order have failed so horribly? To what extent did Iraq continue to pose a threat to its neighbors? Should international efforts be made to remove Saddam Hussein's regime from power? If so, how could Iraq's territorial integrity be guaranteed? What could—or should—be done to reconstruct the shattered official Arab order? What role should relations with the United States play in this order?

While some of these debates spilled out into the media, they were primarily intra-elite arguments, carried out in private, and only tangentially driven by publicity. The arguments that mattered took place at the official level, within the Arab League or the Gulf Cooperation Council, in private diplomacy between governments, at the United Nations, in consultations with Washington. Real arguments took place but in private, far from public scrutiny or participation.

Arab leaders as well as Americans had little reason to believe that public opinion would be especially significant to these debates. Arabism in this period seemed to most observers to be in deep decline. The Gulf War had shattered the Arab order and rendered the Arab League moribund, while the peace process divided Arabs in new ways. The massive street protests against the Gulf War were genuinely new for most Arabs, as protestors from Morocco to Yemen could see each other on CNN chanting the same slogans at the same time.

For all the emotional power of this new recognition of the existence of an "Arab street," however, there was also a widespread recognition that this "street" had failed to sway Arab governments. While Arab regimes might summon the ghost of the street to support their own bargaining positions, or on occasion refrain from provocative actions to avoid domestic unrest, on balance states dominated society. Only Islamism posed a serious challenge to these states, and Islamism through the early 1990s focused primarily on domestic political and social issues in most Arab countries rather than on wider Arab international concerns such as Iraq. In short, Arab states pursued their interests in a broadly realist manner in this period, even as public opinion began to mobilize and converge in unprecedented and unexpected ways.

With regard to my argument about the importance of the new public sphere, chapter 3 tells a negative, counterfactual story: what Arab politics toward Iraq looked like in the absence of the new public sphere. Arab states acted in a realist fashion, except where local conditions intervened, such as in Jordan (Lynch 1999). But even without satellite television, changes were taking place—including both the liberalization of domestic publics and emerging communications and information technology—that facilitated a growing popular consensus on the tragedy of Iraq. Word began filtering out about the human suffering under sanctions—especially in Jordan and in the small neighboring Gulf states, where direct contact with suffering Iraqis through legal and illicit trade networks bypassed a relative media blackout. Word then began to be spread by activists, even if this was not yet a fully fledged social movement. Public discussion in the more liberal domestic medias began to seep into the more mainstream publications and media, reshaping the terms of everyday public debate. Their efforts prepared the ground, establishing a conventional wisdom, so that when al-Jazeera brought the story to a mass public, they were receptive, ready to hear it because the stories "rang true."

The introduction of this identity-based humanitarian narrative radically transformed the incentives facing strategic actors as well as more principled ones. Before this shift, the Realpolitik of Arab states and the high-politics focus on Saddam Hussein, the invasion of Kuwait, and weapons of mass destruction pushed public discussion toward pragmatic questions of various strategies of containment. As the salience of the humanitarian crisis increased in Arab concerns, ambitious elites who hoped to win public approval had an entirely different set of incentives. Finding some way to rescue the "suffering Iraqi people," ending the "blockade," came to be seen as a core concern for any authentic Arab, and the failure to do so a key proxy vehicle for criticizing the performance of Arab regimes. The humanitarian frame also reversed the normative valence attached to supporting American policy. In the early 1990s, support for the containment of Iraq and Israeli-Arab peace agreements had been seen by some as courageous and novel, but as attention focused more and more on the human costs of the sanctions they tended to be seen instead as cheap opportunism, if not moral obtuseness. Awareness of the moral weight attached to the sanctions is crucial to understanding the political potency of a critique that combined identification with suffering Iraqis as fellow Arabs and blaming Arab regimes for their plight.

As described in chapter 2, the half-decade after the Gulf War represented a transitional period in the development of the Arab public sphere. Many key technologies emerged in this time—satellite television, electronic distribution of pan-Arab newspapers—but the public (defined in terms of arguments) remained relatively inchoate. Local politics and a domestic print public sphere took precedence over wider Arab issues such as Iraq or even Palestine. The emergence of these domestic publics had a paradoxical effect on the Iraqi issue. While more liberal media allowed for more open discussion of such issues, as well as for more activism and civil society organization, these newly open publics tended to focus political attention and discourse on long-suppressed local politics, while downgrading regional issues such as Iraq. Over time, however, popular concerns about the sanctions and the wider problem of Iraq began to intersect with wider concerns about Palestine and about domestic repression. Iraq and the Palestinian issue, in particular, served as extremely effective focal points for unifying otherwise highly diverse opposition movements: in Jordan and Egypt, for example, actions in support of the Iraqi or Palestinian people routinely attracted support from Islamists, Arab nationalists, conservative nationalists, liberals, and more. Islamists, in particular, were adopting a more international focus in response to their defeat at the local level. The decline of the Israeli-Palestinian peace process after the 1996 election of Benjamin Netanyahu helped to generate a renewed sense of crisis, which in turn encouraged worried regimes to clamp down on public political action. A series of crises between the United States and Iraq, including airstrikes in 1993, 1994, and 1996, punctuated this increasingly tense situation, although Arab public reaction did not reach the levels that would be seen in the later years of the decade.

As the decade ground on, Arabs protested the official inaction of their regimes in the face of these crises. These protests took place not only in the streets, but increasingly in political salons and in various kinds of media. Temporary press openings in many countries in the early 1990s offered the opportunity for many activists and commentators to publicly discuss the Iraqi issue, which (outside of Kuwait) increasingly meant discussing the impact of the sanctions and the injustice of the status quo. The Iraq story was given substance by opposition political parties and civil society activists, whose travels to Iraq and publicizing of their experiences there made Iraqi suffering viscerally real to elite Arab audiences.

Opinion change in this period, I argue, originated either in face-to-face personal experiences or else within these emerging domestic print public spheres, rather than with states (most of whose leaders prioritized relations with the United States and continued to fear Saddam's Iraq) or with the broader masses (which were far less exposed to information about Iraq). Where state policies changed, it generally came in response to the recognition of the suffering of a fellow Arab people rather than from actual pressure from below. Shaykh Abdullah bin Zayid of the UAE, for example, between 1992 and 1995 changed from staunch supporter of sanctions to critic, not because of the pressure of public opinion but because of his own empathy with the Iraqi people.[1] Yemeni president Ali Abdullah Saleh similarly argued that "it is our duty as brothers in the Arab and Islamic countries . . . to take all necessary steps to ease the severe suffering of the Iraqi people and take a courageous stand to end the sanctions. It is very sad that scenes of misery and suffering of Iraqi children, elderly persons and women which were caused by the sanctions are shown on television . . . which makes it very hard to keep quiet."[2]

Over time, public concerns about the suffering of the Iraqi people began to crack the insular private deliberations of the ruling elites. As they did, this public began to pose different, troubling questions that anxious regimes would have much preferred to avoid. Why did the Arab world fail so miserably to either resolve the Iraq-Kuwait crisis or to resist the American intervention in the region? How were Arab regimes able to so thoroughly ignore a massively mobilized Arab street? Why would—or could—the Arab order do nothing to help the suffering Iraqi people? As the decade wore on, the Iraqi issue was increasingly conflated with the Palestinian one, not only as an example of a suffering Arab people but also as a symbol of the failures of Arab regimes and their refusal to act on the will of the people.

It took time for the Arab public to prioritize Iraqi suffering. Still consumed with the divisions wrought by the Iraqi invasion of Kuwait, and understandably obsessed with the developing peace process with Israel and on the challenge posed by rising Islamist movements, few Arabs had time for Iraq's internal problems. To the extent that Iraq was an issue for the elite print public, the focus was on the Security Council, weapons inspections, and ongoing raw wounds between Iraq and its Gulf neighbors. Kuwait—and to a lesser extent Saudi Arabia—stood firmly against any rehabilitation of Saddam's regime. With this Saudi/Kuwaiti veto on Arab reconciliation with Iraq firmly in place, pragmatic Arab regimes saw little reason to discuss it, to the distress of an emerging Arab public.

Television helped shape opinion by broadcasting powerful images of Iraqi suffering, but in general remained tightly controlled by states or by Saudi owners and offered little opportunity for public debate about the sanctions. The Western media, such as CNN, said little about the sanctions, while for several years state-run Arab television stations did little more. An early exception to this television silence came in February 1994, when Qatari television broadcast a four-part program "highlighting the effect of sanctions on ordinary Iraqis, a welcome break with the refusal of most GCC states to allow such information to be publicized."[3] This documentary caused something of a sensation throughout the Gulf. As Akeel Sawwar observed, "I do not believe people stayed up late in Bahrain debating the sanctions documentary . . . just because of its even-handed and professional production. Rather, their reaction reflects Bahrain's and the Gulf's hunger for a diet other than that offered by CNN. . . . The enthusiasm which the Qatari program generated among the Bahraini people was akin to a referendum on the sources of knowledge available to us, and the results were not in favor of CNN. . . . The outcome of the 'referendum' also shows that the Bahraini and Gulf 'street' is concerned about happenings in Iraq and rejects the picture projected by 'the guided media.' "[4] Kuwait protested bitterly over the documentary, recalling its ambassador to Qatar and formally protesting to the GCC, while the Kuwaiti press denounced the program as "slanderous and distorted." The contrast in the public response to a seven-part Saudi documentary on the Gulf War—which downplayed the effect of sanctions and focused far more on Saddam's evils—broadcast by the MBC satellite station in early 1997 could not be more stark. Unlike the Qatari program, this one largely sank without a trace; few Arab viewers seemed interested by that point in another recitation of the "official" version of the Iraqi story.[5]

Whether in response to audience interest or because of shifting state policies, Arab television stations did begin broadcasting more and more footage of the humanitarian situation in Iraq in the mid-1990s. This usually came in the form of news coverage, without extensive analysis or discussion, but the cumulative impact of the images was devastating. This coverage, however, was not a public sphere as I have defined it. For all the emotional impact, and for all the support the images might have given to social protest against the sanctions, television in this period did not provide a forum for arguments, for disagreements, or for criticism of the political status quo.

The Arab press, by contrast, not only covered the suffering of the Iraqi people but also generated an elite public sphere around the issue by presenting real arguments and a variety of views about the sanctions. This had both the virtues and the drawbacks of a press-centered public: arguably more attention to reasoned arguments and careful thought instead of emotion, but much less mobilizational power and only very indirect influence over state policies. The major Arab newspapers, including the London press as well as the major national dailies, perceived themselves as part of a common argument and discussion, addressing common Arab issues before a common Arab audience while often responding directly to one another—in other words, this was a transnational print public sphere that predated the al-Jazeera revolution.

The London-based *al-Quds al-Arabi*, founded in 1989 and rising to prominence during the first Gulf War with its outspoken opposition to the American-led war largely absent from the other state-run or Saudi-owned media, wrote frequently and passionately about the sanctions.[6] Other London-based Arab papers, such as *al-Hayat* and *al-Sharq al-Awsat*, tended to follow the line of their Saudi owners against Iraq, but even there coverage and criticism of the sanctions began to break through. Unlike in the controlled electronic media, the press offered real disagreement and argument. *Al-Hayat* published numerous essays by both sanctions critics and supporters, with the argument generally staying within the mainstream of official opinion—i.e., rarely challenging the Arab states or the validity of the weapons inspection process itself. *Al-Quds al-Arabi*, while critical of the sanctions and of American policy toward Iraq, routinely published articles by Iraqi dissidents who criticized the Iraqi regime on human rights grounds.

In the newspapers of Jordan and the smaller Gulf states (especially Qatar, the UAE, and Bahrain), open arguments raged about the sanctions and the need for Arabs to find some solution to the crisis. Egyptian and North African newspapers also covered the Iraqi story heavily, again with an emphasis on the human toll of the sanctions. In May 1997 the Bahraini writer Hafez al-Shaykh marveled at the "extremely silly idea" that "some people still believe, even now, that public opinion in the Gulf can be persuaded to turn a blind eye to the agonies of the Iraqis resulting from the sanctions."[7]

Initially, the Iraq issue resonated very differently in these various domestic public spheres. The Jordanian public, for example, saw the issue of Iraq as a rare moment of unity between the regime and the people, and the occasion of great shared sacrifice, and did not hesitate to say so in its relatively free press. The regime's strategic decision to curtail its relations with Baghdad as part of its renewed alignment with the United States and Israel strained this popular unity and contributed directly to the crackdown on public freedoms in that period. The Egyptian press swung between the haughty Realpolitik of *al-Ahram*, which continued to scold Iraq for its behavior, and the sensationalist exposes of Iraqi suffering and official Arab perfidy that dominated the tabloids. In Kuwait, continuing fury with Iraq expressed in its relatively free media and Parliament constrained a regime that at times seemed inclined to move toward a rapprochement for strategic reasons. Popular Kuwaiti anger at Jordan, for example, was so great that the Kuwait government reportedly refused American pressures to compensate the Hashemite Kingdom for lost Iraqi oil subsidies in exchange for a Jordanian role in overthrowing Saddam.

Over time, however, these discordant local narratives began to converge around an increasingly clear Arab popular consensus. The two driving forces were growing horror and outrage over the impact of the sanctions on the Iraqi people, and growing frustration with American and Saudi/Kuwaiti intransigence on the Iraqi file. The emerging transnational media made it easier for Arabs to see common concerns and actions in other Arab states, helping to link them together in a common protest. Arab elites increasingly found themselves in agreement that the Iraqi situation could not continue as it had been going, even if they could not agree as to whether for themselves this meant supporting an aggressive bid to change the Iraqi regime or moving to end the sanctions. At the mass level, stories of Iraqi suffering fit into a common narrative increasingly focused on the United States—with the sanctions on Iraq coming to be equated with American policies in Palestine. This established the baseline against which most Arabs experienced the military confrontations and crises that increasingly marked the Iraqi issue.

While the reality of Iraqi human suffering became a consensus, this did not lead to any agreement—even among the public, much less among states—on what should be done. Given an American policy seen as intransigent and implacably opposed to any real changes, and a widespread belief in the inability of most Arab states to defy American policies, the consensus on the injustice of Arab suffering led to anger and paralysis rather than to any clear plan of action.

It should again be emphasized that this emerging consensus did not prevent considerable dissent and disagreement in the Arab press. The Saudi-owned press, including *al-Hayat* and *al-Sharq al-Awsat*, published a full array of columnists who justified and supported a tough line against Iraq. In July 1993, for example, Abd al-Rahman al-Rashed warned that "lifting the Iraq sanctions now would be seen by Baghdad as a green light to go to war again."[8] Kamaran Karadaghi at one point warned that Iraq "had become a victim of its own propaganda. . . . It tried to persuade [others] that the lifting of the sanctions was in sight and ended up deluding itself," and at another warned sanctions critics that "by challenging the embargo against Iraq they are encouraging aggression and dishonoring themselves."[9]

Many blamed Saddam for the suffering of his people, and took the new concern for them as offering greater urgency for regime change. And the sheer rage felt by Kuwaitis and members of the Iraqi opposition at an unsupportive majority, and their alienation from Arab public opinion, knew no bounds. As one angry Kuwaiti wrote in 2002, "The Arab street did not go out in support of Kuwait when it was occupied by Iraqi forces . . . but it went out supporting Saddam Hussein! In truth I can't trust the Arab street."[10]

Sanctions

> How we wish that humanitarian considerations would also figure into their calculations. . . . Ordinary Iraqis have been impoverished by the sanctions. . . . One thing is certain, that no child of a senior official has gone hungry or had to forgo medical treatment because of the embargo, which gives the lie to the assertion that the sanctions are aimed at the regime and not the people.
>
> —*al-Quds al-Arabi*, November 1993[11]

The Arab public grappled with several interrelated aspects of the Iraqi issue. As noted above, over the course of the 1990s the sanctions on Iraq took on ever greater centrality in Arab public debates. While this section cannot offer a comprehensive overview of the sanctions regime, it attempts to put the Arab arguments into some context.

After the Gulf War ended, the United Nations placed Iraq under comprehensive sanctions that would stay in place until it complied with a set of demands that included the full disclosure and disarmament of its weapons of mass destruction programs (Graham-Brown 1999; Lynch 2001). Most observers expected that these sanctions would quickly bring down the Saddam Hussein regime, and would then be lifted. When Saddam survived post-war uprisings by brutally slaughtering Shia and Kurd rebels the sanctions became institutionalized as a seemingly permanent fixture of the Middle East equation. Their impact on the Iraqi people became evident early on, which initially was generally seen as a sign of success in the effort to undermine and challenge Saddam Hussein's regime rather than as a problem.

As early as March 1991, Under-Secretary-General Martti Ahtisaari reported that "the recent conflict has wrought near-apocalyptic results upon the economic infrastructure"; a follow-up report by Sadruddin Aga Khan expanded on these findings and urged massive humanitarian intervention (Rowat 2000). By 1993, disturbing reports began to filter out of NGOs and UN agencies about the impact of the sanctions on the Iraqi civilian population, including malnutrition and the near collapse of the public health system. The Inter-Agency Standing Committee of humanitarian NGOs began to study intensely the impact of sanctions. Reports by the FAO, UNICEF, the International Committee of the Red Cross, Save the Children, and others painted an increasingly coherent picture of a humanitarian crisis that could not be dismissed as Iraqi propaganda. A 1997 FAO/WFP report found serious deficiencies in the oil-for-food program, including continuing malnutrition, insufficiently balanced diet authorizations, deteriorating agriculture, and severe deterioration of water and sanitation.[12] A 1999 UNICEF report documented escalating malnutrition, child mortality and morbidity, illness, and the breakdown of the educational system, with galvanizing effect. The conclusion by one of the authors of the UNICEF report that "half a million Iraq children have died because of the sanctions," though disavowed by the report's majority, was repeated widely in the Arab media.[13] So was the blunt resignation speech of UN Humanitarian Coordinator for Iraq Dennis Halliday, who told the world, "We are in the process of destroying an entire society. It is as simple and terrifying as that. It is illegal and immoral."[14]

The growing impact of a seemingly endless sanctions regime, and popular fury over the escalating crises surrounding the UN weapons inspections, increasingly forced public opinion onto center stage. Arabs experienced the collapse of Iraqi society under sanctions both directly and vicariously, through the media as well as through stories from migrant workers (in Egypt and North Africa) and the increasing presence of impoverished Iraqi expatriates in the streets (in Jordan).

Stories of impoverished families selling their possessions, babies dying for lack of medicine or infant formula, and untreated water carrying disease began to appear in the Arab press—particularly when United Nations workers or other Western reporters offered supporting data. The Iraqi regime encouraged these reports, providing access and information to reporters who spread the news, but this did not minimize the reality of the humanitarian crisis. Particularly vivid images, endlessly repeated, had a defining impact. For example, a televised procession through Baghdad of thousands of taxis with small, baby-sized coffins tied to their roofs on their way to a symbolic mass burial is an image that few who saw it could ever forget. This reporting framed the issue around the suffering of the Iraqi people, who were a fellow Arab people whatever the faults of their leadership, and pushed political differences as well as the memories of the invasion of Kuwait aside. The consensus that emerged was the result not of the impact of a single story or a single event, but of the impact of a constant stream of converging information from multiple sources.

The consensus did not appear of its own volition, of course: Arabs on all sides of the Iraq issue worked to shape public opinion to their advantage. As the Duelfer report on Iraq WMD concluded, "Saddam's primary goal from 1991 to 2003 was to have UN sanctions lifted, while maintaining the security of the regime."[15] Iraqi officials openly explained that their strategy was to erode the sanctions from below by encouraging Arabs to stop honoring them, since they could never hope to have the sanctions officially lifted by an American-dominated Security Council. By generating the perception that all Arabs opposed the sanctions, the Iraqi regime aimed to spark a self-fulfilling cascade, "through which expressed perceptions trigger chains of individual responses that make these perceptions appear increasingly plausible through their rising availability in public discourse" (Kuran and Sunstein 1999: 685). Iraq hosted countless "popular conferences" for foreign activists and scholars and trade shows for products that it could not yet legally buy, and heavily publicized every visit by a foreign businessman or politician, every statement of support by a foreign government, every demonstration against the sanctions in a foreign or Arab country, every criticism of the sanctions in the UN. Sympathetic Arab commentators picked up on any signal they could find of the imminent lifting of sanctions, pushing for ways to shape expectations in such a way as to generate a self-fulfilling prophecy.

Opponents, in turn, attempted to deflate such expectations by asserting that the United States would not allow sanctions to be lifted under any circumstances. Their success in arguing this point created perverse incentives for what I call "rhetorical free riding." The Clinton administration's credibility was not the issue. Because most Arabs were fully convinced of the American commitment to inflict harm upon Iraq, few questioned the belief that the U.S. would do anything it could to maintain the sanctions. At the same time, Arab leaders did not believe that the United States was serious about regime change, especially after it failed to support the 1991 uprisings and allowed its collaborators in a 1996 coup attempt to be slaughtered by Iraqi forces. This combination—the relative certainty that Saddam would remain in power and that the sanctions would remain no matter what, and the popular unhappiness with the humanitarian and political impact of the sanctions—made talk seem cheap, and encouraged ambitious politicians to indulge in strong rhetoric with little fear of their demands actually being met. This seemingly cheap talk, however, fueled the shifting background beliefs that slowly transformed the strategic environment.

Iraq's adversaries, including Saudi Arabia, Kuwait, and parts of the Iraqi opposition in exile, and not a few other Arab regimes in private, initially denied the reality of the humanitarian crisis and subsequently blamed it on Saddam Hussein. Iraq's friends, on the other hand, blamed America for the sanctions, and demanded their immediate and unconditional lifting. Most Arabs occupied a middle ground of distaste for Saddam Hussein and his regime but a conviction that the sanctions were morally indefensible and bereft of any international legitimacy. They opposed American-imposed regime change, but were ambivalent about the existing regime. They appealed to the legitimacy of the UN Security Council, but were outraged that American manipulations of the council and the UNSCOM weapons inspections process gave Iraq little hope of ever escaping the sanctions. Whatever the faults of Saddam Hussein, the sanctions demonstrated the corruption and failure of the existing Arab order, and the illegitimacy of most existing Arab regimes. Sanctions became an ideal wedge issue that seemed to fully embody the juxtaposition of an embattled, divided Arab people struggling against the United States, Israel, and complicit Arab regimes.

Growing Dissent

By the fall of 1994, dissatisfaction with the sanctions was widespread within the Security Council as well as within the Arab world. Even Arab realists not particularly inclined to support Iraq had begun to worry that Iraq's weakness was emboldening Iran, while also worrying that an Iraqi collapse under the pressure of sanctions might create highly disruptive spillover effects. Many simply wanted to put the Iraq divisions behind them and remove this potentially explosive issue from the mix.

Salama Ahmed Salama, reflecting the emerging view of the Egyptian foreign policy elite, argued that "three years after a war which destroyed the old Arab order without toppling the Iraqi regime or resulting in the emergence of a new Arab order . . . Arabs must seek new ways of bringing Iraq back into their ranks . . . [even though] the US and Britain seek to keep the Gulf war rift among Arabs alive."[16] And, warning that "by insisting that the UN sanctions are kept in place indefinitely and maintaining a posture of intense hostility and hatred to all things Iraqi, the Kuwaitis are fueling a sense of deep resentment among ordinary Iraqis that could come back to haunt them long after Saddam is gone," Riyadh al-Rayyes urged Kuwaitis not to let their passions get in the way of their interests.[17] At the end of June 1994, Gamal Mattar argued that current trends "suggest that the countdown to the lifting of the international siege of Iraq has started."[18] Such Arab pragmatists seemed increasingly reconciled to the easing of the sanctions, and were increasingly critical of Kuwaiti intransigence.

To dampen such expectations, in May 1994 (and again in October) U.S. Secretary of State Warren Christopher stated that "frankly it's not feasible for Saddam to comply (with UN Resolutions) and remain in office."[19] Martin Indyk described the American goal as "to establish clearly and unequivocally that the current regime in Iraq is a criminal regime, beyond the pale of international society and, in our judgment, irredeemable."[20] Christopher's successor, Madeleine Albright, repeated this position on the sanctions in March 1997.[21] That Saddam himself came to believe this is suggested by a letter sent to Saddam by his European envoy Barzan al-Tikriti. According to this memo, after meeting with numerous European and Arab leaders, Barzan found "a near consensus that even if Baghdad complied in full with all the UN resolutions relating to the sanctions regime, the embargo on Iraq will not be lifted as long as the present regime remains in power."[22] As if to confirm this sense, Iraq's November 1994 recognition of Kuwait had little impact, despite Russian, French, and Chinese suggestions that this might allow them to more effectively argue Iraq's case. Arab critics used instances such as this to loudly question whether there was anything Iraq could do that would lead the sanctions being lifted.

By early 1995, pressure to ease the sanctions on Iraq had developed to a near-fever pitch. Russia and France both publicly expressed their impatience with the sanctions and their skepticism about American objectives and arguments. China, not usually a state that took the lead on Iraq issues, declared that "given recent developments, the international community should now consider the gradual lifting of sanctions against Iraq so as to ease the Iraqi people's sufferings."[23] The divergence between American policy and the mandate expressed in Security Council resolutions had become a central theme of public debate. At the same time, public discourse suggested that the international community must respond to the humanitarian crisis regardless of Iraqi compliance or noncompliance with UNSCOM. Tareq Aziz made a major push in the days before the March 1995 sanctions review, meeting with all council members except the United States and United Kingdom to push for an end to the sanctions on the basis of full Iraqi compliance. After a fierce debate, however, the status quo was maintained, to the considerable frustration of Iraq and much of the Arab public.

It was in this context that the United States pushed for an "oil-for-food" Security Council resolution to respond to the humanitarian concerns that were undermining support for the sanctions without giving up the core components of the pressure on Iraq. American officials readily admit that Arab public opinion was the primary reason for the passage of the Oil-for-Food resolution.[24] As Under-Secretary of State for Political Affairs Thomas Pickering explained to the U.S. Senate, "without the oil-for-food program . . . the Iraqi government would continue to exploit the suffering of its people to force the international community to lift sanctions. . . . The oil-for-food program is the key to sustaining the sanctions regime until Iraq complies with its obligations."[25] National Security Adviser Sandy Berger's explanation that "we have a moral duty to [feed the Iraqi people]" rang false after the United States had spent years rejecting any recourse to humanitarian arguments with regard to the sanctions.[26] That the Clinton administration had been forced to accept the legitimacy of the humanitarian critique represented an important victory for transnational activists and, to a lesser extent, Arab public voices who had long struggled to bring such issues to the forefront (Lynch 2001).

Security Council Resolution 986 represented the minimum necessary to maintain the status quo of the sanctions, and also offered substantial benefits in terms of providing funds for the compensation committee, the administration of the Kurdish areas, and UNSCOM operations. The unanimous passage of the resolution on April 14 allowed the United States and United Kingdom to attempt to shift the burden of responsibility for the humanitarian problem onto Saddam Hussein's regime (or, later, the United Nations). Initially, the Iraqi regime decided to reject the resolution in the hopes of winning a total lifting of the sanctions, arguing that "it is quite clear to the members of the Council that the United States did not intend in pushing this resolution to help alleviate the humanitarian hardships of Iraq."[27] In June Iraq launched another round of lobbying to ease the sanctions, calling on Russia, France, Germany, Turkey, and others to take the lead.

The passage of the oil-for-food resolution, and Iraq's initial refusal to accept its terms, posed a significant challenge to Arab public opinion: to support a program that might alleviate Iraq's human suffering, or to support Saddam Hussein's political strategy. Arab argument was encouraged by internal disagreements within the Iraqi regime about the resolution's merits, and reflected real uncertainty as to whether the interests of the Iraqi people would be best served by implementing the resolution or by holding out for the complete lifting of sanctions.

In general, Saudi, Kuwaiti, and other hawkish commentators cheered the passage of resolution 986, assuming that Saddam would reject it and thereby place himself in confrontation with his own citizens. Resolution 986 seemed to be a no-lose proposition: either the

humanitarian crisis would be alleviated, reducing the demand for easing containment, or else Saddam could more credibly be blamed for
the suffering because of his rejection of the program. Either way, "the
attempt to provoke international public opinion to lift the embargo
will [now] not succeed."[28] 986, by this argument, would respond to the
real humanitarian concerns without handing Iraq a strategic victory.
Members of this group tempered their enthusiasm with the possibility that oil sales might "create practical and psychological momentum
that is bound to have long-term influence on the eventual complete
return of Iraqi oil to the markets."[29]

More dovish Arabs seemed genuinely torn between the potential
opportunity to help the Iraqi people and the Iraqi political demand
for the total lifting of the sanctions. Fear that the American strategy of
using "oil-for-food" to deflect pressure to lift the sanctions would succeed was compounded by Iraqi complaints about the substance of the
resolution. Since all oil revenues would go not to the Iraqi government
but to a UN escrow account, "oil-for-food" suggested direct Western
control over Arab oil. In all, Arabs sympathetic to Iraq welcomed resolution 986 for its recognition of the needs of the Iraqi people and were
hopeful that it would improve their condition, but remained deeply
skeptical of American intentions.

The late summer 1995 defection of one of Saddam's key military aides,
Hussein Kamel, and his revelations of systematic Iraqi deception toward
UNSCOM, took the wind of out of the sails of efforts to lift the sanctions.
Commentators, perceiving that the end of the Saddam regime might be
imminent, began to openly speculate about the best future for Iraq. The
idea of a Hashemite restoration was mooted—mostly by Jordan—and
rather quickly dismissed by more powerful Arab players. Almost all Arabs rejected any role for the American-backed opposition. Arab intellectuals identified ethnic federation schemes, preferred by much of the
Iraqi opposition in exile, with presumed Israeli interests in replacing
strong, centralized Arab states with weaker, ethnically defined entities.
Most neighboring states feared the potentially destabilizing effects of a
weak or collapsed Iraqi state. Finally, most everyone—the United States
included—worried that such a decentralized or divided Iraq would invite Iranian expansion into the Shia-dominated areas of Iraq and would
remove the main check on Iranian influence in the Gulf area.

The overwhelming sense of this debate was real uncertainty—the defection disoriented what had become a fairly well-entrenched set of positions. Most agreed that Kamel's revelations made the lifting of the sanctions unlikely, in contrast to the general expectation prior to the defection that lifting was inevitable. Indeed, some Arab commentators immediately assumed that Kamel's defection was an "American masterstroke" executed precisely because the sanctions were about to collapse.[30]

In February 1996, amid this blocking of moves toward reconciliation, increasingly vocal Jordanian hostility, and rapidly deteriorating internal conditions, Iraq agreed to begin negotiations on the terms of implementing the oil-for-food resolution. These talks set in motion a quick debate among both Arab camps. Sanctions supporters now worried that Saddam might be able to exploit clauses in resolution 986 if it went into practice. Concerned that Saddam might be able to spin it as a victory and thereby generate a pro-Iraqi bandwagon, they now emphasized the limits of the oil-for-food program, even if this paradoxically supported the Iraqi claim about its inadequacy. Sanctions opponents worried that the resolution had been carefully crafted to maintain American pressure on Saddam and would harm longer-range Iraqi interests, but generally welcomed an agreement because it would provide much-needed relief to the Iraqi people.

In the end, Iraq's agreement on May 20, 1996, to implement the oil-for-food program produced rare consensus between the two camps, although they welcomed it for different reasons. The creation of the oil-for-food program altered the strategic and normative environment dramatically. While the program contributed significantly to improving the lives of the Iraqi people, it strengthened Saddam Hussein's internal position and gave him considerable leverage with the outside world through his ability to negotiate contracts and to distribute lucrative oil vouchers.[31] As the Duelfer report on Iraqi WMD concluded, "OFF rescued Baghdad's economy from a terminal decline created by sanctions. The Regime quickly came to see that OFF could be corrupted to acquire foreign exchange both to further undermine sanctions and to provide the means to enhance dual-use infrastructure and potential WMD-related development."[32]

Shortly after Iraq accepted the resolution, U.S. Defense Secretary William Perry revealed that the United States, Jordan, and other regional actors were working "to accelerate the demise of the regime in Iraq."[33] Many Arab analysts wondered why these groups were speaking so publicly about their regime-change activities, since this would seem to reduce their prospects of success. One answer, suggested by Ragheda Dergham, was that they were attempting to provoke Iraq into a foolish act that would again undermine its international support.[34] Either way, regime-change talk deflated when a coup attempt led by the Iraqi National Accord's Iyad Allawi (later interim Prime Minister) failed spectacularly.[35]

On October 2, 1996, Iraq used a UN General Assembly debate to again argue that it had met all the conditions for the sanctions to be lifted.[36] Tareq Aziz repeatedly declared that Iraq had done everything required by the UN resolutions and demanded that Iraq be declared in compliance and the sanctions be lifted. But in sharp contrast to the widespread expectation in 1994 that the sanctions would inevitably soon come to an end, it now seemed that all the major players, including the United States and Iraq "were content to keep both Saddam and the UN embargo in place" indefinitely.[37]

Throughout this entire period, the United States proved sadly deaf to the changing Arab attitudes toward Iraq. In part this was due to a focus on states rather than on a public opinion assumed to be both hostile and ineffective, and in part it was due to the higher priority of American domestic politics, where no policy toward Iraq could possibly be too tough. The Clinton administration failed to recognize the significance of rising Arab hostility to the sanctions until it was too late, leaving Americans to wonder how the United States had possibly lost a moral argument with a mass murderer (Pollack 2002). American diplomats could argue all they wanted that the dying babies on Arab television sets were Saddam's fault, or that there weren't as many as he claimed, but these arguments carried little weight compared to the horrifying pictures coming out of Baghdad.

Mobilization Beneath the Surface

To this point, I have focused primarily on the high politics of the Iraqi issue in the 1990s, with the Arab public playing only a minor role in

the analytical narrative. While this accurately reflects the overall balance of forces, the narrative above also suggests that Arab public opinion toward Iraq was evolving in this period. This happened differently
in various Arab countries, with mobilization beneath the surface of
events. Over time, these various national mobilizations increasingly
viewed themselves as a coordinated movement. While planes carrying humanitarian goods and political activists to Baghdad had very
little material impact on the circumstances of the Iraqi people, they
graphically focused attention on the contradictions and human costs
of a strategically motivated sanctions regime. Looking at several specific countries will help to flesh out the picture of how these domestic
publics dealt with the Iraqi issue.

Jordan was the epicenter of mobilization on behalf of Iraq. With
both massive economic interests at stake and important bonds of
identity, Jordanian politics was often dominated by disagreements
over Iraq policy; as noted above, the governments of Abd al-Karim al-
Kabariti and Ali Abu Ragheb rose and fell upon the former's anti-Iraq
profile and the latter's closer relations with Baghdad.[38] In September
1998, forty-seven (out of eighty) members of Parliament signed a non-
binding resolution calling on Jordan to stop honoring the sanctions,
and in December fifty-three representatives backed a similar resolution.[39] Support for Iraq was based not only on the very real economic
interests of the Jordanian state, but also on deeply held dimensions of
Jordanian national identity—mobilized by a wide range of civil society actors in the vibrant Jordanian public sphere of the early 1990s.
Liberalized press laws allowed a plethora of independent newspapers
to emerge, many of which published extensively on the sufferings of
Iraqis under the sanctions. Since support for Iraq extended deep into
the heart of the Jordanian regime, even the government-dominated
daily press published a large number of pieces in support of Iraq.

Jordanian public support for Iraq had deep roots. During the 1980s
the economies of the two countries became tightly interlinked, while
Saddam reportedly cultivated ties with many Jordanian journalists
and politicians. After the Iraqi invasion of Kuwait in 1990, popular
committees formed throughout the kingdom to support Iraq and to
prepare to defend the country in the case of an Israeli incursion into
Jordan on route to Iraq. The Committee to Defend the Nation, com-

prising activists at the popular level (political parties became legal only in 1992), linked the defense of Iraq to the defense of Jordan, articulating this as a single national issue. The leftist political party *Hashd* published a weekly newspaper, *al-Lajna al-Shaabiya,* which publicized the activities of the popular committees and issued some directives.[40] In May 1991 the Higher Committee to Defend Iraq brought together some three dozen popular figures and national personalities, establishing branches in all of the kingdom's governorates and collecting funds to distribute charitable contributions to Iraq. These activities tailed off in 1996, after the Iraqi government became reluctant to accept charity because of the beginning of the oil-for-food program and its preference to force the lifting of the sanctions.

Jordan's peace treaty with Israel signed on October 26, 1994, also shifted the strategic environment (Lynch 1998/99). As it built relations with Israel and grew closer to the United States, Jordan ostentatiously turned against Iraq in 1995. King Hussein gave a series of emotional speeches complaining of Saddam's treachery and arguing for an urgent need to bring the Iraqi stalemate to an end in the greater interests of the Iraqi people and the wider Arab order. Because of Jordan's importance to the Iraqi economy, its switch to the anti-Iraq camp harmed Iraq materially and signaled a decisive switch in regional expectations. Immediately after the signing of the treaty, President Bill Clinton toured the Gulf to hold discussions about Iraq, endorsing the GCC hard line, urging Gulf states to take a more proactive role in lobbying the Security Council, and warning against Arab slippage on enforcing the sanctions.

Jordanian Prime Minister Abd al-Karim al-Kabariti had staked his political fortunes on his ability to translate his highly unpopular turn against Saddam into generous Saudi and Kuwaiti compensation. But neither proved forthcoming, and in August 1996 serious disturbances broke out in the southern city of Maan. Frustrated over the failure of the American regime-change efforts it had so publicly backed and by the unfulfilled promises to secure Gulf oil to replace Iraqi oil, Jordan looked to rebuild its relations with Iraq. In March, King Hussein removed Kabariti from office in favor of more Iraq-friendly politicians, and renegotiated oil and trade protocols with the Iraqi regime. That these moves received tremendous popular acclaim graphically demonstrates the extent to which Jordanian public opinion remained impervious to attempts to change attitudes toward Iraq from above.

The professional associations, the primary civil society organizations representing the politically frustrated Jordanian middle classes most exposed to the new media, were extremely active on the Iraq issue even before 1998. In addition to holding regular political rallies and making statements, the associations collected charitable donations and offered functional expertise on behalf of the Iraqi people.[41] Bassam al-Dajani, a former president of the associations, explained that the associations had always been very active on the Iraq issue, collecting charitable donations, food, bread, and medicine. According to Dajani, these programs to help Iraqis enjoyed very wide support: "We collected a lot, but it was just symbolic. . . . What could we do, really, for a big country like Iraq? It was a drop in the sea, but it made for good feelings."[42] According to numerous activists, the Committee for the Defense of Iraq was one of the most active political committees of the professional associations. The government responded defensively to popular mobilization, periodically banning proposed rallies and pro-Iraq activities, and blamed Iraq for riots in summer 1996 which virtually everyone else attributed to economic and domestic political complaints.

In December 1998, in the face of the U.S.-U.K. bombing of Iraq, Jordanian activists formed the National Mobilization Committee for the Defence of Iraq with a more political than humanitarian mission. The NMCDI included both independent personalities and representatives of political parties, professional associations, unions, and popular organizations, and established branches in every governorate in the kingdom. Sulayman Arar, the first head of the NMCDI, and Hakem al-Fayez, who replaced Arar after his death, were senior Arab nationalist figures who lent stature to the efforts.[43] This offered a broad front; according to Hamza Mansour, Secretary-General of the Islamic Action Front, who served as the committee's vice president, "we cooperate with everyone with no problems—Arab nationalists, communists, centrists, liberals, women's groups—everyone who cares about Iraq. . . . For us, issue #1 is Palestine, issue #2 is Iraq, these two above all others."[44] The NMCDI, in coordination with antisanctions groups in other Arab countries, pushed for Arabs to unilaterally cease honoring the embargo.

Outside the NMCDI framework, popular committees in support of Iraq also formed in a less coordinated, grassroots fashion among activists frustrated with the shortcomings of the political parties.[45] In October 1999 these groups launched a coordinated campaign against the sanctions, the most prominent aspect of which was a large-scale pencil drive that ultimately collected 3.5 million pencils and generated great excitement among schoolchildren and ordinary people. A petition drive collected 171,000 signatures: "the goal of the campaign is to unite public opinion against the sanctions and encourage the conscious defiance of the embargo."[46] In September 2000 the committee began the Iraqi Book Campaign, collecting scientific and academic books to highlight the intellectual effects of the embargo and to rebuild Iraqi academic life.[47] The NMCDI also sponsored peaceful protests, conferences, visiting speakers, and art showings, while also issuing a regular stream of press statements and declarations. The coalition of eleven Jordanian opposition parties regularly included the Iraqi sanctions in their joint declarations, calling for "a strong popular movement to end the Arab countries' sanctions on Iraq and to open their borders to supply its people."[48]

Yemen also saw considerable activity against the sanctions and vocal expressions of solidarity with the Iraqi people. Like Jordan, Yemen refused to join the Gulf War coalition in 1990–1991, earning it considerable hostility from Kuwait and punishment by the United States. And as in Jordan, Yemen witnessed popular demonstrations on behalf of Iraq before and during that war. The Yemeni media covered the humanitarian impact of the sanctions heavily, with a broad consensus across the political spectrum supporting lifting the sanctions. While Yemeni Baathists had some role in coordinating these protests, a wider sense of identification with the Iraqi people transcended political lines. In a country struggling with unification and then civil war, such a rare point of consensus is not to be dismissed lightly.

Individuals and groups in Bahrain, Qatar, Oman, and the UAE also engaged in extensive mobilization against the sanctions. Each sent numerous ships loaded with food and medicine to Iraq in the mid-1990s, with the UAE the last to do so, in February 1996. In January 1997 the UAE sent its first official humanitarian mission to Iraq to great public approval, taking over $400,000 in charitable donations through a widely publicized campaign.[49] In May 1997 a regular shipping line between Iraq's port of Umm Qasr and the UAE was established to carry medical supplies, food, and humanitarian assistance—although the UAE was at pains to emphasize that sanctions violations would not be tolerated. A Kuwaiti professor lecturing in an unidentified Gulf state was shocked in early 1994 to be "rebuked by people attending one of his lectures who demanded a lifting of sanctions 'for the sake of the innocent children of Iraq.'"[50]

Societal activism in Egypt began in 1993, "as the price of the sanctions started to become clear, as people began to learn and understand what was happening in Iraq."[51] Egyptian opposition parties, like their counterparts in Jordan, regularly issued joint statements and held rallies calling for a lifting of sanctions.[52] These efforts were again led by NGOs, political parties, professional associations, the media, and activists, while the government tolerated, if not actually encouraged, them.[53] Private activists sent humanitarian flights to Iraq carrying medicine and, often, high-profile artists and cultural figures, such as the film director Youssef Chahine. Women's group's played an important role, focusing upon the impact of sanctions on families, children, and the vulnerable in society. The Arab Women Solidarity Society, headed by the well-known writer Nawal al Sadawi, led an effort by the Egyptian syndicates to collect a million signatures against the sanctions. This organizing led to a massive march through the streets of Cairo in January 1998, with protestors holding baby-sized coffins, ending in a rally at the Cairo football stadium. One organizer claimed that the campaign had collected 18 million signatures across the Arab world.[54] These efforts were not as organized as the Jordanian ones—rather more informal, spread out, without centralized groups—but by the end of the 1990s there was, according to several Egyptian activists, "a very strong popular and elite consensus against the sanctions."[55] In December 1998, fourteen opposition parties and civil society groups released a joint statement with the ominous (for the Mubarak regime) title: "Free the Egyptian people to cooperate with the Iraqi people."

Morocco had a surprisingly large focus on Iraq as a core Arab issue, despite its physical distance from the Gulf. Marches with more than 100,000 participants declaring solidarity with Iraq were not uncommon. During the first Gulf War, more than half a million Moroccans

had marched in support of Iraq. The National Committee for Supporting Iraq called for noncompliance with the sanctions in January 2000,
and the speaker of the House of Representatives led a delegation of
Arab Parliamentarians to urge the European Parliament to challenge
the sanctions. The committee, combining political parties, civil society, professional associations, and prominent individuals, coordinated
marches, rallies, petitions, and humanitarian aid collections.

Even Syria dramatically shifted its position toward Iraq in the second half of the 1990s after many years of extreme hostility between the
two Baathist republics, although this clearly had less to do with popular opinion from below than with strategic calculations on the part
of the regime. Syria opened up to Iraq beginning in early 1997, with
a large Syrian business delegation visited Baghdad in May with great
publicity. In 1998 Iraq began pumping oil through a Syrian pipeline, to
considerable international concern. Syria formed its own Arab Committee for Lifting the Siege Imposed on Iraq, made up of intellectuals
at the Arab Writers Union, in November 2000.[56] Its marches, such as
a massive rally in Damascus in November 2003, were authorized and
coordinated by the Syrian government, reducing their authenticity as
expressions of public opinion.

Participation in the annual Baghdad Trade Fair (see table 3.1), which
resumed in 1996, offers one glimpse into the growing economic allure of
the Iraqi market—or at least the perceived attractions of a public endorse-
ment of a potential return to Iraqi normality. This was as much public diplomacy as it was economic diplomacy, given the reality of the sanctions,
although Iraq certainly dangled the prospects of enormous contracts in
the postsanctions environment in front of potential supporters.

Still, the Iraqi regime pursued a wide range of economic opportunities inside and outside the oil-for-food program that no doubt contributed to at least some of the support for the Iraqi position. In at
least one instance—the opening of an air link between Baghdad and
Damascus by Qatari Hamad bin Ali al-Thani—secret Iraqi payments
through oil vouchers have been publicly revealed.[57]

Cultural activists also brought the Iraqi issue into the public sphere.
Nur, a journal focused on women's issues, published a special issue in
the fall of 2001 focusing on the concerns of Iraqi women facing the
embargo.[58] Numerous popular films and documentaries focused

TABLE 3.1. Baghdad Trade Fair Participants

Date	Number of Countries Represented
November 1996	16
November 1997	26
November 1998	30
November 1999	36
November 2000	45

attention on the suffering of the Iraqi people. For example, the Lebanese director Sayid Kaado's film *Taqasim min Baghdad* used graphic footage from hospitals to illustrate health problems among mothers and children in embargoed Iraq, while the Egyptian director Hossam Ali made several films about the lives of women and children under the embargo.[59] Art galleries and cultural centers hosted numerous shows of Iraqi artists and writers to raise consciousness of the Iraqi situation. Luminaries such as Nobel Laureate Naguib Mahfouz declared that "the embargo on Iraq now is illogical. . . . It is not logic to continue the siege until children die of hunger."[60] Even sports provided an arena for challenging the Arab isolation of Iraq. In 1999, for example, Jordan hosted the ninth annual Arab sports day. With Iraq invited, and even Saudi Arabia committed to attending, Kuwait found itself in a difficult position.

Functional inter-Arab organizations provided another venue for discussions and the issuing of Arabist documents. Professional associations cooperated in their realm of expertise—for example, doctor's associations from various Arab states coordinated campaigns to send medicine to Iraq.[61] In January 1999, representatives of Arab professional associations met in Baghdad to coordinate efforts against the embargo and created an executive committee based in Amman.[62] In 1998, the Arab Parliamentary Union held an emergency session in Amman, producing a consensus document calling for a lifting of sanctions and for determined Arab action to assist the people of Iraq. At the level of political parties, several conferences of Arab Popular Forces met in Baghdad to express solidarity with Iraq.[63] All of this demonstrates how mobilization crossed state lines, contributing to the manifestation of a public Arab consensus, even in the absence of al-Jazeera and the satellite television revolution with which the new public sphere is often equated.

States Strike Back

To say that few Arab regimes welcomed these signs of life in public opinion around the Iraqi issue would be a vast understatement. Arab regimes regularly repressed public demonstrations, and in virtually all instances sought to keep their freedom of maneuver intact. In December 2002, for example, Tunisia prevented a planned march in downtown Tunis that was to be led by eleven opposition parties. The Jordanian government violently suppressed pro-Iraqi demonstrations in the summer of 1996, and banned all public rallies during the crises of 1998. The Palestinian Authority prevented expressions of sympathy with Iraq in November 1998. Such responses to a mobilized public were entirely typical.

Where public opinion could not be repressed, Arab regimes looked to exploit it for their own interests. The cynical approach that states took to this emerging public opinion can be vividly seen in Egypt's two-year term on the Security Council, beginning in January 1996, where it hoped "to appear as championing the alleviation of the Iraqi people's plight."[64] As it sought to win Arab approval without actually challenging American policies, for example, Egypt called for the implementation of resolution 986 without compromising Iraqi sovereignty—a clear attempt to find a middle ground acceptable in the inter-Arab context—and urged the United Nations to "deal more objectively with the suffering of the Iraqi people."[65] *Al-Ahram* called for an Arab League "mechanism to help the beleaguered Iraqi people," and urged Iraq to cooperate with UNSCOM in order to "earn relief from sanctions and rehabilitation in the Arab world."[66] Despite these initiatives, however, Egypt did not invite Iraq to the Arab summit held in June to discuss Netanyahu's election.[67] Its media regularly highlighted the suffering of the Iraqi people and the injustice of the Security Council practices. But for all of its public talk, according to several diplomats who worked with the UN Sanctions Committee, Egypt did virtually nothing to challenge the sanctions regime.[68]

The crucial point here, besides the hypocrisy, is that by 1996 virtually every Arab political figure—no matter how hostile to Iraq in practice—felt the need to publicly declare sympathy with the Iraqi people. Such sympathy had become a core reference point, a defining quality of Arabness that was more firmly established with every iteration. The consensus bridged wide political divides. When Prince Saud bin Faisal began an interview by saying "We all sympathize with the Iraqi people in their ordeal," his sincerity was not the issue—it was that he felt compelled to say so at all.[69] Countless examples could be provided. Egypt's *al-Ahram* wrote that "regardless of [our] opinion of the ruling regime in Baghdad, [we urge] greater efforts to save the Iraqi people from famine, malnutrition, and epidemics."[70] Jordan's information minister affirmed that "Jordan supports all efforts aimed at alleviating the suffering of the Iraqi people."[71] Arab League Secretary-General Ismat Abd al-Meguid stated that "he felt deep sympathy with the Iraqi people, whose continuing suffering due to the sanctions was in no one's interest."[72] Oman's foreign minister declared that "everyone knows that the Iraqi people's suffering has exceeded extremes that no one can bear."[73] Even Kuwait made half-hearted efforts to offer assistance to the "suffering Iraqi people," even if such aid usually took the form of support for the opposition to Saddam Hussein. Saad Ajami, Kuwait's minister of information, for example, defended Kuwait on al-Jazeera by arguing that it had offered the assistance of the Kuwaiti Red Crescent to the victims of Saddam's chemical weapons, an offer Saddam refused.[74]

This did not mean that Arab states had reconciled their opinions on Iraq; on the contrary, Arab divisions were as sharp as ever. But sympathy for the suffering Iraqi people had become a core point of consensus on which very little dissent could be heard. Iraqi dissident Ghassan Attiyah warned as early as 1993 that "the pro-sanctions stance adopted by the bulk of the Iraqi offshore opposition groups had become a political and moral liability," isolating them from mainstream Arab opinion.[75] Such sympathy, and the changing strategic context it created, could only go so far, however. Iraqi officials complained that "it is meaningless for any Arab official to profess sympathy with us and declare an understanding of our suffering under the unfair sanctions while at the same time reiterating the U.S. attitude."[76] While the ground of Arab politics gradually shifted from below, Iraq grew impatient for deeds to match the words.

Military Strikes: The Perverse Consequences

While the sanctions issue percolated from below, American attacks on Iraq offered galvanizing moments for Arab public opinion, both demonstrating and consolidating the emerging popular consensus. The military crises focused attention and crystallized the public consensus; one Arab ambassador explained, "The sanctions are worse than the bombing in what they do to the Iraqi people, but the bombings are dramatic and galvanize the public."[77]

The first unifying moment came with the late June 1993 American cruise missile attack on Baghdad that killed Iraqi artist Layla al-Attar. Most of the Arab world, except Kuwait, expressed skepticism and anger. Few believed the claim that Iraq had plotted to kill former President George Bush; this was instead seen as a pretext for Clinton to demonstrate his toughness to Saddam. Arabs complained bitterly about American double standards, and at the U.S. willingness to bypass the Security Council when it saw fit. As Abd al-Bari Atwan, editor of *al-Quds al-Arabi*, put it: "Arab opinion is disgusted at the way the United States keeps demonstrating its military prowess against Iraq while allowing the Serbs and Israelis to get away unpunished for murder on a grand scale."[78]

At this point some Arab observers were already arguing that the American action demonstrated that there was no value in cooperating with the UN inspections, since the United States would always find some excuse to maintain the sanctions.[79] They also argued that American military strikes inevitably strengthened Saddam Hussein by increasing popular sympathy with Iraq.[80] *Al-Hayat* editor Jihad al-Khazen worried that the attack "was a blow to Arab moderates" and that Kuwait had isolated itself even further by backing the Americans against an Arab consensus.[81] *Al-Ahram* asserted that "the raid won virtually no support in the Arab world, while the announcement that Washington had contacted some of its Arab allies to discuss the attack with them only increased those governments' embarrassment."[82] And for Atwan, the silver lining of the attack was that "it put America's Arab allies on the spot. . . . Unable to justify it, they were with the sole exception of Kuwait reduced to an awkward silence, . . . [making clear that] the viewpoint of ordinary Arabs is completely at odds with that of the governments."[83] The response to the bombing offered a first demonstration of evolving Arab background beliefs, and thereby moved to shape expectations about the likely normative reward for adopting positions sympathetic to Iraq.

The muted response of Arab states to the 1996 American bombing of Iraq's south after Saddam's armies wiped out an Iraqi National Congress operation based in the Kurdish areas bears attention. Arab writers were quick to note the disparity between the official caution of the Arab regimes and the vocal opposition of other states and of the Arab public. As European states opposed the airstrikes, but "Arab leaders stay mum," writers in the pan-Arab press suggested that Arab states "ha[d] shown themselves to be the weakest party in the international community's response to blatant aggression against an Arab country," despite clear popular demands for a public response. A prominent writer in *al-Ahram* noted the "contrast between the vocal international criticism . . . and the meek silence maintained by most Arab countries. . . . Apart from the voice in the wilderness of Arab League Secretary-General Ismat Abd al-Maguid, all that was heard was an embarrassed whisper of protest from Cairo and a deafening silence in most other Arab countries."[84]

Most writers explained this silence in terms of American pressure, but more seemed to be going on. To the extent that Arab leaders had been engaging in rhetorical free riding, winning points with public opinion while publicly falsifying their preferences, the prospects of Iraqi success were far less appealing to these leaders than their public profiles would suggest. The surging Iraqi initiative worried Arab states as much as it emboldened Arab public opinion, leading many Arab regimes to tone down their rhetorical free riding, which now seemed to carry unnecessary costs.

The GCC: Reconciliation or Regime Change?

Efforts to overcome the Gulf crisis and to resolve the ongoing divisions in the Arab world proved fruitless, in part because of Kuwait's hardline stance toward those who had been inclined toward Iraq. The absence of a genuinely independent public sphere capable of mobilizing against these powerful states handicapped such efforts. Kuwait (and to a lesser extent Saudi Arabia) exercised a veto over any Arab gathering that might rehabilitate Iraq, and worked to focus attention on Iraqi perfidy rather than on Iraqi suffering. Kuwait aggressively policed public discourse to keep the focus on Saddam's evil. Over time, unyielding Kuwaiti rhetoric and policy became counterproductive, particularly as the new Arab public found its voice.

This part of the chapter takes the Gulf Cooperation Council (GCC) as a microcosm of Arab politics, and explores the repeated efforts by various smaller members—the UAE, Bahrain, Qatar—to adopt a more open policy toward Iraq. Concerned with the impact of the sanctions, and with the public's increasing anger, they advanced a series of initiatives that challenged GCC unity.

As early as June 1993, some Gulf newspapers began to call on the GCC "to abandon its obsession with the 1990–1991 Gulf crisis and the regime of . . . Saddam Hussein, and to throw its lot in with efforts to reunite the Arab world and reconcile with Iraq."[85] These early popular appeals had little impact on Kuwait and Saudi Arabia, however, who still perceived Iraq as a threat and were adamantly opposed to any softening toward it. Kuwait in particular was fiercely opposed to reconciliation even with what it termed "adverse states" such as Jordan, much less with Baghdad itself, and would consider mending fences with other Arab states only if they clearly adopted a rigorous array of hard-line anti-Iraq policies.[86] Mohammed al-Rumayhi spoke for many Kuwaitis when he rejected calls to "let bygones be bygones" as an insult to Kuwaiti suffering.[87] As Abd al-Wahhab Badrakhan noted, Kuwait's parliament, media, and public opinion were far more emotional and enraged with the Arabs than was the more pragmatic royal family—a striking example of public opinion working against Arab rapprochement.[88] King Hussein's calls for change in Baghdad beginning in 1993 did not satisfy Kuwaitis, who noted Jordan's continuing economic relations with Iraq and took a vindictive line against Jordan under any circumstances. Tunisia's foreign minister cut short the first official visit to Kuwait since the war in June 1993 "after coming under a barrage of abuse from the emirate's press and legislators."[89]

In September 1993, the GCC rejected moves toward rehabilitating Iraq, "hold[ing] the Baghdad regime responsible for the suppression and sufferings being sustained by the brotherly Iraqi people as a result of the practices of the regime and its noncompliance with Security Council resolutions." There were already clear divisions within the GCC, however, with half its members hoping for a softer line.[90] Hopes that these expressions of concern might foster reconciliation with Iraq were routinely disappointed, however, as expectations of change in policy based on the positions of the UAE, Qatar, Oman, and Bahrain were dashed by the hard line of Kuwait and Saudi Arabia. In December 1993 King Fahd made short work of the hopes for a rehabilitation of Iraq with a firm speech at the GCC summit condemning the Iraqi regime, demanding its compliance, and insisting on the maintenance of the sanctions.[91] Nevertheless, Qatar "rejected a direct request from the Clinton administration to stop contacts with Iraq." [92]

All these maneuvers by the small Gulf states took place within clearly circumscribed parameters, as GCC policy depended on Saudi Arabia and Kuwait. Nevertheless, the smaller states established a tone of humanitarian concern and impatience with the ongoing Arab divisions that helped consolidate the background frame of a popular Arab position confounded by self-interested powerful Arab states and outside forces.

Over the winter of 1993–1994 the Arab—and especially Gulf—press increasingly took up the issue of the sanctions as an urgent Arab concern.[93] The two camps struggled to reconcile tough containment with humanitarian relief. In April 1994 the GCC reiterated that they "agree[d] on a common resolve to stand vigilant and determined" to enforce the sanctions despite the publicly expressed concerns of its members.[94] In August Egypt, the UAE, and Morocco each took futile initiatives to seek Saudi and Kuwaiti agreement on reconciliation with Iraq, but in September the GCC officially "praised the United Nations Security Council's decision to maintain economic sanctions on Iraq until it complies fully with U.N. resolutions."[95] In this context, GCC members actively lobbied the Security Council to maintain a hard line on sanctions, despite the growing expressions of Arab dissent.[96] This hard public line—along with the Security Council's renewal of sanctions—had the desired effect on expectations, convincing most Arabs that there was little hope for the sanctions being lifted in the near term. But changes were beginning to break through the wall. In the same month that Kuwait Parliamentary Speaker Ahmed al-Saadoun said Kuwait would continue to press the international community to "accelerate its pressure and tighten the economic blockade on the Iraqi regime to force it into unconditional submission to all UN Security Council resolutions related to its aggression on Kuwait,"[97] the GCC for the first time expressed "total sympathy with the fraternal Iraqi people in their humanitarian sufferings."[98]

In December 1994 GCC dissension burst into the open as Bahrain publicly called on Kuwait to be more open to dialogue in the expectation that the UN Security Council would be easing the sanctions relatively soon.[99] Expectations of change at the global and Arab levels fed on each other, as trends against the sanctions suggested that "the GCC ought to brace for Iraq's eventual rehabilitation in the Arab world."[100] Numerous authors pointed out the need to adjust Arab positions to the likely changes at the international level, and warned of the political consequences of being seen as obstacles to the easing of the sanctions. They also pointed out the unacceptability of Arabs lagging behind other, non-Arab states in challenging the sanctions.

Even Kuwaitis recognized that their vigorous efforts to assign responsibility to Saddam were falling flat: "Despite all attempts to show that Saddam is to blame for that suffering, Arab public opinion increasingly calls for the question of sanctions to be decoupled from that of the Iraqi regime's behavior or survival."[101] After Kuwait's dismissal of a Moroccan reconciliation initiative, the Arab press filled with criticism of Kuwaiti intransigence: "By its behavior, Kuwait is not only antagonizing a growing number of Arab and Islamic states who consider the retention of sanctions against the Iraqi people unconscionable, but also damaging its ties with its five GCC partners."[102] Kuwait's refusal to reconcile with Jordan after its peace treaty with Israel played into the perception of its irrational intransigence.

In the run-up to the December 1994 GCC summit, Qatar pushed to have the GCC recognize the need to deal with the humanitarian dimension of the sanctions, within the limits of the Saudi and Kuwaiti hard-line approach.[103] After the GCC ministers' meeting was—quite exceptionally—delayed because of the difficulty of reaching consensus, the final communiqué did acknowledge the changes in Iraqi behavior toward compliance, but attributed this to the tough line endorsed by the GCC, which appealed "to [the Security Council] to continue in these principled and firm stances and in their effective efforts to compel Iraq to take similar steps toward the serious implementation of all Security Council resolutions."[104] Egypt, while agreeing with the need for Iraq to comply with the resolutions, stated that it "was very annoyed by the suffering of the Iraqi people resulting from the blockade" and asserted that "there is a common feeling that we must do something."[105] Egyptians hastened to clarify that sympathy for the Iraqi people did not extend to Saddam's regime, however; *al-Ahram* editor Ibrahim Nafei's late September front-page commentary entitled "God save the Iraqi people from Saddam" was widely seen as standing in for Hosni Mubarak's personal sentiments.[106]

In January 1995 moves toward reconciliation with Iraq picked up steam, as Egypt worked to convene an Arab summit to discuss Iraq's return to the Arab fold. "We should extend the bridges of care for Iraq, whose people are suffering. We should not forget our history and pan-Arabism," UAE Defense Minister Sheik Mohammed bin Rashed al-Maktoum said, echoing calls from Qatar and Oman.[107] The Egyptian media, which had been filled with anti-Iraqi rhetoric, now opened to humanitarian and political critique of the sanctions. Omani Minister of State for Foreign Affairs Yousef bin Alawi said, "I and friends on the Security Council are looking for ways and means of lessening the sufferings of the Iraqi people" while maintaining the demand for full Iraqi compliance.[108] King Hassan of Morocco warned President Clinton of the dangers of ignoring the long-term consequences of the sanctions on the population of Iraq.[109]

Tellingly, when Warren Christopher came to the Gulf to discuss the eroding consensus, he dealt only with heads of state, with virtually no effort to engage Arab public opinion in any kind of direct dialogue.[110] The impact of Christopher's message to the GCC states could be seen in the June ministerial declaration, which took a remarkably tough line and contained hardly a hint of the struggles behind the scenes. Still, the Gulf press continued to fill with articles criticizing the United States, Saudi Arabia, and Kuwait for their inflexibility.[111]

In October 1995 an initiative by the UAE for reconciliation with Iraq—"whether the West wants it or not"—met with strong resistance once again from Saudi Arabia and Kuwait. Shaikh Zayed bin Sultan al-Nahyan of the UAE argued that "it is time to lift sanctions because it is the Iraqi people who were paying for [Saddam Hussein's] mistakes," a call endorsed by Ismat Abd al-Meguid, secretary-general of the Arab League, Yemen, Oman, Bahrain, Qatar, and Egypt.[112] Alarmed, Kuwait took unusually strong measures to reinforce GCC discipline, with mixed success. In January 1996 GCC states again publicly argued over the terms of a rehabilitation of Iraq. Some reports indicated splits within the Saudi royal family on Iraq policy, suggesting that some Saudis were being swayed by Egyptian and Arab arguments that the sanctions were actually strengthening Saddam's internal position while harming the interests of Iraq's Gulf opponents.[113] These debates were reflected in the GCC communiqué of March 1996: "While the Council feel regret on deterioration of living and health conditions of the brotherly Iraqi people, it holds the Iraqi regime full responsibility due to its ill-conducted policy all the time and calls Iraq to implement resolution 986 with articles aimed at handling humanitarian needs of this people to alleviate its bitter suffering."

The UAE's November 1996 proposal for a route to normalizing Iraqi-Arab relations erupted into a major debate among GCC countries, playing out in opinion pages across the Arab world. The usual Gulf states stepped up their efforts toward rehabilitating Iraq, while Kuwaitis and Saudis traveled around the Arab world and Europe trying to shore up support for the sanctions. The UAE, reportedly with support from Egypt and Bahrain, "took issue with the sanctions on both humanitarian and political grounds."[114] Kuwait and Saudi Arabia insisted (following the American line) that the reason for the suffering of the Iraqi people remained Saddam, and not the sanctions. When the GCC secretariat asserted that the UAE ideas did not change official GCC policy, one Bahraini commentator responded that "the call for Iraq to be relieved of sanctions serves the strategic interests of the

Gulf states and expresses the feelings of their peoples. The secretariat's rejection of that call is, accordingly, damaging to GCC interests and contemptuous of public opinion."[115]

While it remained impossible to forge a political consensus, booming illegal trade in the Gulf suggested that many individuals as well as governments no longer felt any normative adherence to the sanctions regime.

On the Brink of Change

This chapter has tracked the interaction between Arab states and an emerging public dismay with the sanctions on Iraq in the period before the satellite television revolution. Public debates about Iraq remained primarily confined to domestic print publics and the elite transnational press, while states mainly argued in private over strategic issues rather than humanitarian ones.

Over the course of the decade, however, real developments could be seen in the cohesion and influence of Arab public opinion toward the sanctions. By 1996, virtually no discussion of Iraq could omit reference to sympathy with the suffering Iraqi people. As frustration grew with what was widely perceived as an unjust and devastating sanctions regime, Arab states found it harder to ignore or to repress the issue. When Richard Butler replaced Rolf Ekeus as chairman of UNSCOM in June 1997, a more confrontational period between Iraq and the UN immediately commenced.

4

The al-Jazeera Era

On December 20, 1998, after the final withdrawal of UNSCOM, four days of American and British bombardment of Iraq, and massive Arab protests, al-Jazeera broadcast an episode of *Sharia and Life* featuring Yusuf al-Qaradawi.[1] The host, Ahmed Mansour, began by invoking the outrage felt by Muslims at an attack on Iraq during Ramadan, and quoted former Algerian Prime Minister Ahmed Ben Bella asking whether the attack on Iraq was "an extension of the crusader campaign which began against the Islamic world after the fall of Granada." But Mansour was dubious: "Is this the truth of what happened to Iraq at American and British hands?" Carefully framing the debate, Mansour wondered: "If there are those who blame the Iraqi regime for the crisis which the *umma* has lived through since 1990 because of the invasion and aggression against Kuwait, will they object to this destruction now of the regime or the capabilities of Iraq? . . . But at the same time, what responsibility does the Iraqi regime bear for what has happened to Iraq since 1990?"

Qaradawi endorsed Muslim outrage that in 1998 "Ramadan begins with fear instead of hope, with war instead of peace, with destruction instead of birth, with death instead of life." Openly identifying with the Iraqi people, Qaradawi bemoaned that "this is what our brothers the Iraqi people suffer under. . . . We find ourselves now attacked during Ramadan." He blasted the United States for setting itself above God in determining matters of life and death, while explaining the attack on

Iraq as primarily about defending Israel. Qaradawi praised the Arab street for protesting, even if it had no effect on American actions, in an exquisite illustration of the expressive logic of action discussed in earlier chapters. There was value, he argued, in simply declaring that even where "the weak cannot stand in the face of power . . . he is able to say no. . . . With our limited capabilities to say no, we say to America no, we don't accept this."

But Qaradawi refused to offer a simple pro-Iraqi stance. Far from defending Saddam Hussein, Qaradawi repeatedly and insistently distinguished the Iraqi people from a regime he despised. "We are against Saddam Hussein, but we are not against the Iraqi people," he explained. "We consider the Iraqi regime a criminal and harmful regime for its people." Directly addressing Saddam, Qaradawi said, "I call on the Iraqi president to allow freedoms inside of Iraq and to allow the Iraqi people a voice. . . . If he is truly a strong ruler then he would know that the people are confident in him . . . and if not . . . " But he nevertheless condemned the bombings: "I do not permit a hostile power to use this to attack the Iraqi people."

Did the al-Jazeera audience take umbrage at Qaradawi's hostility toward Saddam Hussein? The first question to Qaradawi came over fax from Iraqi opposition figure (and former head of Saddam's military intelligence) Wafiq al-Samarrai: "What is the position of the Sharia on this: if there is an unjust ruler as is the case in Iraq, is it permissible to leave a killer to kill and a criminal to commit crimes, which is what will happen if Arab states don't intervene?" Qaradawi agreed that "we cannot leave the killer in place, we must use force to remove him," but insisted that such action must come from within and not from American-backed opposition groups: "It is not permissible for a Muslim to make himself an agent of a power that is hostile to Islam." A debate ensued over the phones, with several callers blasting Samarrai for his Baathist past, and Qaradawi ultimately defending Samarrai's right to change his views. Ahmed Mansour explained to a seemingly confused Qaradawi that "this question is always posed to Samarrai in every dialogue we have, that he was a part of the regime . . . and he participated in great crimes against the Iraqi people"—which must surprise the vast array of commentators who later accused al-Jazeera of ignoring the crimes of Saddam's regime.

Some callers echoed the position of the Iraqi opposition: "The whole Iraqi people beg to be rescued from this repressive regime, I call on our beloved Shaykh to see that there is a solution to this problem for the Iraqi people, which is to save the Iraqi people from Saddam Hussein, who has done far worse to them than has the United States." Others bemoaned the sanctions, and Arab inaction in the face of Iraqi suffering: "Is it permissible for the Muslim to leave his Muslim brother suffering under the blockade and not help him?" Over the course of an hour and a half, virtually every position was expressed, as Arabs openly grappled in public over an issue about which they clearly disagreed. The only point on which all seemed to agree was that Arab regimes had failed miserably to deal with the Iraqi situation, to listen to their people, and to stand up for Arab interests—however those interests might be defined.

These open dialogues—heated, contentious, and contemptuous of the political status quo—constituted a public sphere very different from the one described in chapter 3, of private deliberations of elites and carefully modulated editorial debates in the elite press. These new public arguments were open, heated, and unrestrained. If anything, critics worried that they focused too heavily on confrontation and polar opposition. In their pursuit of entertaining television, the talk show hosts much preferred high intensity arguments between an Iraqi official and a Kuwaiti parliamentarian to a calm discussion between detached intellectuals. One of the first high-profile controversies generated by al-Jazeera's talk shows came in March 1997, when Faisal al-Qassem hosted a program asking why Kuwait refused to reconcile with Iraq, leading Kuwaiti officials to angrily protest to the Qatari government and sparking dozens of hostile commentaries in the Kuwaiti press (Zayani 2005: 95). In January 1999 *More Than One Opinion* pitted the Arabist editor of *al-Quds al-Arabi* Abd al-Bari Atwan against the Kuwaiti information minister Saad al-Ajami and the Egyptian journalist Mahmoud Attallah.[2] The next month, Faisal al-Qassem hosted a debate between Sami Mahdi, editor of the Iraqi newspaper *al-Thawra*, and Egyptian academic Gihad Awda on the question of whether "the blockade on Iraq is an Arab conspiracy more than an American or Zionist one."[3] In March *More Than One Opinion* returned to contemplate "the war of attrition against Iraq" with Iraqi professor of military science Mazen al-Ramadani and former American ambassador David Mack.[4] In August Qassem hosted a discussion of the sanctions on Iraq featuring a pro-regime Iraqi expatriate and a member of the Kuwaiti parliament.[5] In another program, the Jordanian radical Layth Shubaylat squared off against Ayad al-Manaa, a leading Kuwaiti journalist.[6] Such direct, impassioned arguments offered a stark change from decades of Arab public politics. They tapped into the raw emotional identification many Arabs felt with the Iraqi people, giving an outlet for the anger and frustration built up by the graphic news coverage on the station.

The period from 1997–2002 well deserves the much-abused title of "the al-Jazeera Era." Building on its successful coverage of Iraq, as well as the second Palestinian Intifada and its exclusive access to Afghanistan after 9/11, al-Jazeera dominated Arab public discourse for these crucial years, before—as described in chapter 2—competing stations emerged to challenge its hegemony. Its live coverage of these contentious events, in real time, with graphic imagery and openly supportive and engaged commentary, defined those conflicts for viewers in intensely personal and vivid ways.

Over the course of the period described in this chapter, the Palestinian and Iraqi issues increasingly merged into a common narrative, with the United States playing the villain's role in each. This convergence was graphically embodied by the juxtaposition of the Israeli reoccupation of the West Bank and the American push for a confrontation with Iraq in the spring of 2002. It is often forgotten that the initial Arab response to 9/11 was marked by considerable ambivalence, with a wide range of important Islamist and Arab figures condemning those attacks and expressing profound sympathy with the victims, even as significant numbers of Arabs doubted al-Qaeda's responsibility for the attacks. The debates over the invasion of Afghanistan were similarly ambivalent, with public debates marked by intense disagreements between those who rejected any American military action in the Muslim world and those who saw it as a justifiable response to al-Qaeda's assault on America. Anti-American sentiment spiked only after the combination of President Bush's "Axis of Evil" speech, the Israeli reoccupation of the West Bank—during which Bush famously declared Ariel Sharon to be a man of peace—and the beginnings of the campaign against Iraq.

The Arab public sphere thus literally defined the response to the American mobilization against Iraq in 2002–2003 by placing it within this particular context. In the narrative that developed and hardened over the course of the 1990s, American arguments were automatically discounted and nefarious motivations ascribed. The profound differences in American and Arab perceptions of the relationships among events in Israel, Iraq, and the war on terror opened what al-Jazeera host Ghassan bin Jadu called "an epistemological chasm between the Iraqi opposition and Arab elites"—a gap that was even greater between the United States and the Arabs.[7] Participants in the Arab debates routinely invoked articles published in the Western press, reports issued by the United Nations or Western think tanks, and interviews with Western officials or personalities. The Arab public paid close attention to American politics, and could not help but note Congressional and media criticisms of the Clinton administration's alleged lack of seriousness in moving against Saddam. At the same time, Clinton's ostentatious public support for the Iraqi opposition—as a way of deflecting this Congressional criticism—rebounded against that opposition by heightening the sense of many Arabs of its inauthenticity. But Americans largely ignored Arab debates, which left them painfully unaware of how their initiatives would be received, how much their credibility had eroded, or how toxic America had become in Arab eyes.

Another major difference between the American and Arab understanding of Iraq has to do with its salience. After the collapse of the UN inspections and the four-day bombing campaign against Iraq, the Iraq issue transformed in a number of ways. The Clinton administration sought to remove Iraq from the headlines, with a low-intensity bombing campaign that rarely reached levels deemed newsworthy by American media. It proved slow to appreciate the new importance of Arab public opinion. Most of 1999 was taken up with the tortuous negotiation of resolution 1284, which ultimately passed over the abstention of three permanent members of the Security Council. Ironically, given later events, George W. Bush's initial approach to Iraq emphasized a revamping of the sanctions regime—"smart sanctions" rather than military confrontation. Only after September 11 did American attention turn again to Iraq as a front-burner issue.[8]

For Arabs, on the other hand, Iraq never retreated to the periphery of their concerns. As Mohammed el-Nawawy and Adel Iskander argue, "Al-Jazeera first realized it had the opportunity to consolidate Arab audiences when it covered the Desert Fox U.S. military operations against Iraq in 1998. . . . From that point forward, footage from the raids and extensive discussion of the sanctions on Iraq fed Arab fury. The UN-sanctions economic embargo seemed, in a word, unjustified" (2001: 58). Iraq by this point had been well established as an Arab core concern, with the United States increasingly placed at the center of the problem. Well before September 11, more and more Arabs openly talked about the plans of "the American Enemy" to attack Iraq.[9] Discussion of a coming American attack on Iraq was common in the summer of 2001.[10] After September 11, arguments about al-Qaeda and the war in Afghanistan quickly merged into fears of an American expansion of the war into Iraq. As early as October 16, 2001, *The Opposite Direction* discussed whether America would "widen the war on terror to Iraq"; on November 28 *No Limits* focused on "American plans on Iraq after Afghanistan"; and a December 4 *The Opposite Direction* asked whether America could "Afghan-ize Iraq."[11] Untold numbers of writers in the Arab press similarly asked whether—often, simply when—the Bush administration would turn toward Iraq.[12] When Osama bin Laden invoked the suffering of the Iraqi people in a tape broadcast by al-Jazeera in November 2002, he clearly saw the usefulness of tapping into this widespread Arab conviction.

Perceived American double standards stood at the heart of Arab complaints. Arabs constantly pointed out that Israel routinely ignored UN resolutions, while Iraq was expected to live up to the letter of these resolutions. These double standards became increasingly central as the Palestinian uprising began in the fall of 2000. The no-fly zones were a particular example, especially after the United States began a punishing campaign of bombings, ostensibly to enforce them, after Desert Fox. The no-fly zones were not established by the Security Council, Arabs pointed out, and as such had dubious legal justification. American manipulations of the UN Sanctions Committee fed the outrage.

At the same time, Arabs constantly pointed to American regime-change declarations as evidence that the United States itself had little regard for UN resolutions. Assertions by officials such as Madeleine Albright that the sanctions would not be lifted as long as Saddam remained in power (see chapter 3) quickly solidified into an absolute conviction—one which damned the United States, while at the same time in Arab eyes justifying Iraqi refusals to cooperate with the inspectors.[13] The Iraqi Liberation Act, passed with bipartisan support in October 1998, served as a final proof for most Arabs of their belief in American intentions on this point. Lebanese columnist Raghid Saleh summarized this widespread interpretation: "The position of the United States on the embargo is not based on international law. The US says that it will not lift the blockade and will not revisit the questions of sanctions until the regime in Iraq falls, and international law does not say that."[14]

Between 1998 and 2003 the emerging triumphalism of the new Arab public sphere, as it recognized its own growing influence, gave way to a dangerous frustration when its efforts failed to translate into real political outcomes. The public witnessed startling successes: the Arab street did protest in force, an Arab public consensus did form, and all states—from America to the Gulf—were forced to alter their strategies to the new reality. But for all the "victories," the Palestinian uprising failed to accomplish its goals, instead sinking into nearly unfathomable violence. Arab governments refused to become more democratic; indeed, in response to the crisis atmosphere generated by the Palestinian uprising and then by September 11, many governments clamped down and became even more repressive. And not only did the sanctions on Iraq remain in place, but in 2002 the United States began mobilizing the region and the world for a war to topple Saddam Hussein. In all the areas of greatest concern to the new Arab public, then, movement and argument and even consensus failed to translate into real political success. Such frustration—which may be structurally endemic to a weak international public sphere—had an inevitable effect on the tone, content, and pitch of argument in the Arab public sphere. By the end of the period discussed in this chapter, the Arab public sphere had passed from a moment of enthusiasm to a grinding despair and a resurgent politics of identity.

The New Public Sphere and Iraq

The emergence of al-Jazeera coincided remarkably with the beginning of the collapse of the system of sanctions and inspections maintained over the previous six years. Chapter 3 argued that the years 1991–1997 followed roughly realist lines of state behavior, while opinion slowly shifted from below. The major states dominated the action, as they pursued strategic interests in private diplomacy and at the United Nations. While the beginnings of public discontent over the human costs of the sanctions could be seen distantly, this emerging Arab public opinion had no effective outlets to express itself or to influence policy. Arab states, like the United States, largely ignored this Arab sentiment.

The emergence of al-Jazeera radically transformed the political and strategic environment, bringing into the public eye not only graphic footage but also arguments that had previously taken place only in the elite press and in private forums. The hothouse environment of an Arab public sphere dominated by questions of identity and a sense of subordination nurtured a particular kind of Arabist identity and sense of interests. al-Jazeera did not create Arab views toward the core shared policy issues, but it did reshape the background assumptions and the intensity of Arab views (Nisbet et al. 2004; Telhami 2005).

Building on the ideas spread from below (as described in chapter 3), the suffering of the Iraqi people became a core touchstone of debate, one which all speakers hoping to be taken seriously had to acknowledge regardless of their personal beliefs. For example, as a preface to a discussion about the strategic aspect of the sanctions, one al-Jazeera host described the sanctions as "this embargo which has imposed harsh suffering on the Iraqi people, which weighs heavily on the souls even of Washington's friends in the region, this embargo which continues without any legal or moral excuse."[15] This led even Kuwaitis to change their argumentative style. Within the domestic Kuwaiti media, the standard fare was attacks on "those who oppose overthrowing the Iraqi regime[, who] embody a repressive style and a culture of dictatorship, and give tyrannical regimes the legitimacy to continue in dominating their peoples and stealing their wealth."[16] But when appearing on al-Jazeera, Kuwaitis would preface their remarks with concern for "the long suffering of the Iraqi people."[17] Even Kuwaitis found it necessary to position themselves as defenders of the Iraqi people, however improbably, as in the following hallucinogenic exchange on *The Opposite Direction*:[18]

> ABD AL-MUHASSAN JAMAL: I speak with the tongue of the Iraqi people . . .
>
> FAISAL AL-QASSEM: [*interrupts*] You speak in the name of the Iraqi people?
>
> JAMAL: In the name of the Iraqi people, because I am part of the Arab people.
>
> QASSEM: [*incredulous*] You are a member of . . . a member of the Kuwaiti Parliament!

For all their centrality to Arab debate, the Iraqi people themselves lacked any real voice. This was not because of a conscious attempt by al-Jazeera to exclude them: Iraqis living in exile appeared frequently, and were a constant presence calling in to the programs. But the tyrannical nature of Saddam's regime made it impossible for Iraqis living inside Iraq to freely speak their minds to the Arab media. The unpopular opposition in exile could not credibly speak on their behalf, despite their efforts to do so, while few accepted the representativeness of Saddam's tyrannical regime. As a result, all parties felt free to speak on behalf of the Iraqi people, to claim to authentically represent them. The frustration this engendered among the actual Iraqi people would only be genuinely exhibited after the fall of Baghdad, as ordinary Iraqis vented their rage at the Arab media and at the Arab political system as a whole. But from the early 1990s through 2003, Arabs of all political persuasions were free to project their own preferences onto this object of identification and sympathy. As Iraqi opposition figure Abd al-Halim al-Rahimi tellingly described it, everyone in Arab debates "ignores the opinion of the Iraqi people . . . while at the same time pretending that their positions express the interests of the Iraqi people. . . . This ignores the opinion of Iraqis, deputizing themselves to speak on their behalf." Rahimi, equally tellingly, then did exactly what he accused others of doing, assuring readers that "the reality is that the vast majority of the Iraqi people, inside and outside, of all political and ideological trends, and all nationalities and religions, not only want but are working to overthrow Saddam's regime."[19]

While al-Jazeera covered the humanitarian side of the Iraqi issue intensely and sympathetically, and gave a platform to voices highly critical of the United States, this does not mean that al-Jazeera was an Iraqi instrument or "pro-Saddam." Intense and fierce arguments about the regime of Saddam Hussein punctuated its programs. Almost every program on Iraq featured Kuwaitis or Iraqi opposition figures, as well as live callers, who insistently turned every issue—whether a confrontation with the United States or the effect of the sanctions—into accusatory dissertations on the evils of Saddam's tyranny (*al taghiya*). Of twenty-three guests who appeared on Iraq-themed al-Jazeera talk shows in 1999, for example, five were Kuwaiti (including the minister of information and several members of Parliament), five were pro-regime Iraqis (including Tareq Aziz), seven were figures identified with or sympathetic to the Iraqi opposition (including Wafiq al-Samarrai, Ghassan Attiyah, and Hamid al-Bayati), three were Arab journalists who tended to side with the Iraqi opposition, and six were Arab writers who tended to be critical of the sanctions and the United States (including several appearances by Abd al-Bari Atwan, editor of *al-Quds al-Arabi*).

When Iraqi officials appeared on al-Jazeera talk shows, they usually received tough questioning quite unfamiliar to them in the tightly controlled Iraqi media. For example, in January 2000 host Jumana al-Namour repeatedly challenged Iraqi Foreign Minister Mohammed Said al-Sahhaf.[20] When Sahhaf claimed that other governments knew "that Iraq has implemented all the demands in the Security Council resolutions," Namour interrupted him to say, "But this is not what the Security Council says." When Sahhaf claimed that current Security Council demands exceeded the terms of the original resolutions, Namour demanded specific examples, and was visibly unsatisfied with his responses. "If there are no weapons present," she demanded, "then why are you afraid of an inspections team entering Iraq?" On another program, Namour interrupted Riyadh al-Qisi's defense of Iraq's oil policies to ask whether he had any documentation to back up his claims, or any proof for viewers who doubted what he was saying.[21] When al-Qisi cited "UN officials" as blaming the United States for the suffering of the Iraqi people, Namour reminded him that the same official (Hans von Sponeck) had also accused the Iraqi government of some responsibility for that suffering.[22] To be consistently challenged on facts and arguments in public, by a beautiful young woman no less, was not the norm for a senior Iraqi official.

In his program discussing the ninth year of sanctions, Faisal al-Qassem noted the UNICEF report stating that sanctions were responsible for the death of more than half a million Iraqi children, but also noted that the report showed that children were doing better in the areas outside the control of the regime. "Does this not show," asked Qassem, "that the regime plays some role in the worsening of conditions? . . . Isn't the regime primarily responsible for the suffering of the children?"[23] When a supporter of Saddam's policies claimed that Iraq had been placed under an embargo for no reason, Sami Haddad openly mocked him: "Do you really expect to convince me that . . . [despite] the invasion of Kuwait . . . [and Iraq] not implementing UN resolutions . . . to which it agreed, . . . do you really expect to convince me that [the embargo] came out of nothing?!"[24] Listening to another, Haddad threw up his hands: "After ten years, you have a blockade and sanctions, containment, so many losses . . . isn't it time to speak in a realistic fashion, not with sentiments about the poor Iraqi people suffering under blockade?"[25]

Not every encounter was so contentious, of course. On a September 17, 1999, program, for example, host Jamal Rayan openly identified with the Iraqi regime, repeatedly coming to its defense against criticisms voiced by the guests, and sharply challenged anyone who did not support the immediate lifting of sanctions. Ahmed Mansour—later to become notorious among Americans as the al-Jazeera correspondent in Falluja in April 2004—tended to be far more forthcoming with Iraqi official guests on his program *No Limits*. In a program broadcast in June 2000, Mansour posed tough questions to Nabil Najm from the Iraqi Foreign Ministry, such as "What does America really want from Iraq?" and "How can there be a dialogue [with the United States] when the United States is spending tens of millions of dollars to overthrow the Iraqi government and declares that goal openly?"[26]

But the key to what made al-Jazeera different is that in their live broadcasts, even a friendly environment could quickly turn heated.

A caller to Mansour's program began by affirming the reality of Iraqi suffering under the sanctions, but then said that "this unjust blockade imposed on our people has only one cause and that is Saddam Hussein because of his invasion of Kuwait and his opposition to international society." Mansour quickly responded that he would not permit any head of state to be discussed in such an inflammatory way on his program, and told his viewers to frame their questions in a respectful fashion, but the challenge had been issued and heard by all viewers. And even Mansour infuriated his guest by asking about a rumored deal to resettle Palestinian refugees in Iraq, and by saying that "there are many accusations that you entrench and deepen the embargo, because it allows you to exercise greater control over the Iraqi people." When Najm tried to browbeat Mansour for raising such subjects, Mansour stood fast: "I represent the other opinion, I'm sorry, and I am presenting to you what others say, regardless of whether it pleases you" (*No Limits*, June 28, 2000).

In addition to al-Jazeera, the elite Arab press debated Iraq furiously, with dialogue taking place both within single newspapers and between the different widely read newspapers. While my analysis draws on dozens of Arabic newspapers, for the purposes of systematic analysis I focus here on two major London-based newspapers: *al-Hayat* and *al-Quds al-Arabi*.[27] I collected 643 op-eds about Iraq in these two newspapers between January 1999 and July 2002, making every effort to include all relevant essays.

TABLE 4.1. Op-Eds on Iraq in *al-Hayat* and *al-Quds al-Arabi*, January 1999–June 2002

	al-Hayat	al-Quds al-Arabi	TOTAL
January–June 1999	59	80	139
July–December 1999	43	44	87
January–June 2000	23	46	69
July–December 2000	30	44	74
January–June 2001	42	84	126
July–December 2001	18	29	47
January–June 2002	47	54	101
Total	262	381	643

To give a sense of the extent to which Iraq became an "Arab" issue, in these two newspapers 158 different writers from 19 countries (as well as a number of self-described "Arabs") contributed their opinions on the Iraqi issue. Fewer Kuwaitis appeared in this press than on al-Jazeera, with only 23 columns by self-identified Kuwaitis appearing in the two papers in this period—of which 15 were by Mohammed al-Rumayhi in *al-Hayat*; by contrast, 136 essays by self-identified Iraqis appeared. *Al-Quds al-Arabi*, while fiercely critical of American policy, published a surprisingly large number of Iraqi critics of Saddam Hussein—including Ghassan Attiyah, Abd al-Amir Rikabi, and Burhan al-Jalabi. The regular columnists of *al-Quds al-Arabi*, such as Muta al-Safadi, Adli Sadeq, and Rashad Abu Shawar, as well as the chief editor, Abd al-Bari Atwan, all tended to take a highly critical line toward the sanctions and a pro-Iraqi orientation in general.

In *al-Hayat*, by contrast, far more pro-sanctions voices were routinely published. *Al-Hayat* aspired to be the *New York Times* of the Arab world, and as such sought to present an authentic "mirror" of respectable Arab debates—which meant both pro-sanctions and anti-sanctions voices. On the ten-year anniversary of the invasion of Kuwait, for example, *al-Hayat* invited Madeleine Albright to explain and defend American policy toward Iraq, with the counterpoint offered by the Kuwaiti Mohammed al-Rumayhi.[28] Regular columnists such as Ragheda Dergham and Jihad al-Khazen were often critical of American policy, but were also scathingly critical of Saddam Hussein; al-Khazen famously once wrote that Saddam was personally responsible for virtually every ill of the Arab world for two decades.

The Arabist hope that "taking a firm stand on Iraq could usher in the regaining of conscience to the Arab order" was not realized, however.[29] The reconstruction was limited to the popular level. As chapter 3 demonstrated, the Iraq issue remained divisive at the official level, as states aligned with the United States or genuinely fearful of Iraq clashed with those interested in rehabilitating Iraq for political or economic reasons. Arab states lagged behind European and Asian states in challenging the sanctions. When Iraq was invited to participate in the Arab summit of October 2000, it explicitly promised not to raise the divisive issues of the sanctions or its disagreements with Kuwait, in order to prevent these differences from destroying the summit.[30]

Arab League Secretary-General Amr Musa's visit to Baghdad in January 2002—the first such visit since the invasion of Kuwait—failed to persuade Kuwait to pursue reconciliation, despite widespread hopes and expectations that it would.[31] The impact of Iraq was far greater at the level of the public sphere, generating a unified Arab dialogue and identity rather than consistently driving state policies.

Normalizing Iraq

> Is it rational that the horrible Arab silence about the escalating destruction of an Arab country such as Iraq continues? About the slow death of the Iraqi people? About a war of mass extermination unprecedented in human history against an Arab and Islamic society? Why do some Arabs not mind the death of Iraqis and the absence of Iraq from the Arab arena? . . . Why is it upon Iraq, a country with a million killed, to implement Security Council resolutions to their letter while ignoring Israel's real violations of resolutions half a century old? . . . Why are foreign voices raised to lift the blockade of Iraq while the Arab regimes compete to demonstrate their fealty to the monstrous American position against Arabs?
>
> But on the other side: isn't the blockade of Iraq an international blockade before it is Arab? Isn't it a mistake to violate international resolutions? How can we call on the UN to deal with situations [like Israel] and then ignore its decisions? Doesn't Iraq have its own role by not co-operating with Arab or international initiatives to end the suffering of its people? Didn't one Iraqi official say that if forced to choose between keeping the blockade and readmitting inspectors it would choose the former? Doesn't the regime benefit from keeping the blockade because it consolidates its hegemony over its people . . . and gives it an excuse to not carry out reforms? Isn't the regime responsible before anyone else for the suffering of its children, because it has not given their mothers and fathers anything but torture? . . . Is it possible to reevaluate the Iraqi regime when it is increasing its terrorizing of the Iraqi people?
>
> —Faisal al-Qassem, December 2000[32]

Qassem's introduction to a December 2000 program nicely captures the frustrations of the Arab intellectual and political stalemate over Iraq. In a May 2000 episode of *More Than One Opinion*, host Sami

Haddad raised the possibility that a seminar hosted by the Kuwaiti parliament on the future of relations between Kuwait and Iraq might signal a new willingness to talk about normalization—a taboo in Kuwaiti politics. His first guest, Mohammed Jassem al-Saqr, immediately corrected him: the Qatari foreign minister "was the lone voice which called for normalization; . . . Americans and Iraqis and Kuwaitis all by complete consensus were against normalization."[33]

More interesting than the Kuwaiti's defense of his country's position was the highly public character of what would in the past have been a private discussion among elites. The "private" seminar received extensive coverage, not only from al-Jazeera but from numerous commentators in the Arab press. *Al-Hayat* alone published essays by half a dozen writers discussing the seminar and its implications. Similarly, after an Iraqi opposition figure in *al-Hayat* criticized an Arab Nationalist Conference held in Baghdad in May 2001 for its implied alignment with Saddam Hussein, the newspaper published replies from several participants, and commentaries from a variety of perspectives appeared in numerous Arab papers.[34] In the age of the new Arab public sphere, nothing related to Iraq could remain private, and everything was up for discussion before an intensely engaged audience.

The entrenched consensus on the suffering of the Iraqi people defined the terrain of legitimate Arab political debate. Popular sympathy with the Iraqi people made opponents of the reconciliation appear heartless and cruel, and as fundamentally detached from the sensitivities and concerns of "real" Arabs. But, as powerful as this consensus was, it did not foreclose debate. The anti-Saddam camp responded by affirming their sympathy for the Iraqi people, but focused attention on Saddam Hussein as the cause of that suffering. The Kuwaiti writer Mohammed al-Rumayhi's concern about this trend in the Arab media was palpable: "Yes, the Iraqi people are suffering, . . . but whose fault is that? Saddam's. . . . And the Arab media should say so."[35] Rumayhi attempted to turn the suffering of the Iraqi people back against critics of the sanctions, by asking a series of questions leading toward a plea for regime change: can Saddam Hussein be accepted or ignored? Can the sanctions continue forever? Can the sanctions overthrow Saddam?[36] If Arabs really wanted to save Iraqi children, argued Rumayhi, they should do so by backing the overthrow of Saddam—which would save all Iraqis, not only the children.[37] One al-Jazeera caller articulated the oft-heard refrain, "There is a solution to this problem for the Iraqi people, which is to save the Iraqi people from Saddam Hussein."[38]

Emotions ran high in these arguments about Iraq. It was not uncommon for talk shows devoted to Iraq to degenerate quickly into screaming matches and insults.[39] These public arguments were not always the highest examples of critical rationality—though they seldom failed to provide entertaining television. Many Arabs, desperate for a reconciliation, found themselves frustrated by the extreme polarization. In an al-Jazeera poll taken in January 2002, more than 90 percent of respondents supported the efforts of the Arab League to bring about an Iraqi-Kuwaiti reconciliation. When Saddam Hussein lashed out violently at Saudi Arabia in August 2000, even *al-Quds al-Arabi* was taken aback, while the usually sympathetic Mohammed al-Musaffir begged for an end to the "media wars between Riyadh and Baghdad."[40] In a September 2000 program dedicated to the "crisis in relations between Iraq and the Arab League," Qassem sharply questioned his Iraqi guest about "this senseless media campaign against the Secretary-General of the Arab League," and asked, "Why doesn't Iraq know anything other than the language of escalation and hostility?"[41]

In short, the interests of the new Arab public and those of Saddam's regime were not identical: for most of the Arab public, alleviating the suffering of the Iraqi people was the overwhelming priority, with backing Iraqi diplomacy a means to that end; for the Iraqi regime, on the other hand, easing the sanctions—or promoting the evidence of their devastating impact—was only a means to the end of staying in power.

Official Arab *silence* was a prominent theme in these public sphere discussions, with many seeing its primary mission to be forcing Arab leaders to take some position about the "noise of the silent war over Iraq."[42] "When will the voices of Arab officials rise up over the misery of 26 million Arab Iraqis?" asked Amar Najib.[43] The United States, argued Yusif Nur Awadh, did not fail to gain public support for American policies from Arab rulers, but only "to guarantee Arab silence and to prevent the raising of voices of protest in the event of an attack."[44] In addition to the heartfelt anguish over the sanctions, the new Arab public expressed outraged over official Arab silence about the regular bombings of Iraq through 1999. This media coverage put considerable pressure on governments that clearly would have preferred that the bombings remain "silent."[45] Others were outraged at "the silence of Arab rulers about the scenarios for dividing [partitioning] Iraq," especially after the American-backed Iraqi National Congress endorsed the principle of federalism for the Kurds.[46] For Burhan al-Jalabi, "every Iraqi cries, 'how long will the embargo last,' . . . but the Arabs support the United States."[47]

Others were more struck by hypocrisy than by silence—not only the hypocrisy of Arab states sympathizing with Iraq in public but supporting America in private, but also the hypocrisy of Arabs who claimed to detest Saddam Hussein but who strengthened his hand in practice. As Kuwaiti Ahmed al-Rubai complained, "There is a contradictory Arab language toward Iraq, a language that is sympathetic on the surface but tortured beneath it; a language that cries tears of compassion for Iraq and demands no attack against it . . . but at the same time fails to distinguish between the tyrannical regime and the oppressed people."[48] Others complained that Arabs could hardly demand that Israel live up to UN resolutions while "encouraging Iraq to violate them."[49] And, on the other side, staunch defenders of Iraq complained that Arabs said all the right things, but in the end did nothing. A cartoon in *al-Quds al-Arabi* portrayed an Arab leader shouting "No to USA" to an angry crowd, but with "Yes to USA" written across his back.[50] Subhi Hadidi marveled that "American officials openly say that the public positions of some Arab states, especially Saudi Arabia, do not resemble their private positions which they express . . . away from the lights of the cameras."[51] 85 percent of more than 37,000 respondents to a January 2003 online al-Jazeera poll said that Arab leaders were insincere when they publicly proclaimed their refusal to participate in a war on Iraq.[52] Did breaking the wall of silence mean only producing more hypocritical rhetoric?

The arguments over Iraq increasingly revolved around *identity* as much as around interests. These critiques insistently equated the hugely unpopular American policy with the support—tacit or vocal—of that policy by Arab regimes. With the dying Iraqi children having become the "greatest Arab issue," complained Abd al-Wahhab al-Affendi, "the Arab regimes have become the primary defenders of the interests of the West against the interests of the Arabs."[53] The sanctions survived only because Arab states enforced them, these critics pointed out. "Even the cultural embargo on Iraq is Arab," complained Abdullah al-Hourani.[54] It became increasingly common to refer to the sanctions as "an American and Arab aggression against the Iraqi people."[55] Frustrated with Kuwait's rejection of Amr Musa's reconciliation efforts in early 2002, Jordanian writer Fahd al-Fanik observed that "Musa should realize that Arab reconciliation is an American affair decided in Washington and not in Arab capitals."[56] The equation of direct American intervention with the Arab opposition to rehabilitating Iraq framed the issue as "Arab" versus "not Arab"—a deadly equation in the new Arab public. As Mohammed Abd al-Hakim Diyab put it, "The Saudi-Kuwaiti veto [over Iraqi participation in an Arab summit] translates the American desire to isolate Iraq . . . and is clearly against Arab public opinion."[57]

Support for the Iraqi people became a key marker of Arab identity—which implicitly defined those who publicly supported the sanctions as *non-Arab*. In April 1998, a writer in *al-Quds al-Arabi* set off a controversy with a series of articles questioning whether Kuwait could still be considered Arab given its position on Iraq; while numerous people complained that the newspaper had "no right to raise such sensitive issues," Kuwaitis themselves fiercely debated the same question.[58] A Saudi writer worried about this new trend, in which positions on the attack on Iraq, for example, were used to say, "this one is an Arab and this one is not an Arab and this one is a semi-Arab, . . . this is less Arabist, this is more Arabist."[59] The new media proved particularly conducive to this politics of identity, as the images on television stations conveyed a powerful emotional impact. Vivid footage of the suffering of fellow Arabs broke through the abstractions of strategy and high politics, which empowered those speakers who could tap into those emotional connections of identity and authenticity.

That the new public sphere enabled both a new kind of open public argument and a more potent politics of identity would over time develop into a major contradiction. During the American invasion of Iraq in 2003, the struggle between the politics of identity and the public sphere imperative of rational discourse would come to define much of the debate over the performance of the Arab media.

The Iraqi Opposition

How fortunate Saddam is in his opposition. . . . How miserable Iraq is in its *umma*.

—Khalid al-Shami, *al-Quds al-Arabi*[60]

We expected from our Arab brothers and sisters a clear position toward the mass extermination, . . . at least some observation of the crime of chemical weapons in Halabja, the crimes of Anfal, the crimes of draining the marshes, the killing of 400,000 people in the intifada of 1991, the killing, the attacks, the repression . . . all of this without a word of condemnation from the Arab League.

—Biyan Jabar, *Behind Events*[61]

Many Arabs bemoaned the absence of good choices, complaining about the impossibility of the options presented them—intolerable Iraqi suffering, a despised Iraqi regime, a distrusted America, an ineffective and silent official Arab order, a widely ridiculed opposition. For many of these voices, moreover, Saddam's regime was only a slightly harsher face of the tyranny of almost all Arab governments. As Egyptian journalist Mahmoud Attallah explained, "The Arab people go down into the street to protest attacks on Iraq, but this does not mean that they support the Iraqi regime, but this confusion is exploited by extremists on both sides, those that want to support Saddam Hussein, and those who hate everything Iraqi."[62] Ragheda Dergham's formulation captured a vital sense of this Arab middle ground: "The Iraqi people are victims of both Washington and Baghdad."[63] Or, more starkly, Mohammed Abd al-Hakim Diyab described "the difficult choice between the Satan of the rulers and the Satan of the opposition."[64]

The Iraqi opposition was famously divided, torn between competing personalities and agendas, and legendarily unable to unite. These internal struggles consumed much of the opposition's time and effort. Some of the differences were over matters of real political significance: should the Iraqi opposition align itself with the United States, gaining power and resources at the risk of being labeled American puppets? Should it support the sanctions as a means of putting pressure on Saddam, or oppose them out of concern for the well-being of the

Iraqi people? Should it call for a loose federalism or a strong central state? Should it advocate a military coup, American invasion, or popular revolution? How important was democracy as a goal? What role should be played by people who once held high positions in the Iraqi regime? Underlying many of these substantive arguments were personal rivalries and ambitions, to the extent that disentangling them sometimes seemed impossible. These internal divisions and endemic rivalries both made it easy to dismiss the Iraqi opposition as ineffectual and offered entertaining political theater for the new Arab public sphere. Some Iraqi opposition figures proved quite skilled at speaking to Arab audiences, while others did not.

The Iraqi National Congress (INC) was formed in June 1992 under American patronage as an umbrella for the Iraqi opposition. A wide range of groups participated in the early negotiations, which culminated in an October 1992 meeting of some 234 delegates from parties including the two main Kurdish parties (the KDP and PUK) and a major Shia opposition party (SCIRI) in Salahuddin, in Iraqi Kurdistan. This original moment of unity—frequently invoked by all factions—soon gave way to internal power struggles and disagreements. Fierce fighting broke out between the PUK and KDP in May 1994, while in 1995 member groups such as the important Shia Dawa party, the Iraqi Democratic Union, and the Arab Nationalist Party pulled out of the INC and SCIRI suspended its membership in the executive council.

A coup attempt led by Major General Wafiq al-Samarrai failed in March 1995, after the United States pulled out based on intelligence that the coup planning had been badly compromised. In August 1996 Iraqi forces sacked the INC's base in Salahuddin after the KDP invited Saddam's army into Kurdistan to assist it against its rivals in the PUK. By the mid-1990s, much of the American foreign policy establishment, including the State Department and the CIA, had come to despair of the INC's endless internal divisions, its shady accounting practices, and its inability to deliver results inside Iraq. Some preferred the Iraqi National Accord (al-Wifaq; INA), established in December 1990 with the help of Saudi Prince Turki bin Faisal, appealing primarily to Sunni ex-Baathists, and led by Iyad Allawi; the INA's own coup attempt failed in June 1996, again compromised by Iraqi intelligence. A wide range of other factions operated outside the INC umbrella, refusing to be publicly aligned with the United States and fiercely critical of those who were.

For all of its organizational incompetence and unpopularity on the ground, the Iraqi National Congress—with help from the American public relations firm the Rendon Group—proved masterful at producing and distributing propaganda in the American and global media (McCollam 2004). While ineffective in influencing Arab opinion, Chalabi and the INC very effectively shaped American public opinion in what the editor of Lebanon's *al-Safir*, Joseph Samaha, describes sarcastically as the most effective Arab public diplomacy campaign in history.[65] Chalabi, by far the least popular of the Iraqi opposition figures among the Arab public (see below), was well connected in Republican party circles, with neo-conservative writers and pundits, and with the neo-conservative civilian leadership in the Pentagon. He was despised by the CIA and the State Department, however, and roundly distrusted by most Arab leaders—particularly in Jordan, where he faced a standing arrest warrant for embezzlement for his role in the collapse of Petra Bank in the 1980s.

The Iraqi opposition faced enormous difficulties moving between the American and Arab public spheres, as the arguments made to win support in the United States rebounded against them among Arabs. The INC proved far more effective in marketing itself to American audiences than to Arab audiences, which only exacerbated its problems in the Arab public sphere. Chalabi's friendly public position toward Israel, helpful for building support among American neo-conservatives, badly damaged his image in the Arab world. For example, in March 2002 Sadiq al-Musawi explained on al-Jazeera that the INC agreed with the international consensus against attacking Iraq, but also agreed with the "very strong" international consensus for changing the Iraqi regime.[66] When host Jumana al-Namour challenged him to reconcile this position with Ahmed Chalabi's statement that he was ready to support America if it attacked Iraq, Musawi retreated to emphasizing the need to overthrow Saddam and create a democratic regime in Iraq. When she pressed him further, he explained that the Iraqi opposition opposed "any attack that does not have the goal of overthrowing the regime" and would support an attack that did target the regime.

Most Arab public opinion condemned or ridiculed the official Iraqi opposition as pawns of the United States who commanded little real support inside of Iraq: "They wake up in America and breakfast in Kuwait."[67] The alleged "inauthenticity" of the Iraqi opposition was their Achilles heel; as Joseph Samaha warned, "The United States' designating some Iraqi opposition as its protégés weakens them."[68] The INC was routinely mocked as the "supported Iraqi opposition," as being "outsiders," as "failing to understand Iraqi realities."[69] Calls by some members of the Iraqi opposition to intensify the sanctions made them seem heartless toward their own people.[70] For Abd al-Wahhab al-Affendi, that parts of the Iraqi opposition supported the sanctions at a time when people all over the world were doing everything they could to help the suffering children of Iraq proved "its isolation, not only from Iraq and its realities, but from humanity."[71] In short, the Iraqi opposition over time not only lost the argument about Saddam, but came to be seen as fundamentally non-Arab. Such views were reinforced by calls made by Iraqi opposition figures such as Kanan Makiya and Ahmed Chalabi for a post-Saddam Iraq to be "a federal, *non-Arab*, demilitarized Iraq."[72]

Few in the Arab public sphere criticized opposition to Saddam Hussein in principle. A desire to overthrow a hated dictator was not out of line in the new Arab public sphere, which prided itself on its comprehensive rejection of the repressive Arab status quo. Mohammed al-Musaffir acknowledged, "There is no controversy that there are noble Iraqi opposition figures . . . who live in exile out of hatred for what has happened and is happening to their comrades and who do not want their Iraq to be destroyed, . . . and they can hold their heads high. . . . The regime in Baghdad should respect them and listen to them when they call for reforms."[73] But these noble figures, Musaffir asserts, should not be confused with those opportunists who sell out their country to the United States and beat the drum for a war against their own people. How could such well-intentioned figures fail to see the contradiction between American declarations of love for the Iraqi people and "the reality that every Arab can see," of the American role in the violence against the Palestinian people?[74] Change, for this line of thinking, must come from within and not from American support.

The new Arab media served as a vital forum for the Iraqi opposition factions to bring their arguments directly to an Arab public. Competing editorials in Arab newspapers, or public arguments on al-Jazeera, offered a powerful tonic to the back-room politicking and secretive deal-making commonly attributed to the Iraqi opposition (especially Chalabi and the INC). In 1999 alone, *al-Hayat* and *al-Quds al-Arabi* published some forty essays about the Iraqi opposition. Each encouraged dialogues and challenges to its own editorial line. When a regular columnist denounced Iraqi opposition figures who supported attacks on Iraq, for example, *al-Quds al-Arabi* published a lengthy response by Ala al-Lami, which insisted that "friendship with the Iraqi people cannot mean friendship with the Iraqi regime."[75] At almost the same time, two columnists debated each other on the editorial page over the urgency of demanding democracy in Iraq before supporting the Iraqi regime.[76] Writers such as Ghassan Attiyah and Haroun Mohammed wrote sympathetically about efforts to unify the Iraqi opposition and to give it a message that could appeal to an Arab public opinion that had little use for Saddam but even less confidence in the United States.[77] Entifadh Qanbar, Hamid al-Bayati, and Ghassan Attiyah were among the most frequent guests on Iraq-related al-Jazeera programs. Iraqi opposition voices were hardly silenced in the new media, even if they convinced few.

The press allowed Iraqi exiles to openly speculate about the future of Iraq, to lay out their aspirations, and to wage their private battles. For example, Abd al-Amir Rikabi wrote in February 1999 wondering about the commitment to democracy of the Iraqi nationalists in the opposition. A November 2001 essay in *al-Hayat* by Abd al-Halim al-Rahimi frankly dissected the different trends within an Iraqi opposition deeply conflicted over the possibility of an American invasion of their country.[78] Rahimi identified three major opinion groups: those who opposed any attack which did not remove Saddam, since such a weak attack would only strengthen Saddam and mobilize public support in his favor; those who opposed any attack on Iraq from the outside, preferring that change come from within; and those who supported any strike against Iraq.

The crucial point here is that the new Arab media brought publicity to the closed world of the Iraqi opposition, making their private arguments and disagreements more visible to a suspicious Arab public. Portraying these differences within the opposition served a useful purpose in distancing the opposition to Saddam from generic support for American policy. Indeed, what emerges from the Arab public sphere is less a distaste for opposing Saddam as for the American-backed Iraqi National Congress and its leader, Ahmed Chalabi.

Two American-sponsored Iraqi opposition meetings in 1999, in London in March and in New York in October, offered a revealing public window into the personalities and political struggles inside the opposition. The meetings received a great deal of attention in the new Arab media, and were the occasion of considerable discussion and debate. After the New York meeting, for example, *More Than One Opinion* hosted a discussion that pitted Iraqi participants in the meeting against dissidents who had either chosen to not participate or had not been invited, giving ample time for both INC members and their critics from other factions of the Iraqi opposition to defend their positions.[79] In the press, Adil al-Qiyar voiced a common complaint, noting that "despite the material, media, and political support that American intelligence has contributed to help the Iraqi National Congress and the factions of the so-called Iraqi opposition in exile, it was not able to unify their ranks."[80] Ghassan Attiyah noted a dramatic change from the unified, inclusive vision of the Iraqi opposition embodied in the 1992 Salah al-Din meeting in Kurdistan to the restrictive, controlled, and—in his view—American-orchestrated meetings in New York.[81] The exclusionary and undemocratic quality of those meetings received a great deal of attention: power was centralized in the hands of a small number of figures with close relations to the United States while other Iraqi opposition factions complained of being shut out.

Members of the Iraqi opposition bitterly resented their perceived treatment by the Arab media—but this had less to do with their access to the media than with the hostile reception to their ideas. In the INC newspaper *al-Mutamar*, for example, Daoud al-Basri complained that in his own recent appearance on *The Opposite Direction*, Faisal al-Qassem had asked him to avoid insulting the Iraqi regime—which Basri interpreted not as an attempt to maintain civil discourse but as an "absurd" and biased attempt to protect Saddam from criticism.[82]

This particular episode, in December 2001, offers an instructive example of negative interactions between a very present Iraqi opposition and a hostile Arab public sphere. Fa'iq al-Shaykh Ali of the Iraqi opposition had been invited to present the case for an American invasion of Iraq against Maan Bashour, president of the Arab Nationalist Forum. After Shakykh Ali had held the floor for the first segment, Qassem took a phone call from former Iraqi ambassador Salah al-Mukhtar, who denounced any opposition that took money from the United States and rejected any claim they made to speak for the Iraqi people on those grounds. Shaykh Ali responded by yelling, "Why don't you go back to Iraq and be killed!", and then accused al-Jazeera of being on the payroll of the Iraqi mukhabarat and of being an insult to the sacrifices of the Iraqi people. As the discussion degenerated into a screaming match, Shaykh Ali repeatedly accused al-Jazeera of insulting the Iraqi people because "most of your guests are from the Iraqi regime or are friends of it." An exasperated Qassem challenged him: "Why do you always run away from the question and change the subject? . . . We have presented many programs on this topic, and every time you resort to avoiding the topic of the discussion."

Basri called in to the program to defend Shaykh Ali and to object to the form of Qassem's question: "Of course no sincere Iraqi supports bombing or destroying his country, but such slogans as 'Afghanizing Iraq' . . . are just false slogans inflamed by the Iraqi regime and its Arab supporters. . . . We are of course pleased at the absence of officials from the Iraqi regime [on the program], but they leave that task to their well-known allies and friends in the Arab arena." Basri then launched into a personal attack on Bashour and accused the Arab Nationalist Forum of being "against the Iraqi people and against the Arab umma," along with a fierce attack on Saddam's regime and anyone who failed to back the Iraqi opposition against it. It was at this point that Qassem invoked al-Jazeera's consistent rule of avoiding personal attacks, urged Basri to stick to the topic, and finally took a different caller.

This incident captures a number of essential points: that the Iraqi opposition had ample opportunity to make their case in the Arab media, that they largely failed to persuade, that they bitterly resented this failure, and that they often blamed that media for their own failures.

As Kanan Makiya of the INC complained, "The Iraqi opposition is ostracized in the Middle East. It's worse than not having support. It's an actual sort of an assumption that it doesn't even exist, that it's not relevant. When the Arab world talks about Iraq, it excludes the fact that there is an opposition."[83] While Makiya exaggerates the exclusion of the Iraqi opposition from Arab debates, this self-perception among the Iraqi exiles was widespread and deeply held. The opposition denounced the Arab League for refusing to meet with it or to support its calls for regime change in Iraq; Arab League spokesmen pointed out in response that the League represented the Arab states who were its members.[84] Virtually every appearance by an Iraqi opposition figure on al-Jazeera soon degenerated into a catalogue of grievances against the Arab states, the Arab media, and all of those they described as supporters of Saddam.

The Iraqi opposition, frustrated at the lack of public enthusiasm for war, did not lack for opportunities to challenge Arab leaders. But the distinction drawn by most Arabs between the Iraqi regime and the Iraqi people posed a nearly insoluble dilemma for opposition figures. Ghassan Attiyah wondered whether the Arabs declaring their sympathy with the Iraqi people really wished Saddam Hussein on them, or were they perhaps simply ignorant of the suffering imposed on them by Saddam?[85] Others expressed less doubt, reducing the question to its barest terms: "Do you support Saddam or the Iraqi people?"[86] But most Arabs simply did not accept the claim that opposition to an attack on Iraq "came on behalf of the interests of Saddam and at the expense of the interests of the Iraqi people."

Iraqi Arguments

Opinions about Saddam Hussein in the new Arab public sphere varied widely, from uncritical praise for a perceived hero holding out against American power to bitter attacks against a reckless lunatic who persecuted his own people. Sanctions critics and regime critics alike found Saddam's behavior baffling and exasperating, repeatedly undercutting his own presumed objectives. In the words of long-time Saddam critic Hazem Saghiyeh, "nobody can understand Saddam's behavior"—neither his supporters nor his enemies.[87] Even *al-Quds al-Arabi* declared Iraq's decision to cease cooperation with UNSCOM in August 1998 as "suicidal."[88] But at the same time, the powerful impetus in the Arab public sphere toward sympathy with the Iraqi people served as an important strategic asset to the Iraqi president. Iraq tailored its rhetoric with an eye toward the priorities of the Arab public sphere, nurturing Arab public sympathy with a clear eye toward its strategic value and attempting to leverage it into pressure on other Arab leaders and to undermine compliance with the sanctions regime.

Iraq argued that its rehabilitation served Arab strategic interests and that only Kuwaiti and Saudi intransigence stood in the way of achieving a united Arab front. A strong Iraq would benefit Arab power and security, against Iran, against Turkey, against internal division, and against Western domination: "For Iraq to resume its regional and international role would be in the interests of all the [Arab] brothers. . . . We must move toward the future and whatever is in everyone's interests. We should realize that what happened between us is not the first in the history of the nations, in order to enable ourselves to turn the page of the past and open a new page based on all that is in everyone's interests."[89] Rhetorical attacks on Gulf states undermined these arguments about collective security, however, by casting doubt on the sincerity of Iraqi reassurances. Tariq Aziz argued that despite the remaining differences between Arab states, "many say, mostly in secrecy and sometimes in the open: Iraq's absence has humiliated and weakened us; we need Iraq to return and play an effective role in Arab life and affairs. This has been reflected everywhere. Of course the masses had a clear stand. Even official stands of Arab leaderships and decision makers reflected this: the press, research centers, and influential political figures."[90]

The Iraqi regime attempted to manipulate and use the Arab public sphere to its own ends, with direct efforts at propaganda as well as more subtle strategies of manipulating and controlling information. As described in chapter 3, it encouraged reports on the sanctions, providing access and information to reporters who spread the news, but this did not minimize the reality of the humanitarian crisis. Iraq appealed to Arab brotherhood to work to end Iraqi suffering, pointing out dual standards with regards to Israel, challenging the integrity of

UN operations, and calling to rally Arab forces against the West. Iraqi argumentation improved over time, perhaps as Iraqis gained a better sense of the resonance of different frames, and as sympathetic Arabs outside Iraq helped to spread their message.[91]

Establishing that "authentic Arab" public opinion was with Iraq was central to the Iraqi regime's strategy. As Tariq Aziz put it, "all the people of the Arab nation call for lifting the siege. Most Arab governments—with the exception of two governments whom you know—are calling for lifting the siege. . . . Our calls for lifting the siege . . . are in line with the Arab people's will as well as that of the international community."[92] Establishing that the Arab public sided with Iraq was a major component of Iraqi strategy, and to that end it did everything possible to overload the system with information to that effect. One method was to host "popular summits" in Baghdad that would bring together popular (and less well-known) opposition figures from all over the Arab world to build pro-Iraqi coalitions; the largest of these, in July–October 1999, included delegations from more than half a dozen Arab states. To establish a since of progress and momentum, Iraq heavily publicized every visit by any delegation. Another method was to work through a wide array of pan-Arab organizations, such as the Arab Parliamentary Union, which regularly issued statements of support for Iraq. Yet another was to invite Arab journalists to visit Iraq, showering them with attention and gifts. The cash awards for Palestinian suicide bombers was part of this strategy (see below), aimed far more at Arab public opinion than at the Palestinian arena itself.

American military attacks against Iraq that left the regime in place generally served Iraq's interests by mobilizing a sense of Arab outrage, and putting pressure on Arab governments to distance themselves from American policy.[93] In general, Iraq proved far more successful when working to shape this Arabist worldview than when it attempted direct appeals for Arab political action. Whenever Saddam Hussein attempted a Nasser-style direct appeal to the Arab people to rise up against their rulers, he not only failed to win support, but generated significant opposition. In January 1999, for example, Iraq launched a violent rhetorical attack calling for the Arab street to rise up against rulers who continued to support the sanctions. The chief editor of Egypt's MENA responded: "Don't labor under the illusion that un-

leashing your media apparatus ... would get you off the hook. ...
The sympathy and outrage felt by the Arab street in the wake of the
U.S.-British bombings were motivated by support for the Iraqi people
and feelings of disillusionment and revulsion. ... Neither this anger or
sympathy was meant to support you."[94]

Iraq's violent rhetorical attacks on other Arab state were generally
counterproductive. When Uday Hussein threatened Kuwait in January 2001, *al-Quds al-Arabi* complained that "there is no excuse for
this ... it sets back all our efforts against the embargo."[95] Iraqi calls for
the masses to overthrow regimes that continued to support the sanctions—as in January 1999—almost certainly drove wobbling states
back toward a hard line by enhancing their perception of threat. After
the Arab Summit in Cairo in October 2000, Iraq celebrated its return
to the Arab order by calling for the masses to rise up against the Arab
regimes: "Some Arab rulers have again submitted to the will of the
enemies of the Arab nation and disregarded the Arab masses. ... We
urge the masses of our nation ... to undertake the responsibility of
exposing those who betrayed the nation ... to stage a revolution and
punish the traitorous rulers."[96] While it is hard to imagine how such an
argument could fail to persuade said traitorous rulers, most remained
curiously unmoved.

Iraq, Israel, and the Palestinians

The belief that the Iraqi and Palestinian issues were related is almost
universal in the Arab public sphere. Most Arabs believed that American policy toward Iraq was—to a greater or lesser extent—motivated by
its pro-Israeli sympathies. The power of the "Jewish lobby" over American Middle East policy was a matter of faith, as was the hostility of this
lobby to Arab identity and interests. Since a weak or divided Iraq served
Israel's interests in the regional power equation, it seemed plausible that
Israel played some role in driving the containment of Iraq.

Arabs picked up on American media discussions of "neo-conservative" influences on Bush's foreign policy as confirmation of these
suspicions. From time to time, controversies broke out over alleged
Israeli plans to resettle Palestinian refugees in a post-Saddam Iraq.[97]

Chalabi's widely reported promise that an Iraq led by the INC would recognize and have friendly relations with Israel, and would be willing to resettle Palestinian refugees in Iraq, fueled these speculations, while also doing much to discredit Chalabi in the eyes of Arab public opinion. Richard Butler's warnings in January 1998 that Iraqi chemical weapons could reach Tel Aviv immediately suggested to many Arabs that Israeli security was the real motivation behind the Iraqi file.[98] The revelation of Scott Ritter's reliance on Israeli intelligence in his UNSCOM inspections confirmed what had been widely alleged in the Arab media—with many commentators declaring themselves vindicated against Western denunciations of their "conspiracy theories."[99] When Iraq was bombed by the outgoing Clinton administration in January 2001, one writer described the attack as "fifty-six cruise missiles on Iraq to prevent it from supporting the Intifada."[100]

Saddam understood that Iraq could benefit by linking the Iraqi issue to the Palestinian one, about which Arabs were far more unanimous and politically mobilized. When Palestinians were the first to publicly protest the possibility of an attack on Iraq in early 1998, it had a greater effect than protests almost anywhere else would have. Palestinian activists formed a Palestinian Committee for Solidarity with the Iraqi People in January 1998; the sight of Palestinian children, with all of their difficulties and with all their symbolic weight, collecting humanitarian supplies for Iraqi children struck a powerful chord.[101] Iraq's opposition to the Palestinian-Israeli peace process won it gratitude among Arab and Islamist critics of the negotiations, even if Iraq's centrality to that opposition has been vastly overstated by Americans who saw "the road to Jerusalem leading through Baghdad."

Some Palestinian hard-liners actually worried that Saddam might offer peace with Israel as an incentive to reconcile with the United States, while Palestinian supporters of the peace negotiations resented Iraqi support for the hard-liners. In this environment of violence and despair, Iraq did what it could to keep the "Arab street" agitated and to be seen as doing what it could to assist the Palestinians. Its much-publicized payments to the families of Palestinian "martyrs" were expressly aimed at Arab public opinion—to demonstrate that Iraq, even as it suffered under sanctions, would still do more to support the Palestinian struggle than did other Arab states. Similarly, its decision to stop pumping oil temporarily to "support the Intifada" in April 2002 was widely seen as a publicity stunt, but as a valuable and praiseworthy one all the same.

After September 2000, growing numbers of Arabs believed that they could effectively support the Palestinian uprising only by closing ranks and putting the Iraq war divisions behind them. Divisions over Iraq, according to this argument, must be set aside in the face of a greater common threat to Palestine—over which a genuine consensus existed. Some Palestinian and Iraqi partisans worried that more concern for one issue would detract from the other. But the opposite seems to have been the case within the new Arab public sphere, as the two issues together created a multiplier effect, strengthening Arab public support for both Palestine and Iraq.[102] Rather than making a choice between the two issues, the Arab public insisted on the intimate linkage between the suffering of the two peoples, with the United States being the key actor in each.[103] As Mohammed al-Musaffir scathingly complained, "The United States of America deals with Arabs with the worst and most vicious kind of terrorism just as Israel does toward the Palestinian people and the Lebanese people. . . . America is doing the same thing with its near daily bombings."[104] The Arab public drew direct comparisons between the suffering of Iraqis and Palestinians, while blaming their governments for doing too little about either. As Ghassan Attiyah noted with some concern in the spring of 2000, "Iraqi suffering is joining Palestinian suffering as a card in the hand of the Islamists."[105] Such an equation could be found in the state media as well as the new public sphere, with a growing focus on the American role linking the two crises.

As the United States began pushing for war with Iraq in 2002, the Arab public sphere drew ever tighter linkages between Iraq and the Palestinian issue. Contrary to the arguments of many American conservatives that displays of American power would win Arab respect, it is clear that American support for Israel deeply undermined its credibility with Arab audiences (Gerecht 2002). As one writer bluntly put it, "After all that the United States has done for Israel, how can it possibly have good intentions in attacking Iraq?"[106] The grinding violence in the West Bank, and especially the bloody Israeli re-occupation in April 2002, ensured that any American moves on Iraq would be viewed through the lens of Palestinian suffering.

U.S. Vice President Dick Cheney's visit to the region in March 2002 brought all these trends to a head, and serves as an excellent window into a transformed normative and strategic environment that the United States badly failed to understand. While Cheney came to marshal support for action against Iraq, he found instead a region consumed with concern over the escalating war between Israel and the Palestinians (Woodward 2004: 111–112). As Jordanian columnist Fahd al-Fanik put it, "Cheney said to the Arab leaders: Iraq, and they said to him: Palestine. He said to them: Saddam, and they said to him: Sharon."[107] A cartoon published in *al-Hayat* showed Cheney walking through a puddle of blood in the West Bank; looking down at the bloody footprints tracking behind him, Cheney says "I'm sure that Saddam did it."[108]

In an almost unprecedented acknowledgment of the new power of public opinion, even pro-American Arab leaders made clear that they could not be asked to publicly support a war against Iraq while the United States supported the Israeli re-occupation of the West Bank. Even Saudi Arabia and Kuwait demurred from supporting an attack on Iraq at that time, "because it would harm the Iraqi people and not its regime."[109] Even Kuwaiti writers who had long strongly supported overthrowing Saddam's regime refused to step forward. For example, Ahmed al-Rubai, while affirming the deep Kuwaiti gratitude to Cheney personally, complained that "you know that you have many friends in Arab governments who find themselves always in a difficult position toward the United States, for one simple reason, which is that the American position toward Israel cannot be defended."[110] As Said al-Shihabi observed, "Despite the efforts of some Arab rulers to conform to the American agenda, there is a general feeling of deteriorating conditions because of the crimes committed by 'Israel' against the Palestinian people, and the unlimited American support for that aggression. . . . Washington realizes the existence of popular anger against its policies, which is why one of the goals of Cheney's visit was to put pressure on Arab governments to support its policies toward Iraq and Palestine."[111]

The Arab public, astounded by its own success, celebrated its newfound power in frustrating Cheney's mission—although at the same time, most of that public assumed that war with Iraq was inevitable nonetheless. Most simply assumed their leaders would be hypocritical: "Cheney did not expect to receive public support from Arab states. . . . Arab media support is not what he wanted, but rather tactical and logistical support for the American war machine . . . and that, in private, he probably received."[112] Expressions of opposition to a war on Iraq, complained the skeptics, "were strictly for local consumption."[113] Even where leaders scrambled to meet the expectations of the new public, the gap between regimes and publics remained vast.

The UN Weapons Inspections: From Crisis to Crisis

From the summer of 1997 onward, a more-or-less perpetual crisis between Iraq and the UNSCOM weapons inspectors kept Iraq at the front of the Arab and international publics. When tensions began to rise over a series of controversial inspections, the most common interpretation was that the United States was seeking a confrontation.[114] From the American perspective, the crumbling sanctions and insistent divisions in the Security Council were making the containment policy unworkable, leading to a difficult choice: to keep sanctions or to keep inspections (Byman 2000). Worried that the inspections might prove ineffective without a Security Council united in backing them with force, the Clinton administration chose to sacrifice the inspections in order to keep the sanctions and to pursue regime change options. The culmination of these crises—the withdrawal of UNSCOM and four days of massive bombing by the United States and the United Kingdom—followed by revelations of American and Israeli misuse of UNSCOM vindicated many Arabs in their convictions. This served Iraq very well in the Arab context, as public opinion grew first frustrated and then infuriated at the seeming intransigence and irresponsibility of the United States, which deflected attention from Iraq's own continuing defiance of the inspectors.

By the time of the UNSCOM crises of 1997–1998, many Arabs had already been convinced of the political bias of UNSCOM. Richard Butler's style certainly aggravated these convictions. Even the Saudi newspaper *al-Sharq al-Awsat* complained that Butler "did not bother on any occasion to win the good opinion of Iraqi citizens or ordinary people anywhere in the Arab world. . . . Butler's words were music to Baghdad's ears."[115] Arab support for easing the sanctions most likely entered into Saddam's strategic calculations in his decision to challenge the inspections process beginning in late 1997. Each successive crisis strengthened the general popular background consensus among Arab publics about American unilateralism and the injustice of the sanctions.

Most actors, both Arab and Western, expected the "Arab street" to be controllable by Arab regimes, which were expected to cooperate with the ongoing American demand for Iraqi cooperation with UNSCOM inspectors. Most expected Arab opinion to be against bombing, but doubted that this opinion could be expressed effectively or that Arab leaders would respond to public opinion. Adli Sadeq articulated the general public sentiment, "It seems clear that the official viewpoint of the GCC and other Arab states is . . . that bombings of Iraq that do not remove Saddam are inflaming the public mood" but that they would "support a U.S.-U.K. attack that successfully targeted Saddam personally."[116] Or, in the words of another critical writer, "The main concern of Arab regimes is how to best submit to America's demands."[117]

As the year progressed, an unusual Arab consensus emerged "on the need to lift the blockade on the starving, tortured Iraqi people. . . . The United States imagines that it can separate the Arab regimes from their people . . . and force them to act against the peoples' feelings, . . . but the gap [between regimes and the people] is not nearly so great as imagined by current American policy."[118] As *al-Quds al-Arabi* explained, "With the exception of Kuwait, the Gulf states are hesitant to back any U.S. military action against Iraq that would not bring about the hoped-for change at the helm. . . . Limited strikes have been proven to strengthen the Iraqi leader and boost his popularity both inside and outside Iraq, while weakening Gulf governments and putting them in an embarrassing position vis-à-vis their citizens and other Arabs."[119]

In February 1998, however, Arab political behavior took a different turn—because, I argue, of the new strategic and normative environment created by the new Arab public sphere. While the resurrection of "the street" in most Arab countries is often believed to have begun with the Palestinian uprising of September 2000, it actually dates to these February 1998 protests against an American strike against Iraq. In mid-February, after a period of surprisingly little public mobilization, large rallies in support of Iraq began to break out throughout the Arab world. The February 12 rally in the Palestinian territories received the greatest notice, but there were also protest rallies in Jordan, Lebanon, Egypt, Yemen, Tunisia, and Morocco. As one observer put it, "Arab opinion expressed itself by any means available despite the obstacles placed before it by the Arab officials. . . . The greatest contradiction was between the direction of the Arab street and the official direction."[120] Arab regimes were no less shocked than was the United States, as many Arab writers and commentators noted, by this sudden appearance of popular mobilization. Citing these demonstrations, Arab commentators overwhelmingly concluded that "Arab public opinion is beginning to move with force and to put pressure on its governments."[121] CNN, as well as the emerging Arab satellite television stations, played an important role by broadcasting footage of these rallies across the Arab world, inspiring imitation demonstrations and encouraging ordinary Arabs to act in ways that in the past would have seemed too dangerous.

This new Arab public opinion shaped the strategic calculations of all actors in the escalating Iraq crisis, even if the Arab media itself failed "to realize the importance of the political success it accomplished in frustrating the project of a third Gulf War."[122] Arab rejection of the legitimacy of the sanctions, and their insistence on action to rescue the Iraqi people from their misery, fatally undermined the status quo in spite of the preferences of most Arab regimes. As Ghassan Attiyah warned, "Pictures of Saddam Hussein are raised today in protests in Gaza and Jordan, and some Arab leaders are presenting themselves as sympathizing with the ruler of Baghdad in order to be closer to that street."[123] The open arguments on al-Jazeera could not be restricted to just the television screen, and soon began to spill out into open political mobilization in almost every Arab country. These protestors used a common language and employed similar imagery, with their actions in turn rebroadcast on the Arab media—providing inspiration for others in a virtuous circle of activism. It was quite common for guests and callers on al-Jazeera to directly address this "Arab street," to call on the street to rise up, or to invoke its desires. And, in this period, the "Arab street" did reappear, giving political substance to the consensus emerging in the public sphere.

In response, not a single Arab state—not even Kuwait—agreed to participate actively or passively in an attack on Iraq. Even those regimes that longed to be rid of Saddam were "forced to use two voices, one in public and one in private," by the strong Arab consensus.[124] In response, Arab regimes moved swiftly and firmly to regain control before the next crisis, banning demonstrations and establishing redlines for public demands on their policies. But an important signal had been sent, which gave much greater political weight to the opinions and arguments now being heard on satellite television and in the press. When crises hit in Iraq Arab states had little choice but to take into account the very real presence of a mobilized and angry Arab street.

The February 25, 1998, "Memorandum of Understanding" negotiated by Kofi Annan that defused the crisis was received enthusiastically by Arabs desperate to avoid a war. As al-Quds al-Arabi pointed out, however, it was striking that the crisis was resolved "with the near-complete absence of official Arab diplomacy."[125] Iraq, worried Ghassan Attiyah, had "succeeded in mustering Arab public opinion, benefiting from sympathy which far exceeded that of the Arabs who traditionally support the Iraqi regime."[126] Beyond the concessions about inspection protocols encoded in the MOA, Iraq had broken its Arab isolation, driven a wedge between Washington and its Arab allies—or else between those regimes and their publics—focused global attention on the sanctions, and (in some eyes) humiliated the Clinton administration. While few doubted that the United States would look for another opportunity to attack, the unexpected outcome—and the role played by Arab public opinion—surprised everyone. The lesson taken away from this crisis for the new Arab public was the stark contrast between an effective Arab street—one which protested vigorously and captured the attention of the global media and of the United States—and silent, ineffective Arab regimes.

Arab public opinion played a key role throughout the year of crisis, as all strategic actors attempted to manipulate or position themselves in response to it. Even if many Arabs believed that America had sought out a confrontation, savvy observers saw that Iraq "welcome[d] missile strikes because this convince[d] the Arab street of American hostility, . . . and Saddam Hussein [saw] the Arab street as key to his strategy."[127] When the Clinton administration contemplated military action against Iraq, therefore, it received virtually no public support from Arab regimes—in sharp contrast to years past, when its efforts received public backing from the Gulf Cooperation Council states and, often, Egypt. Many Arab commentators saw it as an attempt by Clinton to distract attention from his domestic political problems—a notion that Operation Desert Fox, coinciding exactly with Clinton's impeachment trial, did little to dismiss. Few believed that Iraqi weapons of mass destruction were the real issue in this crisis, or those to follow. Most considered the American goal of overthrowing Saddam Hussein to be the real driving force. This consensus, established through years of intense public argument in the new Arab public sphere, would return to shape the Arab reception of the Bush administration initiative in 2002.

The February crisis framed expectations for the next major crisis, which erupted in November 1998. In contrast to the earlier period, when Arabs overwhelmingly called for Iraqi defiance, this time Arabs desperately urged Iraq to cooperate with the inspections. Convinced of the American intent to attack, Arab leaders scrambled to avoid war. With the memory of the February protests vivid in Arab minds, there were virtually no major demonstrations or protests. Many regimes clamped down hard on protests. In Palestine, for example, there were "efforts to limit protests. . . . Arafat has told police and top political activists that this is not a good time for such public displays."[128] While Iraq did back down, preventing war for another month, many Arabs grew ever more bitter at their impotence in the face of the Iraqi-American power struggles: "As developments have come to a head, Arab citizens—whether ordinary people or officials—discover that Arab feelings, interests, security, or sovereignty do not carry any weight in American decision making. . . . Arab sovereignty, dignity, and lives are so cheap in the eyes of U.S. arrogance," complained one Palestinian writer.[129]

In December the Desert Fox bombings announced the American-British decision to abandon the UN Security Council, sacrifice the inspections, and to simply use military force. That Saddam Hussein survived the four days of bombing was taken by many Arabs as an Iraqi victory and an American defeat. A bombing campaign that left Saddam in power while inflaming the Arab street fulfilled the worst fears of many of America's Arab allies. In response to the bombings, massive protests broke out across the Arab world. These demonstrations served to punctuate the radically transformed role of Arab public opinion—which in turn served as a clear precedent for the behavior of Arab publics and governments during the Palestinian uprising and the war in Iraq. Saudi writer Fawzia Abu Khaled noted in *al-Hayat* that for the first time since the 1991 Gulf War there was "clear American concern about the movement of the Arab street. . . . American policy makers have realized the political weight of the Arab street and the need to take it into account."[130] This newfound concern extended to Arab rulers, argued Abu Khaled, who "had themselves not valued these popular forces adequately, . . . [which] followed from their policies of marginalizing that street." Al-Jazeera and other satellite television stations played a crucial role in this, she argued, by showing the simultaneous demonstrations in one Arab capital after another to protestors themselves fixated on the television coverage.

These demonstrations targeted not only the United States and Great Britain, but also Kuwait, for allowing its airspace to be used in the campaign and—tacitly—all other Arab governments who failed to act effectively in response to the attack. Observers of the protests and of the subsequent post mortems all agreed on the remarkable impact of al-Jazeera and other television coverage in the crisis. In Kuwaiti *diwaniya* (political salon) discussions, according to one writer, "Al-Jazeera had a large share of the dialogue and commentary and discussion. . . . I did not attend a single *diwaniya* in Kuwait in which al-Jazeera was not on the television. . . . But there was some displeasure with the style of al-Jazeera, which they saw as not objective . . . and as contributing to the incitement of the Arab street against Kuwait. . . . And they had some objections to the objectivity of some of the presenters and some of the regular guests."[131] Even al-Jazeera's critics, he noted, had to admit that its undeniable success shed cruel light on the shortcomings of the traditional Arab media. In contrast, a former GCC secretary-general lambasted al-Jazeera across the board as "harming Gulf relations."[132]

The contrast between an Arab street that had acted to the limits of its ability and Arab governments that stood weakly by and did nothing could hardly have been more prominently aired.[133] Yusuf Nur Awadh powerfully expresses this sense of possibility and the reach of the Arab public critique: "A new stage of Arab consciousness began to appear after the latest attack on Iraq, a stage imposed by the Arab street, which raised its arms against the policy of Arab governments. . . . But do not understand from that that the Arab street demands only a change in the positions of governments toward Iraq or toward holding an Arab summit. . . . The Iraqi crisis points rather toward holding up a mirror to force the Arabs to see their own monstrous face reflected, . . . and the Arab street demands a comprehensive review of the entire Arab condition."[134]

Hopes that this mobilized Arab public might push Arab regimes to take action were quickly frustrated, however. The negotiations that began immediately after Desert Fox—to hold an Arab summit that would finally formulate a unified Arab position regarding Iraq—while in line with the agenda pursued by Egypt and others for several years, clearly responded to highly mobilized Arab public opinion: "The momentum for holding such a summit was provided by the impressive display of public opposition throughout the Arab world to the latest Anglo-American strikes. . . . By spontaneously taking to the streets in solidarity with the Iraqi people, the Arab peoples showed they are more politically mature than their rulers. . . . They also reaffirmed their shared sense of Arab identity."[135]

More skeptical observers saw the Iraqi government's demands, building on its perceived victory, to be "yet another theft and cynical exploitation of genuine Arab feelings about the suffering of the Iraqi people."[136] When the Iraqi regime lashed out at Arab rulers, calling on the Arab street to rise up against them, it triggered a powerful backlash. Saddam's regime overreached and, as Ragheda Dergham argued, badly misread the Arab public, whose intense sympathy for the Iraqi people and rejection of the bombing campaign simply did not translate into support for Saddam Hussein, or make the Arab street into a political weapon he could wield.[137] In the end, no Arab summit was held to commence Arab reconciliation, nor did a push begin to lift the sanctions. Ultimately, the Arab foreign ministers' meeting in Cairo in late January produced a document that pressed tough demands on Iraq and offered little concession to the public demands about the sanctions. Much of the Arab public blamed this failure on American pressure.[138] As one Arab writer despaired, "The meetings behind closed doors at the Arab League in Cairo showed the lengths to which the bootlickers would go to escape the extraordinary consensus of the

Arab people . . . [and] showed the difficulty in translating an Arab position into resolutions that express the united Arab will."[139]

Over the course of 1999, UN diplomats struggled with what would eventually become Security Council Resolution 1284—an attempt to comprehensively rethink the Iraqi issue in all of its dimensions: disarmament, sanctions, and the internal problems of Saddam's regime. In December 1999, a nine-month effort by the United States and United Kingdom to rebuild Security Council consensus on the weapons inspections regime failed, with three permanent members of the Security Council (and Malaysia) abstaining from the key resolution and Iraq refusing to cooperate with the new UNMOVIC inspection team.

The Arab debate about these negotiations offers a window into how the new public sphere had changed Arab politics. In earlier UN debates, Arab publics had little information about deliberations in New York beyond the highly controlled snippets offered in the official media or else the highly partisan information to be found in Iraqi propaganda. In 1999, however, the new Arab media reported on and discussed these ongoing negotiations vigorously. In June 1999 Tariq Aziz appeared on *More Than One Opinion* to discuss the negotiations.[140] As in the examples noted above, Sami Haddad vigorously challenged Aziz on both factual claims and on his arguments. Haddad asked Aziz how Iraq could reject a plan that could immediately relieve much Iraqi suffering, and interrupted him to correct inaccurate claims Aziz made about the contents of the draft resolution. When Aziz tried to stand on the principle of sovereignty, Haddad refused to back down, pointing out that Iraq had accepted other deals, such as the oil-for-food program. Throughout, Haddad demanded that Aziz explain how Iraq could place political considerations ahead of the humanitarian crisis, which most concerned the Arab public. Such an encounter demonstrates the ways in which the new Arab public sphere challenged Iraqi diplomacy at the same time that the focus on the humanitarian crisis helped it.

The Sanctions

While street protests against American military strikes in Iraq demonstrate one aspect of the new public's concrete political impact, another crucial aspect was the delegitimation of the sanctions regime and the growing pressure on Arab states to challenge the embargo. The mobilization from below described in chapter 3 blossomed in this period, with the suffering of the Iraqi children publicized across the Arab and Muslim world in a variety of creative and evocative ways. From collection boxes outside mosques, to dramatic posters of starving Iraqi children covering the walls of professional association offices, to cultural exhibits featuring Iraqi artists and poets, to screenings of brilliantly polemical documentary films, Iraqi suffering permeated the cultural consciousness. The business sector, aware of the vast economic opportunities on the horizon, often supported these efforts, while governments that preferred such quiet activity to dangerous demands to act against Israel largely stayed out of the way. Both formally—through Arab professional associations or popular conferences or official committees to coordinate solidarity with Iraq—and informally, Arabs organized themselves to bring relief to the Iraqi children.

Concern for the Iraqi people was not limited to Arabs and Muslims, of course. Those involved directly with the UN humanitarian program in Iraq were "traumatized" by the humanitarian catastrophe related to sanctions (Minear et al. 1998: 9). Reports by the FAO, UNICEF, the International Committee of the Red Cross, Save the Children, and others painted an increasingly coherent picture of a humanitarian crisis that could not be dismissed as Iraqi propaganda. Dennis Halliday forced the internal UN dissatisfaction into the public arena with his highly publicized resignation in September 1998. Distressed by the inability of the humanitarian program to alleviate the suffering of Iraqi society, largely because of political interference from the Security Council Sanctions Committee, Halliday unleashed a highly public blast of moral outrage that generated considerable public attention. Halliday's successor, Hans van Sponek, resigned a year later for identical reasons and joined Halliday in publicly attacking the UN for its role in the humanitarian problems in Iraq, as did Jutta Burghardt of the World Food Programme. These critiques received support from UN Secretary-General Kofi Annan, who implored the Security Council to improve its procedures and allow humanitarian work to proceed. In August 2000 Belgian law professor Marc Bossuyt stirred up a diplomatic storm with a report commissioned by the UN Human Rights

Subcommission that attributed the humanitarian disaster in Iraq to the sanctions and called them "unequivocally illegal."[141] A quote attributed to a senior UN official, saying that "the Americans are, I'm afraid, the real villains in all this," captures the prevailing sense of anger and frustration within the UN bureaucracy.[142]

The UNICEF report concluding that half a million Iraqi children had died as a result of the sanctions was prominently discussed in the new Arab media. Even on the suffering of the Iraqi people, the new Arab public sphere refused to uncritically accept assertions, particularly on the question of who bore responsibility for the tragedy. The August 24, 1999, episode of *The Opposite Direction* explored at great length the difference between infant mortality rates in the northern Kurdish areas and in the areas under Saddam's control. On the October 4, 1999, *More Than One Opinion* program, Sami Haddad challenged guest Abd al-Bari Atwan when he invoked the figure of 8,000 Iraqi children dying a month due to the sanctions, noting that "it is strange, though, that the level of infant deaths in northern Iraq is much less than in the south."[143] Even defenses of the sanctions could still be heard, albeit infrequently. For example, Raghid al-Saleh, a frequent critic of Saddam, cited a range of American scholars to argue that despite the problems, sanctions often did work and could be justified in the case of Iraq.[144] Dozens of columns in the press blamed Saddam, often noting that a major problem with the imposition of sanctions was that it strengthened his regime even as it harmed Iraqi civilians.

As Western activists began to openly question the sanctions, the Arab media pointedly asked why Arabs were doing less than non-Arabs to challenge an embargo they claimed to despise. When an Italian plane landed in Baghdad, *al-Quds al-Arabi* pointedly asked, "Why couldn't the plane be Arab instead of Italian?"[145] The Arab media lingered over visits by Venezuela's Hugo Chavez, Indonesia's Abd al-Rahman, and Malaysia's Mohammed Mahathir, each time pointedly noting the absence of their Arab counterparts. During a controversy over a scheduled visit to Iraq by the Pope, Abd al-Bari Atwan told Sami Haddad, "I had hoped that if the Pope visited Iraq in December he would be joined by the Shaykh of al-Azhar, and Ali Khameini ... and Shaykh Hussain Fadlallah, and all religious leaders in the Arab world ... to go to see the suffering of more than 22 million Arabs and

Muslims and Christians suffering from starvation and poverty and killing and blockade."[146] Publicizing non-Arab activities shone an indirect but glaring spotlight on official Arab inaction, which mobilized pressure on them to match words with deeds. Arab opinion, which had coalesced over the 1990s (as described in chapter 3), now became a primary concern for even powerful states. Even Kuwait and Saudi Arabia reluctantly acceded to the premise that Iraqi suffering could not continue indefinitely.

As Mohammed al-Musaffir urged, "We will break the embargo peacefully, through trade and noncompliance."[147] Perhaps the most visible example of this strategy came with a series of "airplane challenges" to the sanctions. In 1993, at a time when the normative consensus supporting the sanctions remained strong, Pakistan petitioned the UN for permission to fly worshipers to Iraq to visit important religious centers. This request received considerable support from the Islamic world, given its humanitarian and seemingly nonpolitical mandate. After the UN grudgingly allowed one flight, several other states followed suit. Attempting to exploit the wedge, states tried to send flights full of dubious "pilgrims"—politicians, journalists, movie stars, businessmen. When the UN barred one of these flights, Pakistan backed down and the pilgrimage flights ended. In April 1997 Iraq sent an airlift of pilgrims to the Haj in Saudi Arabia in defiance of the southern no-fly zones. When the United States abstained from shooting down planes full of religious pilgrims, some hastened to describe this as a weakening of the sanctions. *Al-Quds al-Arabi*, for example, described it as "another small but significant step in the process of loosening the political and economic noose."[148] Even more, it argued, "even while hungry and besieged, Iraq has succeeded in drawing attention to Washington's hypocrisy and double standards, . . . which has earned it the sympathy of millions of Arabs and Muslims and earned the United States yet another dose of revulsion and hostility from the Arab street."

In 2000, at a time when the normative consensus had dramatically shifted against the sanctions, a challenge had a dramatically different outcome. On August 17, 2000, Iraq announced the reopening of Baghdad International Airport for the first time since the Gulf War. Two days later, Russia dramatically flew the first flight into Baghdad, pointedly not requesting permission from the UN on the grounds that nothing in the Security Council resolutions prevented humanitarian flights. Over the next month, a heated debate took place concerning the appropriate response to the Russian flight and about the procedures by which such humanitarian flights might be governed. With no consensus reached in either direction, France sent a second flight on September 22. This triggered a cascade. On September 27, Jordan sent the third flight—and the first Arab flight. It was followed in short order by Yemen (September 28), Morocco (October 4), the UAE, Algeria, and Tunisia (October 6), Syria (October 8), Turkey (October 9), the Sudan and Lebanon (October 13), and Bahrain (October 16).

Once the precedent was established, states that hoped to demonstrate their support for Iraq against the sanctions felt urgent pressure to act—and to act quickly, before the flights became routinized and therefore carried little political value. Many states sent multiple flights, or attempted to innovate in some way in order to stand out from the thickening crowd: on October 6, the UAE trumpeted the fact that its flight was the first from a GCC state; on October 17, Syria sent the first large jet; Jordan always tried to have sent the most flights. The second airplanes challenge demonstrates well the cascade dynamics that could be triggered under conditions of systemic hypocrisy. It also shows how such a cascade could overwhelm the power of the United States, which was reduced to focusing its energies on establishing that allowing the flights was not a signal of the impending collapse of the sanctions regime. As Salah al-Nasrawi argued, the sanctions would actually end only when Arab governments directly challenged the United States, but in the interim such a public initiative would "create a psychological atmosphere helpful to the Iraqi leadership in its efforts to rally Arab and international public opinion on the necessity of lifting the blockade."[149]

By 2000 the sanctions on Iraq were collapsing from below, losing legitimacy and facing increasingly public challenges. Sanctions violations were skyrocketing, and American officials frankly recognized that the sanctions could not be sustained indefinitely (Cortright and Lopez 2000: 2). As Kofi Annan put it, "The humanitarian situation in Iraq posed a serious moral dilemma for the United Nations, which was in danger of losing the argument—if it had not already lost it—about who was responsible for the situation: Saddam Hussein or the United Nations."[150]

In the spring of 2001 the United States and the United Kingdom expended considerable political capital on an effort to reform the Iraq sanctions in ways precisely calibrated to respond to the humanitarian critique of the anti-sanctions network while retaining more tightly focused military sanctions. The efforts followed from widespread recognition that the sanctions were becoming unsustainable as they lost legitimacy: smuggling increased, Iraq worked out deals with "middlemen" to gain oil revenues outside the UN framework, and humanitarian missions from dozens of nations challenged U.S. interpretations of the UN rules to travel to Baghdad to demonstrate solidarity with the Iraqi people.[151]

From an American policy perspective, "smart sanctions" had many merits. This seemed to respond to European and Arab concerns about Iraqi suffering, which would presumably blunt pressures for lifting the sanctions. It could potentially rebuild a Security Council consensus behind American goals of containing and undermining support for Saddam's regime. It maintained what Washington saw as vital: control over the disposition of Iraqi oil revenues, effective prevention of potential military imports, and enhanced surveillance over what passed through Iraqi borders. The smart sanctions proposals responded to growing pressure in international civil society, and drew heavily on ideas developed in a wide range of international agencies and working groups concerned with making sanctions more effective and less deadly. Despite all of these merits, however, the smart sanctions proposals failed (Lynch 2001). In part, they were simply a casualty of great power politics, as Russia held out in defense of its own self-interest and other countries looked ahead to vast profits if the sanctions were lifted rather than refined. A significant number of states, including three permanent Security Council members, along with an increasingly vocal international civil society, challenged U.S. justifications for the sanctions.

But even if they had won Security Council support, smart sanctions would still have failed because they commanded no support among the Arab and other neighboring states that would have to enforce them for them to succeed. Across the board, Arab states rejected the enhanced monitoring and border control demanded of them in the proposed smart sanctions regime. This rejection was almost entirely a product of the dramatic shift in the public sphere consensus about the sanctions and the United States. In short, the Arab debate about smart sanctions revolved not around whether they would make the containment of Iraq more effective and sustainable. Instead, Arabs focused on the injustice of the sanctions and the need to remove them entirely.

Toward War

When U.S. President George W. Bush announced his determination to combat an "axis of evil" in his 2002 State of the Union Address, it seemed clear that Iraq would be the primary target in the new campaign. The administration's mobilization of support was initially derailed by the violence in the West Bank, which led to the failure of Vice President Dick Cheney's March visit to the region. But in the early fall, the Bush administration began an aggressive campaign to muster support for a decisive confrontation with Iraq. After winning Congressional support, Bush turned to the United Nations to attempt to build an international consensus for military action. His failure to do so—discussed in the next chapter—profoundly shaped the course of the conflict that followed.

The emergence of the Arab public sphere at the end of the 1990s, and its growing emphasis on the United States as the cause of Iraqi and Palestinian suffering, deeply shaped the reception given the American drive toward war with Iraq. As described above, the Arab public sphere had for years been arguing about American support for Israel, the hypocrisy of American enforcement of the sanctions and no-fly zones, American indifference to the deaths of Iraqi children, the unprecedented American military presence in the Gulf, and official Arab subservience to American policies. American support for Israel and for Arab dictators left Arabs almost universally skeptical of a moralizing American rhetoric about democracy and human rights. The enormous public attention to American manipulation of UNSCOM and the Security Council in the late 1990s ensured Arab incredulity over American claims to be motivated by the need to enforce UN resolutions. And the Bush administration's nonresponse to Israel's reoccupation of the West Bank cemented deeply felt resentments about American policy and doubts about American intentions. In short, the developments in this period established the narrative context for the great arguments about the invasion of Iraq.

5

Baghdad Falls

During the invasion and occupation of Iraq in 2003, the performance of the Arab media became the subject of intense debate. Whereas it had already been singled out as a source of anti-Americanism and political radicalism after 9/11, now it seemed to pose a major and direct obstacle to the American military campaign. The protests over the Israeli-Palestinian issue had made Americans and Arab regimes alike painfully aware of its mobilizing protentional and its influence on Arab public opinion. The Arab media therefore itself became a central front of political conflict during and after the war.

Al-Jazeera in particular was accused of actively supporting the Iraqi regime with its skeptical reporting on the case for war and its heavy coverage of the conflict's human impact. The complexities of al-Jazeera's coverage of Iraq (see chapter 4), and the diversity of opinions found on its talk shows, faded away in the eyes of many observers in the harsh light of war. Almost every aspect of its coverage came under criticism: the word choices of news presenters who used terms such as "invasion" rather than "liberation"; the guests on the talk shows, many of whom were fiercely critical of the war; the broadcasting of footage of Iraqi civilians in agony or of American prisoners of war. After the war, al-Jazeera came under even more intense scrutiny, accused of aiding and abetting the Iraqi insurgency and of undermining the transition to Iraqi democracy.

The Arab public sphere did play a major role in shaping the political and normative environment, but in more complex and ambiguous ways than its critics recognize. For one, 2003 represented precisely the point of transition away from al-Jazeera's hegemony in the Arab media realm. While it remained the most popular and influential satellite television station at the time the war broke out, al-Jazeera now faced potent competitors such as al-Arabiya, as well as smaller but effective rivals such as Abu Dhabi TV and al-Manar. Their struggles for market share meant that they both led and followed public opinion, as they competed to position themselves within a rapidly evolving political environment.

The ways in which the Arab public sphere discussed the possibility of a war with Iraq can be understood only in the context of the emergence of the new public and its engagement with the Iraqi issue over the preceding years. The issue of Iraq had by 2002 been well established as a core aspect of an Arab identity about which every Arab should and did have an opinion. While Arabs disagreed and argued intensely over the appropriate course of action, American policy toward Iraq generated almost universal condemnation and hostility. The sanctions and regular bombings combined to deeply entrench the Arab conviction of American hostility toward the Iraqi people, which rebounded harshly against the United States when it tried to make the case that its war would be a liberation for the benefit of the Iraqi people. Furthermore, the escalation toward war coincided with intense agitation over the horrifying stalemate between Palestinians and Israel, which led most Arabs to link the question of Iraq to the suffering of the Palestinian people under occupation, American support for Israel, and official Arab impotence. The close identification between the Bush administration and Ariel Sharon in this Arab consensus badly tarnished American credibility on any regional topic, from invading Iraq to spreading democracy. The Arab public sphere interpreted each development through the filter of a narrative that had been finely tuned through years of public argument.

This chapter examines the engagement of the Arab public sphere with the American invasion of Iraq, from its introduction onto the agenda in 2002 through the summer of 2003. As with earlier chapters I do not present a comprehensive history of the war, or of the diplomacy surrounding that war. Far more than the other chapters, this one focuses on al-Jazeera rather than the Arab press, and particularly the remarkable open talk shows aired in the month after the fall of Baghdad, in which uncensored callers debated the meaning of Iraq live night after night in what may be the truest public sphere in Arab history. While I do pay some attention to the news coverage of al-Jazeera, I am more interested here in the evolution of a public opinion through arguments and dialogue within the new Arab public sphere.

Before the War

As chapter 4 documented, Iraq had become a central element of the new Arabist identity that had developed through the public arguments of the new Arab public sphere. In the last months of 2001, at a time when Iraq was hardly on the American public agenda, the Arab public was openly discussing what it saw as the real possibility of an American attack on Iraq. Even before the Afghan campaign had ended, Ahmed Mansour hosted Iraqi Vice President Taha Ramadan (November 2001), and a few days later Faisal al-Qassem hosted a discussion of whether "America could Afghanize Iraq." In January 2002, a program surveyed the question of international inspections and their prospects for avoiding a crisis. Even at the height of the focus on Afghanistan, then, Arabs never lost sight of Iraq.

American credibility, which was a near obsession for many war advocates in the United States (and, reportedly, for some Arab leaders) was hardly an issue in the Arab public sphere: virtually everyone assumed that the Bush administration was determined to invade Iraq no matter what, and most discussion revolved around how this might be prevented (Woodward 2004: 228–231). This included widespread calls for the Iraqi regime to avoid giving the United States an excuse for war. In the November 2001 program, for example, Qassem wondered why Iraq did not simply readmit the inspectors and pull the rug out from under American plans, while on the other hand asking whether America had not already done enough to the Iraqi people with twelve years of sanctions and bombings.

Outside the Arab public sphere, concerns about American credibility had more serious ramifications. Iraqis bitterly remembered the experience of 1991, when they rose up in response to the first President Bush's calls and then found themselves alone to be massacred by Saddam's military. Many Arab leaders similarly feared a replay of the end of the first Gulf War, where the United States defeated Iraq but left Saddam in power. American rhetoric meant to reassure Iraqis and Arab leaders about the "seriousness" of American intentions reinforced the convictions of the Arab public, fueling their deep suspicions about American arguments concerning WMD, terrorism, or spreading democracy.

Bush's "Axis of Evil" State of the Union Address fueled an Arab argument that had already been raging. Numerous talk shows asked about "the American agenda for Iraq" (*First Wars*, February 15), "the possibility of an American attack against Iraq" (*First Wars*, February 18; *First Wars*, March 6), and "the position of neighboring states on an attack against Iraq" (*First Wars*, March 11). In a March 15 program, for example, Robert Satloff of the Washington Institute for Near Eastern Policy and Abd al-Rahman al-Rashed, the pro-American editor of *al-Sharq al-Awsat*, faced off against more critical figures. On March 22, Sami Haddad invited the British military expert Simon Henderson to explain Britain's position. These programs, as well as dozens of op-eds in the Arab press, offer a clear picture of elite public discourse on the topic.

Almost no Arabs took seriously the idea that Iraq was a legitimate front in the war on terror, or that Saddam's regime might have ties to al-Qaeda or have had a hand in 9/11. But after years of criticizing the sanctions and worrying about American regime-change efforts in Iraq, most of the Arab public fully believed that the United States would eagerly exploit the opportunity to go after Saddam. After years of experience with what was widely considered to be an arms inspection process fatally compromised by its subservience to American foreign policy (the opposite of general American views of the inspectors), few Arabs took the Bush administration's demands for Iraqi disarmament or renewed inspections seriously. After years of denouncing American support for dictatorial Arab regimes and hostility to the aspirations of the Arab people, not even the most committed liberals believed that the United States was motivated by humanitarian concerns in Iraq or that it really hoped to spread democracy in the region. The Bush adminstration did not face a generic, irrational hatred and mistrust of America in its campaign against Iraq—it faced a specific, deeply entrenched narrative about the preceding decade that almost guaranteed a negative reception for its arguments. Since almost nobody believed that the campaign to act against Iraq was really about spreading democracy, or about Iraqi WMD, or about ties to al-Qaeda, attention inevitably turned to motives such as oil and Israel. There was near-complete consensus that the Bush administration had long decided on war and that all the rest was only for show.

Public opinion surveys suggest that general views followed the public discourse. In an April 2002 opinion survey, only 3 percent of Egyptians favored an American attack against Iraq and 84 percent were against; 7 percent of Lebanese for and 84 percent against; 11 percent of Saudis for, 80 percent against; 13 percent of Kuwaitis for and 61 percent against.[1] On American policy toward Iraq, 4 percent of Egyptians found it excellent or good, while 83 percent found it so-so or poor; 4 percent and 90 percent in Lebanon; 17 percent and 55 percent in Kuwait; 9 percent and 83 percent in Saudi Arabia. The Zogby poll found that 80 percent of Egyptians said that their opinion of the United States would improve if it lifted the sanctions on Iraq, as did 77 percent of Saudis and 75 percent of Lebanese. The Pew Global Attitudes survey released in March 2004 offered a stark picture of Arab opposition not only to the war, but to American policy more broadly.[2] 66 percent of Moroccans and 70 percent of Jordanians said that suicide bombings against Americans in Iraq were justifiable. 70 percent of Jordanians and 48 percent of Moroccans thought Iraqis would be worse-off post-Saddam, while 76 percent and 72 percent thought that America was "overreacting to terrorism." Only 3 percent of Jordanians and 9 percent of Moroccans thought that their country had done the wrong thing by refusing to participate in the war. Only 5 percent of Jordanians and 27 percent of Moroccans—close American allies—had favorable views of the United States.

The arguments in the Arab public sphere revealed genuine uncertainty and a real variety of viewpoints, despite an overwhelming consensus on the overarching narrative. Al-Jazeera online polls—which are not scientific, but which often receive tens of thousands of responses and can serve as useful snapshots of at least the preferences of al-Jazeera viewers—produced outcomes skewed overwhelmingly (usually about 90 percent to 10 percent) against any American position, but divided much more evenly on internal Arab questions. Unlike questions related to Israel, there was no smothering consensus governing Iraq discussions. For example, asked in January 2003, "Do you support the Iraqi president stepping down from power to save his people from war?," 39.6 percent said yes and 50.2 percent said no (with 56,662 responses). When asked in December 2002 whether Iraq should continue to cooperate with inspectors in the face of American threats, 54.9 percent said yes and 43.4 percent said no (with 40,800 responses). In a poll concluded on March 20, 2003, more than 111,000 respondents divided closely over the question of whether the United States would succeed in overthrowing Saddam Hussein (42.1 percent said yes, 51.5 percent said no). In late November 2004, opinion divided almost evenly (48 percent–52 percent) on the question of whether the Iraqi elections should be postponed. Such results suggest that while the Arab public sphere overwhelmingly accepted a particular identity and narrative, this did not lead automatically to consensus on specific issues or policies.

The Arab public struggled to make sense of American intentions, of the calculations of their leaders, of what could possibly be done. But then the Israeli reoccupation of the West Bank drove Iraq from the headlines and from the talk shows, while transforming everyone's evaluation of the strategic significance of the "Arab street." The furious demonstrations and protests in March and April 2002 startled virtually everybody: not only regimes, but also the Arab public itself, which had come to expect its own impotence. This time, massive street protests exploded across the Arab world, in Bahrain, Jordan, Tunisia, Yemen, Lebanon, Syria, the UAE, Egypt, and the largest demonstration (over a million people) in Morocco's history.[3] Tence face-offs with police and military, particularly in Jordan and Egypt, where protestors sought to march on the Israeli embassy, focused attention on regimes that seemed unable to act. Even Bush administration officials, who had since the 1991 Gulf War been dismissive of Arab public opinion, began to take note.[4] Arab leaders were clearly worried, as Jordanian Foreign Minister Marwan Muasher admitted: "The demonstrations are getting stronger by the day.... The street is literally boiling. We are being forced to take steps we don't want to take because people are angry and public opinion in the Arab world cannot be ignored."[5]

Most observers credited the Arab media with fueling this newfound mobilization, as the Palestinian issue—with graphic images of civilian casualties as well as live footage of protests in other countries—dominated the satellite television broadcasts. As Shibley Telhami observed, foreshadowing the coverage of the Iraq war, "Arab satellite television stations . . . carry live pictures of the horror in Palestinian cities and live phone calls from Palestinian men and women calling events massacres and atrocities."[6] Egyptian analyst Mohammed Sid Ahmed nicely captured the qualitative difference in the intensity of this experience: "The enmity between the Arabs and Israel has been there, but before an Israeli was imagined in Cairo like someone on the moon—inaccessible, unseeable. Now, the hatred is closer."[7]

Concerns about this newly potent Arab public opinion threw the American mobilization toward war with Iraq off track in 2002, at least for a time. As discussed in chapter 4, when Vice President Cheney came to the Middle East in March 2002 to win support for an attack against Iraq, an Arab public as skeptical of their own rulers as of America wondered whether Arab regimes would—in their view—sell out the Iraqi people to the Americans. To everyone's surprise, leader after leader told Cheney that Israel's actions toward the Palestinians made it impossible for them to consider participation in any initiative toward Iraq. Arab leaders took several symbolic steps toward Iraq, including inviting Iraq to an Arab summit for the first time since the 1990–1991 Gulf War and engineering a symbolic (if largely meaningless) reconciliation between Iraq and Kuwait. Egypt canceled regular flights to Israel by its semi-official airline. During a visit with the President in Crawford, Texas, Crown Prince Abdullah bluntly warned Bush about the ramifications of his support for the Israeli actions. But, as Hosni Mubarak frankly said in January 2003, no Arab government could or would stand in the way of an America resolved to go to war—leaving the Arab public with no means by which to act effectively.[8]

For all their public rhetoric, however, Arab states did not act on demands to confront Israel, begin an oil boycott, and expel American diplomats, or other concerns of protestors. As Abdullah Sanawi put it, during the run-up to war Arab regimes "were not even able to support the European position out of fear of angering the United States."[9] The Arab public was left with a baffling but heady mixture: a new self-confidence based on its unprecedented display of strength in April; enormous anger and frustration at the inability to actually help the Palestinians or stop the Israeli offensive; an ever greater sense of distance from their own rulers; and intense fury with the United States for the Bush administration's perceived unqualified support for Ariel Sharon.

As American discussion of a possible invasion of Iraq increased in the late summer, so did the Arab debate. Once again, these debates included a wide range of voices and a variety of perspectives—but all within this evolving narrative of despairing fury with the United States over Iraq and Palestine. When discussing Security Council resolution 1441, for example, Sami Haddad made a point of reminding viewers that resolution 242 (passed after the 1967 Arab-Israeli war) had never been implemented, and emphasized the differences between the American-British and the French-Russian interpretations of the resolution. Some argued that the resolution had prevented a war—the Syrian explanation of its vote—and that the inspections would prevent America from invading. Most Arabs doubted this, arguing—correctly, it turned out—that the Bush administration would wage its war regardless of what the inspectors did or found. Haddad spoke for many in declaring that the choice was "between bad and worse."[10]

It is worthwhile reviewing at some length the programs aired in this crucial period to show the range of discussion that actually characterized al-Jazeera's talk shows. On July 18, Jumana al-Namour hosted the Iraqi opposition figure Mustafa Bazarghan on the subject of overthrowing Saddam Hussein. On July 27, Ghassan bin Jadu explored the regional implications of the Iraqi issue, with guests including the Iraqi opposition figure Mohammed Baqir al-Hakim of SCIRI. On August 2, Hafez al-Mirazi invited Scott Ritter, Iraqi opposition figure Rand Rahim, and former UN humanitarian coordinator Hans von Sponeck to discuss American relations with Iraq. On August 6, Faisal al-Qassem provoked a minor crisis between Qatar and Jordan with a program on Jordan's role in a war, with the leftist Asaad Abu Khalil facing off against Mahmoud al-Khurabsheh from the Jordanian Parliament. On August 8, Edmund Ghareeb appeared to talk about the American perspective on inspections. On August 11, Danielle Pletka from AEI (one of the leading American advocates of an invasion) and a former Egyptian diplomat debated Iraq's future in the face of American threats. On August 22, Jumana al-Namour hosted the Egyptian analyst Hassan Nafia to discuss the Arab position toward an attack, while on August

30 *More Than One Opinion* invited Mohammed Idris from Egypt's *al-Ahram*, Mohassen Khalil (Iraq's representative to the Arab League), and a Russian analyst to discuss the same question. American academic Laura Drake (September 4) and British analyst Rosemary Hollis and Rachel Bronson from the Council on Foreign Relations (September 12) discussed the impact of a war on the future of the Middle East. On September 20, Hafiz al-Mirazi discussed a possible war with *al-Ahram*'s Mohammed al-Sayd Said, Muwafic Harb (who became the director of programming for Radio Sawa and al-Hurra), Amru Musa (Secretary-General of the Arab League), and American Congressman Nick Rahall.

After the United Nations passed resolution 1441 in November, Haddad invited Iraqi opposition figure Majid al-Samara'i to argue with Abd al-Bari Atwan, and a Syrian analyst to explain why Syria did not vote against it. A September 27 program on the confrontation between the United States and Iraq hosted Mike O'Brian, British Minister of State for Near Eastern Affairs, along with a Russian policy advisor and two prominent Arab political analysts. A December 2002 program invited a British government spokesman along with a representative of Amnesty International to present the report on human rights issued in support of war, in which the crimes of Saddam's regime were fully aired, although host Sami Haddad's introduction was frankly skeptical of its timing and intention, and a guest bitingly asked how anyone could take British concern for the Iraqi people seriously after it had spent thirteen years defending the sanctions. Douglas Feith, one of the key architects of the Iraq war in the American Department of Defense, appeared in January 2003 to present the American case for war, while a different program on the same day hosted the prominent Kuwaiti columnist and Parliamentarian Ahmed al-Rubai.[11] And in a remarkable program in early October, Qassem pitted former American ambassador Edward Walker against Iraq's oil minister, Omar Rashid, in a rare direct public debate.

Even before al-Arabiya launched in February 2003, al-Jazeera's talk shows featured a wide range of voices, Arab and non-Arab, for and against the war. These debates featured serious disagreement and often violent argument about what should be done, even as they were structured by an overall Arabist narrative frame that established the kinds of arguments and evidence most likely to persuade. Anger at the United States and fear of the possible consequences of a war permeated these discussions, as did profound skepticism about American justifications for the war and its intentions in the region. The core concern with the suffering of the Iraqi people under sanctions translated into great fears about what would happen to them in a war. Arabs expressed deep fears about the risk of anarchy in a post-war Iraq, of ethnic and religious conflict and civil war. Many Arabs feared that the United States intended to partition Iraq into ethnically defined states—Kurdish, Sunni, Shia—in order to prevent the reemergence of a powerful Arab state in Iraq. Others feared that an invasion of Iraq would be only the first step toward attacks on other Arab states, or that it would establish a permanent American occupation in the Arab heartland.

Calling this Arab consensus "pro-Saddam" is misleading. Most mainstream commentators insistently distanced themselves from Saddam's regime even as they argued on behalf of "the Iraqi people." In late April Ghassan bin Jadu challenged several leading Islamists for claiming to be opposed to tyranny everywhere, asking whether their opposition to the war did not contradict this. One responded: "I think that you would not be able to find among all the demonstrators in the Islamic street, the Arab street, even the global street, anyone who stands with Saddam Hussein. All of their slogans were standing with the Iraqi people . . . with the people and not the regime."[12] While among independent Arabists who despised all authoritarian Arab regimes there was an important undercurrent that welcomed the idea of removing Saddam Hussein, few wanted this to take place by American military means. That these opponents of an American role in toppling Saddam had no real alternative to offer, no pathway by which Saddam might be removed without such an intervention, represented a fundamental flaw in their position. Criticism without offering a practical alternative should be seen as a typical pattern in a weak international public sphere: since the public lacked any means for actually influencing official policy, its incentives pushed toward such expressive critique and away from the hard work of actually developing alternatives, which would likely not be adopted in any case.

That these highly mobilized Arab publics showed so little support for Saddam Hussein, especially compared to their positions in

1990–1991, sharply contradicts a conventional wisdom that confuses their opposition to the war with support for the "tyrant." This, I would argue, was a direct result of the new Arab public sphere. In sharp contrast with 1990–1991, when the Iraqi regime had seemed powerful and modern from afar, the new Arab media had brought Arabs much closer to the reality of the regime. Saddam's tight control over all foreign (and domestic) media prevented al-Jazeera—like virtually all media, Western or Arab—from freely reporting on the internal repression in Iraq or on the horrors of the Iraqi regime's depradations (Katovsky and Carlson 2003). But at the same time, al-Jazeera's reporting on the human cost of the sanctions put the suffering of the Iraqi people at the center of Arab concerns, even as its talk shows gave free voice to the regime's critics. Al-Jazeera viewers regularly heard Saddam's regime described by guests and callers as *al-Taghiya* (the tyranny), and his rule was assigned at least some blame (alongside the Americans, British, and Arab regimes) for the suffering of his people. In contrast to the earlier war, where many Arabs supported Saddam as an Arab hero, in this crisis most such Arabs tried—with mixed success—to detach their real and intense sympathy with the Iraqi people from support for Saddam's regime. Fear of America and sympathy with the Iraqi people now drove Arab opinion far more than did solidarity with Saddam.

The discontent of the Arab public sphere focused on their own regimes as much as it did on the United States. For years Arabs had argued that the embargo on Iraq was really an "Arab" one since it would collapse if the Arab states stopped enforcing it. As the United States and its British ally prepared for war, Arab commentators acidly noted that it would be the tacit or active cooperation of Arab regimes—air bases, staging grounds, overflight rights—that would make the military campaign possible (quite ironically, Qatar—the host country of al-Jazeera—hosted a major American base). Even when Arab regimes took popular positions against a war they tended to be perceived as insincere. While most Arabs accepted that their rulers were genuinely worried about the possible consequences of a war—refugee flows, the partition of Iraq, general instability—few believed that the regimes had any real concern for the Iraqi people, or any ability to or interest in standing up to the United States.

Analysts from across the political spectrum agreed on the hypocrisy of official Arab rhetoric. For example, Ahmed al-Rubai (a prominent Kuwaiti supporter of war) told al-Jazeera in late January 2003, "I have recently visited several Arab states, and listened to officials directly, and what is said in the media is not the reality."[13] Abd al-Bari Atwan, Rubai's polar opposite in Arab politics, frequently said essentially the same thing: "Arab officials don't say in public what they agree upon in private."[14] The complete failure of the Arab League, or of an Arab summit, to prevent the war—as well as what most perceived as the near-complete irrelevance of Arab states to the global debates over the war—fit perfectly within the core Arabist narrative of the incompetence and corruption of their leaders. Several programs explicitly asked whether there was any value at all to Arab rejection (*Weekly File*, September 7). As Arabs failed to act, a growing disillusionment permeated public discourse. In January 2003, for example, Faisal al-Qassem declared it "humiliating" that non-Arab Turkey stood up to the United States while the Arab states collectively did nothing. It was not only the rulers who came in for abuse; an October program on "European rejection and Arab silence" focused on the failure of the Arab people to protest in any significant way, in contrast both to the April 2002 protests over Palestine and the massive marches for peace all over the world.

As the crisis escalated, Iraq overwhelmingly became the topic of discussion on the talk shows, driving out even Palestine as the central issue of debate. In 2003 an astonishing 44 percent of the major talk shows focused on Iraq. These programs covered virtually every possible aspect of the crisis. In the month of March, as war drew near, talk shows discussed such topics as an Arab summit (*Issue of the Hour*, March 1), the Iraqi opposition (*Issue of the Hour*, March 3), Turkey's decisions about American troops (*No Limits*, March 5), the Islamic Summit's position toward Iraq (*Issue of the Hour*, March 6; *More Than One Opinion*, March 7), the role of intellectuals in the crisis (*Open Dialogue*, March 8), divisions in the Security Council (*Issue of the Hour*, March 10), the future of the Kurds (*The Opposite Direction*, March 11), and last-minute diplomacy (*Issue of the Hour*, March 13). In one remarkable program (February 22), Ghassan bin Jadu hosted live from Baghdad a discussion between Iraqi students from Baghdad University and American students from George Mason University (shortly thereafter, bin Jadu left Iraq due to Saddam's attempt to interfere with the content of his program).

Even on the brink of the war, however, a variety of perspectives still appeared on al-Jazeera: on February 21, the Kuwaiti Saad al-Ajami defended the official Arab position on the war as realistic; on March 3, a variety of Iraqi opposition figures discussed their hopes and fears for the future; on March 12, Iraqi Foreign Minister Naji Sabri discussed Iraq's strategy; and on March 17 Iraqi Information Minister Mohammed Said Sahhaf appeared. As war approached, however, the tone of discourse grew uglier, louder, more radical, and more prone to expressions of helplessness and blanket condemnation. Hosts, guests, and callers alike reflected an overwhelming level of anxiety, with reasoned dialogue declining and angry outbursts and wild conspiracy theories noticeably ascendant. When an emergency Arab summit in Sharm el-Sheikh (Egypt) collapsed into angry accusations between Libyan President Moammar Qaddafi and Crown Prince Abdullah of Saudi Arabia, live television coverage of the summit abruptly ended.

With the outbreak of war, al-Jazeera shifted to an all-news format, with the public conversation resuming only after the fall of Baghdad.

The Iraqi Opposition

Even as war drew near, supporters of overthrowing Saddam continued to be well represented in the Arab public sphere. Along with being routinely published in *al-Hayat* and *al-Sharq al-Awsat*, Iraqi opposition figures appeared frequently on al-Jazeera, where they had the chance to present their views and to defend them against challenges.

Iraqi opposition figures cannot honestly claim to have lacked for an opportunity to make their case prior to the war. On July 27 Mohammed Baqr al-Hakim of SCIRI made a powerful case for removing Saddam Hussein. On the same program, Mohammed Sadiq al-Husseini argued that the Iraqi people had every right to demand internal change and reform and even revolution, but that Arabs primarily feared and opposed an American role. When Husseini then complained about the opposition using American support to achieve its goals (to differentiate himself from the INC), Ghassan bin Jadu challenged him: "You talk as though the Iraqi opposition were leading the charge and using the United States, so what is wrong with that? If they can use American power, why shouldn't they?" On August 2, Iraqi opposition spokeswoman Rand Rahim Franke made the case for war eloquently by emphasizing the urgency of removing Saddam by any means available. On the August 11 episode of *Issue of the Hour*, war advocate Danielle Pletka of the American Enterprise Institute espoused the standard arguments made in the American media to a frankly skeptical reception—suggesting in part the striking disparities in the argumentative expectations of the Arab as opposed to the American arena.

The American reliance on the Iraqi opposition to make its case proved highly detrimental to its position in the Arab public sphere. The main advocates of war in the Arab arena were individuals and figures who commanded little respect, and often were met with outright disgust, among Arab audiences.[15] Their unpopularity tarnished the war effort by association, leaving it with few effective public defenders. As this became clear, the long-existing anger felt by many Iraqi opposition figures at their rejection by the Arab public began to simmer over. In an appearance on al-Jazeera in November 2002, for example, Iraqi opposition figure Mawfiq al-Rabii denounced his host for making unwarranted assumptions about what the "Arab street" thought, and for employing an inflammatory and inciting style of argument that harked back to the days of Ahmed Said and Voice of the Arabs.[16] Such hostile encounters built on themselves, so that even as al-Jazeera continued to invite Iraqi opposition representatives onto their programs, their appearances often only made things worse for their cause. On April 16, 2004, the INC newspaper *al-Mutamar* published documents alleging that Faisal al-Qassem's hostility to their cause was attributable to payments received from Saddam's regime—a charge believed by almost nobody (and denied by Qassem), but indicative of the depth of antagonism felt by the Iraqi opposition toward their perceived tormentors.

The dividing lines between the dominant Arab consensus and the arguments of the Iraqi opposition appeared constantly in the al-Jazeera programs, both among the invited guests and in the live phone calls. While the Iraqi opposition insisted that an attack would target the Iraqi regime, most Arabs felt that an attack would target and would primarily harm the Iraqi people. And while the Iraqi opposition described an attack as a liberation on behalf of the Iraqi people, most Arabs called it an attack on the Iraqi people. Heavily laden terms such as "liberation," "invasion," and "occupation" were hotly contested in these programs, with few word choices or arguments going unchallenged. In an entirely typical episode of *al-Jazeera's Platform*, a caller from Qatar declared that "the Arab people oppose and reject an attack on Iraq, because an attack on Iraq means an aggression against all Arabs."[17] An Iraqi caller from London responded that "with all respect for the other Arabs and their feelings toward the Iraqis, I think that Iraqis know their suffering the most, and know their own interests better than do the Arabs." Iraq was already occupied by Saddam Hussein, he argued, and the suffering of Iraqis under his tyranny justified any decisive action to liberate them—even if at American hands. A third caller responded that "with regard to changing the regime, this is the responsibility of the Iraqi people themselves on the inside and not an American responsibility." Such arguments raged almost every night as the war approached, even as positions palpably hardened and few minds remained to be changed.

Impact?

Only two places in the world have not seen protests against the coming American invasion of Iraq . . . Israel and the Arab world!
—Faisal al-Qassem, November 5, 2002

Still reeling from the turbulence of street protests in December 1998, the fall of 2000, and the spring of 2002, Arab regimes were now highly sensitive to any mass mobilization that might get out of control or put untoward pressure on them to act against American interests. As a result, the "Arab street" was rather less visible than might have been expected in the run-up to the war, particularly in comparison to the massive peace rallies across the world. While many American conservatives took this as proof that Arab public opinion did not matter, far more was going on. As Mohammed Krishan observed, "The Arab street remains restless between the fear of repression and feelings of frustration."[18]

The muted public Arab response was partly due the aftermath of this intense activity in the spring, as wary regimes kept a tight lid on political parties, civil society activists, and local media. One caller to al-Jazeera claimed, for example, that after the last round of large protests, "most of the protestors went to prison, most were beaten, tortured."[19] American pressure on regimes, and their repression of public opinion in turn, played a primary role in minimizing public protest. And the exhaustion and trepidation felt by publics weary from their fruitless protests over Palestine should not be discounted. As one Saudi caller complained, "What can demonstrations do if the rulers with their armies and missiles say no, no, no, and America will attack? . . . There is no value to these words or demonstrations."[20]

Most Arab governments took advantage of the long run-up to the war to clamp down hard on political opposition and on the domestic media. Almost every government forcefully suppressed mass protests, with techniques ranging from denying permits to direct repression. In Egypt, for example, after two days of massive protests in central Cairo on March 20–21, the police and the military violently suppressed anti-war protests, using a surprising level of force and arresting thousands of protestors (Schemm 2003; Moustafa 2004). There were regular small demonstrations in most Arab countries throughout the war, but considerably greater unrest than was expressed in public demonstrations. Protests in Morocco punctuated the month of January, culminating in late February with about 100,000 Moroccans protesting in Rabat. But still there was nothing to compare with the massive protests that swept the world on February 15, 2003.

But the absence of protests should not be taken to mean that the new public opinion did not matter. Indeed, the fact that Arab governments felt the need to clamp down as fully as they did offers a counterfactual suggestion about the perceived threat of a mobilized public. The emergence of a powerfully expressed public consensus clearly shaped how leaders approached the realm of political possibility. While most leaders carefully formulated their sense of the national interest with a clear eye on their relations with the United States and general issues of regime survival, most also paid far more attention to public sentiment than they had in previous crises.

Similarly, the anxiety of these regimes to prevent public discussion of their roles in the war and their loud rhetoric—however insincere—against the war both speak to their real concern with the new public sphere. In contrast to the 1990–1991 Gulf War, when a significant number of Arab states—including the major powers Egypt, Saudi Arabia, and Syria—joined the American coalition, in this crisis no Arab state other than Kuwait *publicly* supported the war. Many assisted the war effort in private—Jordan and Qatar being primary examples—but the urgency placed on keeping these actions secret is indicative of regime sensitivity to public opinion. As one Saudi explained, "From the Saudi government's point of view, the ideal situation would be to let the Americans know how much we are cooperating, while keeping the Saudi population completely in the dark. But you can't do that in an age of satellite television and the Internet."[21] Arab leaders, while ultimately avoiding confrontation with the United States, proved more resistant than at any time in memory—an outcome that can be explained only by the rising power of the public sphere. But, in the end, they did cooperate, and often played important supporting roles in the war—suggesting the limits of this power.

One exception to this pattern of showing greater attention to public sentiment was, ironically, the country often considered the most liberal and democratic in the region: Jordan. The Hashemite Kingdom had refused to join the American coalition against Iraq in 1990–1991, a decision that won King Hussein extraordinary levels of public support but cost Jordan significant financial and political relations with Saudi Arabia, Kuwait, and the United States. This time, the young King Abdullah opted to cooperate closely with the American campaign despite the overwhelming opposition of the Jordanian public. This decision reflected several trends, including the increasingly autocratic and repressive domestic political arena and Abdullah's strategic choice to position himself as a key American friend and interlocutor in the region (Lynch 2002b). Jordan was rewarded for its efforts with significant American economic assistance, and largely avoided the feared negative effects of war in its neighbor. When the occupation of Iraq proved difficult, bloody, and expensive, Jordan emerged as one of the main Arab "winners" of the war when its long-time adversary Ahmed Chalabi lost out to Jordan's candidate, Iyad Allawi, in the struggle to become Iraq's new leader.

The War

As demonstrated to English-speaking audiences in the popular documentary *Control Room*, American and Arab television portrayed strikingly different wars. The American media featured "embedded" journalists, news anchors with American flags on their lapels, and a frankly patriotic identification with the American troops (Katovsky and Carlson 2003; Massing 2004). News coverage emphasized the high-tech American war, successful military campaigns, and then the carefully stage-managed toppling of Saddam's statue in Baghdad. In the Arab media, in general, there was far more emphasis on civilian casualties, on the fear and stress of wartime, and on Arab anger and resentment. While the Arab stations ran long interviews with American officials and offered live coverage of American press briefings, they also ran endless footage of grieving, wounded, screaming Iraqis. While this book is not primarily about news coverage, it is important to describe these differences here in order to establish the frame within which Arab opinion about the war formed and developed.

As Rami Khouri put it, "For different reasons, Arab and American television . . . broadly provide a distorted, incomplete picture of events, while accurately reflecting emotional and political sentiments on both sides."[22] But, as Khouri pointedly notes, "We in the Arab world are slightly better off than most Americans because we can see and hear both sides, given the easy availability of American satellite channels throughout this region; most Americans do not have easy access to Arab television reports, and even if they did they would need to know Arabic to grasp the full picture." Nabil Sharif, editor of Jordan's *al-Dustour*, argued that "the air of Western media superiority is gone, as proven by the way they covered the Iraq war. The Arab media did a very remarkable job, while their Western counterparts were dependent upon the U.S. defence and state departments." [23] Many images and footage from al-Jazeera did filter into Western media, given that station's access to powerful and even sensational imagery. Indeed, the seepage of these images into the Western press arguably angered and worried American and British officials more than did the Arabic broadcasts themselves, since they tended to assume Arab hostility anyway but were deeply concerned about losing domestic political support for the war. As al-Jazeera's Faisal Bodi put it, "My station is a threat to American media control. . . . People are turning to us simply because the Western media coverage has been so poor."[24]

The Arab media posed a serious challenge to the American strategic objective of maintaining information control. The bombing of the al-Jazeera offices in Afghanistan—twice—and in Baghdad were widely seen as direct attempts to shut down the station's reporting from the ground. In stark contrast to the 1991 Gulf War, when the coalition forces did manage to maintain near-complete control over information and imagery, in 2003 the Arab media simply made this impossible. With correspondents on the ground and a vast audience, Arab television stations complicated American efforts at information dominance.

For all the problems of its identity-driven and emotional portrayal of events, the Arab media sometimes offered a more accurate portrait of some aspects of the war than did the American media, which more often relied on CENTCOM for its information.[25] For example, when American media repeated CENTCOM reports that fighting had ended at the port of Umm Qasr, al-Jazeera was broadcasting live footage of an ongoing battle. At another point, American officials denied that any U.S. soldiers had been taken captive, while al-Jazeera showed pictures of five captured American soldiers. Al-Jazeera's minimal coverage of the toppling of Saddam's statue in Baghdad is often held up as examples of its reporting bias, but subsequent reporting has largely validated the station's editorial judgment. When rumours of a popular uprising in Basra swept through the American media, al-Jazeera broadcast live footage of a deserted and quiet city center. Tim Judah (2003) evocatively described this process: "At the beginning of the campaign, the Americans and British had made all sorts of overblown claims—about, for instance, having pacified towns on the way to Baghdad and neutralized Basra—which had later been proven to be altogether untrue or vastly exaggerated. By contrast, Mr. al-Sahaf's statements during the first ten days or so of war had given him a measure of credibility, so people came to believe what he was saying. Reality then overtook him. His claims became ever more fantastical, but ordinary Baghdadis did not realize this—until they saw the tanks for themselves."

Coverage of the war was tightly controlled not only by CENTCOM but also by the Iraqi authorities. Al-Jazeera and Abu Dhabi TV were the only stations permitted to operate outside the purview of the Iraqi Ministry of Information, and even they faced considerable pressures. Despite this privilege, al-Jazeera's relations with the Iraqi regime were strained. Al-Jazeera during the war did not have "better access to senior Iraqis than the other channels" (Miles 2003). Taysir Alouni, al-Jazeera's star journalist in Afghanistan, was forced to leave Iraq after only a few days when the regime objected to some of his reporting, as were several other correspondents. At one point in the war, Mohammed Said Sahhaf reportedly stormed into the al-Jazeera offices in Baghdad with a gun and "threatened to kill the station's employees, cut off their arms, and throw their corpses into the desert if they reported that the American forces were approaching Baghdad."[26] Well into 2005, al-Jazeera's promotional clips (aired frequently throughout the day) proudly interspersed footage of Sahhaf raging against al-Jazeera with clips of interim Prime Minister Iyad Allawi and other officials in the interim Iraqi government making similar complaints. When al-Jazeera reporter Majid Abd al-Hadi filed a report that the departure of Western journalists from Baghdad hinted that war might be imminent, he was brought in by the Iraqi authorities and threatened with deportation if the story continued to be aired.[27] On March 8, Ghassan bin Jadu was scheduled to broadcast an episode of *Open Dialogue* live from Baghdad, but was forced to relocate to Beirut after the Iraqi authorities tried to place unacceptable restrictions on the broadcast. The Iraqi regime's attempts to use al-Jazeera as a weapon to mobilize the "Arab street" against the war clashed dramatically with the norms of the new Arab public.

The Arab media struggled to find an appropriate balance between an emotional response to traumatic events, the generic pressures of covering a war in progress, and the relentless pressures of the marketplace. Arab reporters had better access to events on the ground, and regardless of their political sympathies simply had more opportunities to witness civilian casualties. Emotionalism and sensationalism were common accusations against al-Jazeera, and it is quite clear that many Arab reporters found it difficult to separate their coverage from their own deeply held feelings and identities. Its decision to show footage of dead American soldiers and POWs shocked and horrified many observers. Still, it is important to recall that the gap between the war seen by Arab journalists and and that seen by American journalists was not simply an artifact of different mental imagery: embedded American journalists saw far less of the impact of the war than did Arab journalists moving freely through Iraqi streets. Mohammed el-Nawawy points out, "As disgusting as these gory images were, not showing them would have been a denial of the reality witnessed by Arab reporters."[28] Abdallah Schleifer's (2003) summary judgment effectively captures al-Jazeera's reporting: "There is no question in my mind that al-Jazeera does not make up facts or deny them and there is no question in my mind that many of al-Jazeera's presenters indulge their emotional commitments . . . to such a degree that at times the spin they put on the facts can be scandalous."

The focus on Iraqi civilian casualties was both the most controversial aspect of al-Jazeera's reporting and the easiest to explain. The emphasis on portraying civilian casualties, while infuriating to an American military determined to control the information environment, only reported a different side of reality rather than manufacturing untruths. On the other hand, Americans complained that these images often lacked context—i.e., that al-Jazeera showed a bombed out mosque, but not the Iraqi soldiers who had been firing from inside of it. Recall that "the Iraqi people" had become a touchstone of Arabist identity and political argument over the preceding decade. Most Arabs thinking about the war approached it from a perspective molded over these years, which led them to care about some things more than others. That al-Jazeera focused less on the horrors of Saddam's regime was not because it sought to downplay or ignore these unsavory issues. On the contrary, for al-Jazeera viewers this was an old story, which had been thoroughly aired and discussed and which had far less urgency to most Arab viewers than the immediate threat of an American invasion and the current threats facing the Iraqi people.

Word choice also emerged as a major point of contention. As Mohammed el-Nawawy recalled, "When an Iraqi cab driver blew up his taxi, killing four U.S. soldiers at a checkpoint . . . he was described as a 'terrorist' by US networks and a 'freedom fighter' by most Arab networks."[29] In official American discourse the American campaign was insistently described as a "liberation," a war in defense of the Iraqi people against the Iraqi regime. The Arab media described it as an "invasion" producing an "occupation"; while this word choice was a red flag for critics of al-Jazeera, within months even President Bush routinely referred to the American "occupation." Most provocatively, the Arab media applied the same terminology—martyrs, occupation—to the American campaign in Iraq that it had long used with regard to Israel and the Palestinians, thereby subtly equating the two issues, to devastating effect.

The increasingly competitive Arab media market played an important role in shaping news coverage. Just as CNN tailored the domestic version of its broadcast to be more "patriotic" in response to its losing market share to Fox News, Arab satellite television stations increasingly took market pressures into account (Massing 2004). If al-Jazeera chose to abstain from broadcasting sensational images, it now had to fear that it would lose market share to other, less abstemious stations. Al-Arabiya, during the war, battled with al-Jazeera by competitive outflanking, raising the ante for al-Jazeera and all other stations. Even after Abd al-Rahman al-Rashed, a fierce critic of the Arab media, took over the programming of al-Arabiya, that station continued to air graphic videos of violence and gut-wrenching clips of hostages begging for their lives—showing the power of market pressures over editorial decisions. Others, such as Abu Dhabi TV, attempted to establish credibility through a more sedate presentation.

This market competition, based on frank evaluations of what would draw Arab audiences, had as much to do with broadcasting choices as did political preferences or identity. Arab channel surfing was the reality of the war, as satellite television viewers—both at home and in public spaces such as cafes—voraciously consumed and compared not only the Arab stations but also CNN, Fox, BBC, and more. The available evidence suggests that al-Jazeera was considered the most credible news source and remained the most-watched station, albeit with considerable regional variations (Abu Dhabi TV did better in the UAE than elsewhere, for example, and LBC in Lebanon). For example, Mohammed Ayish (2004) found that students at the University of Sharjah (UAE) considered al-Jazeera the most credible source of news in the war, with Abu Dhabi TV a close second and all other stations (including al-Arabiya) trailing far behind.

Discussion of the war passed through three phases with remarkable rapidity, in line with events on the ground. With the immediate outbreak of the war, and the "shock and awe" bombing campaign over Baghdad, Arabs watched with dread, fury, and trepidation. The second phase came with the unexpected resistance to the invading forces, as Arabs almost wanted to believe—even if few really believed—that Iraq might actually win. The early days of the war gave Arabs unexpected hope, as the American and British forces struggled to establish a beachhead at Umm Qasr and made little tangible progress. Arabs were astonished—and delighted—at Iraqi resistance, and talk began to circulate about how Iraq might even in defeat offer a glorious legend of Arab pride. But this hope remained mixed with deep foreboding and horror at the certainty of massive destruction and death. In the third phase this tentative hope gave way to astonishment and humiliation at the sudden fall of Baghdad on April 9. A June 2003 Pew survey found enormous disappointment among Arabs at the rapid end to the war, with 93 percent of Moroccans, 91 percent of Jordanians, and 82 percent of Lebanese expressing disappointment with the outcome. And while 80 percent of Kuwaitis thought Iraq would be better off without Saddam, substantial majorities of Jordanians and Palestinians thought otherwise.

Conversation Resumes: After the Fall of Baghdad

Many who have been following the entry of American tanks into the center of Baghdad ask, where is the Iraqi resistance? Why are the streets of Baghdad empty of Iraqi dead? Where is the political leadership?
—Jumana al-Namour, April 11, 2003[30]

In the first talk show broadcast after the fall of Baghdad, Jumana al-Namour spoke for millions of bewildered Arabs. A few days later Mohammed Krishan began an episode of *Behind Events* with almost identical questions: "Where was the battle of Baghdad that would slaughter the enemy in the streets? Where was the Republican Guard? Where were the Fedayin of Saddam? Where was Saddam himself? What happened to all the pillars of the regime? Did the earth open and swallow them up? Were they all killed? Did they flee? Where?"[31] The sudden collapse of Iraqi resistance around Baghdad was almost unbelievably shocking and deflating after the build-up of the second phase. Al-Jazeera devoted nearly two dozen talk shows in a week to the question of why Baghdad fell. In the remainder of this chapter, I focus primarily on these al-Jazeera programs, for three main reasons: first, because they reached the widest audiences; second, because of the availability of full transcripts; and third, because they were broadcast live and un-censored, offering an unmatchable window into Arab public political argumentation.

On the very first program broadcast after the fall of Baghdad, studio guest Mahmoud al-Muraghi surveyed the disappearance of the Iraqi regime without any immediate coalition alternative, and prophetically voiced his fears of how people would behave in the absence of any au-thority. With the outcome uncertain and a near-complete power vac-cuum, Muraghi feared ethnic and civil strife, and violent struggle for power, but above all feared that various elements would take advan-tage of the absence of authority—a fear amply confirmed by the loot-ing campaign that swept through Baghdad as American forces stood by. But host Jumana al-Namour challenged Muraghi's use of the term "occupation," pointing out that "the Americans present themselves as a liberating power which will surrender authority very quickly, giving authority to Iraqis." Muraghi demurred: "Liberation does not come with bombs. . . . Nobody believes that the issue is one of liberation and modernization, building a democratic society. . . . They went to Iraq to plunder its wealth and to occupy Iraq, and therefore the question: when will the occupation end? When will the Iraqi resistance begin?"

Namour then opened the phone lines, and a remarkable outpour-ing of views unfolded. The first caller to the program began by saying: "Sister Jumana, you grieved over the fall of Baghdad, but I celebrated the fall of the tyranny, I'm sorry I mean the fall of Baghdad. . . .We hope that this tyrant is slaughtered in the streets of Baghdad." Namour interrupted him to point out the uncertainty surrounding the fate of Saddam Hussein, as well as about the future of Iraq, and then asked the caller what he hoped for Iraq's future. He responded: "I have a message from the Iraqi people, with all frankness. . . . We will not be satisfied with an American occupation, not a British and not a Zionist and not any fortress on Arab soil." The second caller, an Iraqi Shia in Germany, declared that he was trapped between two conditions: joy at being released from the tyranny and dictatorship of Saddam Hussein, and fear that the Americans would remain in Iraq. When he admitted that an American presence would be necessary for a short while to prevent communal strife, Namour pushed him on whether he expected violent conflict between Sunnis and Shia. The third caller came from Saudi Arabia and again declared that "we want in every sense of the word to celebrate this victory over the tyranny . . . this liberation of Iraq, this new Iraq." Namour asked him whether he felt any fears or doubts about who might rule Iraq or for Iraqi unity; the Saudi responded, "I fear that the forces came to Iraq to protect the oil, and will abandon Iraq to civil war."

After three successive calls celebrating Saddam's fall, the fourth caller was a Palestinian who mourned that "the issue is not the future of Iraq . . . it is the slaughter of Muslims and Arabs at the walls of Damascus, at the walls of Beirut, at the walls of Jerusalem, and now the slaughter of Muslims and Arabs at the walls of Baghdad. . . . I say to those who follow al-Jazeera who attack the tyranny, who is it, and how does it rule?" A Tunisian caller urged Arabs not to think of the Americans as enemies or friends, but to think in terms of interests and power. A caller from the Emirates worried that what was unfolding on television screens was worse than what had existed before, and hoped only for a rapid solution to restore order and peace to Iraqis. A caller from Jordan declared that he was not satisfied that Saddam had been overthrown, because all the other Arab regimes remained in place, all of which were no better than or worse than Saddam. When one caller mentioned the looting in Baghdad as a form of resistance against the American forces, Namour pointed out that "the thieves are probably Iraqis, but the victims are Iraqis too." As the calls poured in, a rough sense began to emerge of the variety of Arab responses to the fall of Baghdad—most notably, the widely held contempt for Saddam's regime and the fears of American intentions.

A similar story repeated itself on subsequent nights, with the personality of the host and the day's news shaping the character of the discussion. On April 12 discussion revolved around the looting and chaos in Baghdad, with fears of ethnic conflict between Sunnis and Shia emerging as a primary topic of concern. The first caller, from Jordan, denounced the looting as an American plan to destroy Iraqi culture and civilization, and to make the Iraqis look so backward and uncivilized that a long-term American presence would be required. A Saudi caller said that the chaos and looting of Baghdad should be seen as a clear warning to the Arab peoples to "hold on to their rulers and support them, to stay far away from inflaming anarchy [*fitna*]." Host Fayrouz Ziyani responded that many people "see a hidden hand behind the actions," a suggestion with which the caller quickly agreed. An Iraqi living in Saudi Arabia declared that "I express the feeling of many Iraqi Sunnis that I never wanted to see such a dark day as the fall of Baghdad."

Talk Shows as a Public Sphere

During the war, news coverage drove out talk shows. After the fall of Baghdad al-Jazeera dealt with the war by placing most of its regular talk shows on hold and running one program—*al-Jazeera's Platform* [Minbar al-Jazeera]—every night. While its regular host, Jumana al-Namour, appeared frequently, the star hosts of other programs rotated through as well, with the contents often reflecting the personality of that host (Ahmed Mansour tended toward the more sensational and anti-American topics, while Faisal al-Qassem looked for the most controversial and unsettling topics). Al-Jazeera also ran frequent episodes of *Behind Events*, again featuring a rotating cast of its star hosts, as well as *Issue of the Hour*, a program devoted to Iraq that began shortly before the war (March 7). After the war, it created several new programs broadcasting from Baghdad—*Iraqi Voices*, which featured interviews with ordinary Iraqis on the streets during and after the war; *Iraq After the War*, featuring Mohammed Krishan and Maher Abdullah (the regular host of *Sharia and Life*), which ran until early June 2003 and focused on a wide range of topics, from security to the economy to the cultural scene to the media and more; and *The Iraqi Scene*, which continued broadcasting through the time of writing this book. After the regular talk shows resumed in mid-May 2003, a wide range of programs focused heavily on Iraq.

Al-Jazeera viewers were therefore offered at least one live talk show about Iraq, and often two or three, almost every night of the week from March through early June 2003. Between April 11 and May 31, almost one hundred talk shows aired, with some two hundred different guests, ranging from Iraqi opposition figures to prominent Arab and Muslim political figures and journalists to Americans to ordinary Iraqis. Few topics seemed off-limits in these programs, whch featured a wide range of Iraqi guests (although some Iraqis complained about the identity and politics of the Iraqi guests, accusing it of favoring Sunni Arabs and of contributing to ethnic conflict).

Immediately after the war an unusual number of these programs eschewed studio guests in favor of exclusively relying on live callers—perhaps the closest thing to a true public sphere in the history of the Arab world: open to all on an equal basis, unscripted and uncontrolled, in a dialogic format broadcast to an enormous audience. While some calls were clearly prearranged (see Fandy 2000 for a critical account of the management of these callers), this varied by program. *Al-Jazeera's Platform*, which aired nightly for much of this crucial postwar period, was probably in this sense the least "managed" of the programs, which contributed to the openness and unpredictability of the discussion in this uncertain period. All told, al-Jazeera broadcast twenty-eight of these "open" programs between April 11 and May 31, taking calls from twenty to thirty Arabs from dozens of locations from around the world in each program. These dialogues could turn emotional, with exaggerated claims and angry denunciations—but this was an accurate reflection of al-Jazeera's agitated and confused audience rather than something imposed by al-Jazeera's editorial decisions. Indeed, the decision to move in a less scripted and more open direction at this pivotal moment is nothing short of remarkable—and contrasts sharply with the American preference for tighter control over information and a more restrained media. Rather than relying on a limited pool of regular guests, al-Jazeera focused in this first month after the war on introducing Iraqi voices to its Arab audience, even when those Iraqis offered opinions and information sharply at odds with mainstream Arabist opinion. The personality of the host played a large role in shaping these programs, with some seeming to encourage negative, angry arguments and others insisting on more measured, constructive dialogues. Taken as a whole, these programs offer an unparalleled window into an Arab public opinion in flux.

Even if al-Jazeera had wanted to impose an agenda on Arab public opinion, the experience of these live talk shows suggests the difficulty of doing so. In an April 13 program ostensibly devoted to the prospects for democracy in Iraq, the first caller ignored Qassem's introduction and instead asked, "Where is the mercenary opposition in the unfortunate events happening in Baghdad?" Qassem immediately challenged him: "You call them mercenaries, this is a big word." The second caller, from Saudi Arabia, wanted to discuss reports of Saudi volunteers killed in combat in Iraq. The third caller, from France, declared that "Saddam was a tyrant and a dictator, and an American agent, and now the Americans are trying to save themselves from this agent. . . . I think that Saddam will never be tried, because a trial would reveal America's secrets."

Qassem struggled to return to the topic, asking each caller about the possibility of democracy, but had little success in keeping the callers focused. When pressed, one caller was dismissive: "Do you know the first thing the Americans did when they conquered Umm Qasr? They established an occupation of the oil installations, made them secure. . . . Fine. Are oil refineries more valuable than the Iraqi people? Are they more valuable than ancient and Islamic artifacts?" In an April 16 program ostensibly devoted to the Nasiriya meeting, the first caller wanted to talk about al-Jazeera's coverage of Iraq, while the second went into a long rant about Muslim suffering and backwardness. When one caller on April 16 claimed that Kuwaitis had been among the looters sacking the Baghdad Museum, Abd al-Samid Nasir interrupted him: "This is crazy. . . . There is no evidence for this statement, let's stay away from crazy accusations." On April 18 Namour interrupted a guest who began insulting Kuwaitis—telling them to go to the American embassy to thank their masters—by insisting that her program would look only to the future and not allow the settling of old scores. An Iraqi calling from London on April 20 lashed out at al-Jazeera and at Arabs in general as an embarrassment: "You incite Sunni against Shia, with your heretical style of incitement, leave Iraq alone. . . . Go liberate Palestine with your empty words, a million people were killed by Saddam, and you Arabs believe in peace. . . . The Americans are liberators, not invaders, but you are ignorant and your minds are occupied, you are backward and a joke in the West. . . . I hope that Sharon defeats you" (through this tirade, Qassem did not cut him off, and at the end he politely thanked him for his opinion).

These programs took on an enormous range of subjects. The first post-war episode of *al-Jazeera's Platform*, described above, laid out an agenda of the challenges facing the new Iraq. On subsequent nights, the challenges explored included the factions of the Iraqi opposition, "democracy in Iraq," the security situation, the destruction of Iraqi culture, the Nasiriyah meetings to select a transitional government, reconstruction, the future of Iraqi relations with Kuwait, religious movements, the Arab "volunteers" who came to fight in Iraq, health conditions, education, security, the emerging Iraqi media, relations between Iraqi citizens and the American troops, political parties, labor, the role of mosques, the role of tribes, military institutions, the service sector, children and families, banking, the judiciary, electricity, and even athletics. The talk shows made repeated attempts to explain the collapse of the regime, were remarkably open to self-criticism, and were deeply interested in American intentions. Nor did they ignore positive signs or insist on a single, negative storyline; on April 19, for example, Fayrouz Ziyani hosted a remarkably upbeat discussion of "Baghdad's return to life," while a program in May looked optimistically at elections at Baghdad University. There was also considerable self-criticism, with programs on April 20 and April 29 assessing the performance of the Arab media during the war. As time went on, however, and security conditions worsened and the reconstruction stalled, these discussions turned increasingly angry and embittered.

In these remarkable open discussions, it is possible to see Arabs from all over the world struggling to make sense of events, looking both to the past and to the future with a mix of anger and hope. Hundreds of different callers reached the air each week, expressing views from across the political spectrum. The discussions sometimes degenerated into score-settling and abusive comments directed toward particular Arab regimes, toward Kurds or Shia or Sunni Iraqis, toward Saddam Hussein, and toward the United States and the United Kingdom. Many callers aired conspiracy theories, some defended Saddam as a great national hero, and many claimed Zionist motives behind the American campaign. Islamist callers denounced the "Crusader campaign," and called for an Islamic state in Iraq as the only way to avoid ethnic strife or American domination. Many other callers denounced Saddam Hussein and celebrated Iraqi liberation from "the tyranny." Concern about ethnic or religious strife in Iraq was often heard, with many callers and hosts urging Iraqis toward unity—either against the occupation forces or in cooperation with them—and other callers attacking al-Jazeera for inflaming conflict simply by discussing the prospect in public. There was considerable focus on the future, speculation about the possibility of creating democracy in Iraq, and almost universal mistrust of American intentions. In short, these talk shows reveal an Arab public divided and confused on many issues, while sharing a core set of assumptions and concerns that powerfully shaped their responses to specific questions. What the talk shows emphatically do not show in this period is either a stifling consensus or a calculated campaign of incitement or negativism on the part of al-Jazeera personalities.

The possibility of a democratic Iraq was discussed frequently, but skeptically. Most callers and guests expressed great hope for democracy, but deep skepticism that America intended to create democracy in Iraq. Indeed, Faisal al-Qassem, al-Jazeera's most popular personality, chose "democracy in Iraq" as the topic for his first program after the fall of Baghdad (April 13). "Has Iraq become a model of democracy in the Arab region as the Americans promised? What is the likelihood of this happening? Is it only like Iblis' dream of Heaven? Have the Americans carried the project of democracy to the Arabs as they did to the Germans and Japanese after the second World War? Can democracy be achieved in a country such as Iraq with its ethnic and tribal and national divisions?" But most callers were skeptical of American intentions. Most were frightened of the chaos and anarchy unleashed by the fall of the regime, but suspected that this must somehow have been by American design—how could a country able to defeat Saddam's army in three weeks be unable to police the streets of Baghdad? As one Palestinian caller said, on April 29, "I don't see any plans to establish a government in Iraq which represents the Iraqis. . . . It is not possible that a government will be established in Iraq that doesn't represent the interests of America and the interests of imperialism only." A caller on April 20 bluntly told Qassem that "those who dream or imagine that the Americans will bring democracy to Iraq or to the Arab world . . .

are deluded." Why? Because, the caller said, "who will be empowered by democracy in a country such as Iraq or any Arab country? An Islamist regime will triumph, and I don't think that America came to establish an Islamist regime in the region." But when the caller doubted that America would ever really support democratization, Qassem challenged him: "If you ask people in Latin America, they might say yes."

While anger and fear permeated the discussions, positive developments and hopes for the future did come up on al-Jazeera talk shows. On April 14, Ayman Banourah began a program on the security situation by observing that "security conditions seem to be moving toward improving in some ways." Sami Haddad's April 18 program looked frankly but hopefully at the question of rebuilding Iraq, bringing up a range of pragmatic issues such as Iraqi debt and obstacles to investment with an economic expert from the United Nations and with Patrick Clawson, an American expert with close ties to the Bush administration. On April 19, Fayrouz Ziyani led a discussion of "Baghdad returning to life." In the April 21 program on the fate of Saddam Hussein, many guests hoped that his disappearance would allow Iraq to "open a new page." An April 22 program on the future of Iraqi-Kuwaiti relations gave full voice to Kuwaitis great excitement about a more positive future. A Saudi caller on May 10 expressed his confidence that Iraq's future was bright because every country occupied by America emerged better for the experience.

Other programs accentuated the negative, giving voice to sensationalist claims about the American occupation. On April 15, Qassem began a program on "the American project in Iraq" by reflecting on the Palestinian experience: "When the Palestinians signed the Oslo agreement with Israel 10 years ago, the boosters of this agreement spoke of transforming the Gaza Strip into a new Singapore, they promised prosperity and progress and growth, but instead of the promised heaven, Palestinians face hell, they have lost the roof over their heads as their region has turned into devastation. . . . Is this same scenario to repeat itself in Iraq?" In an April 15 discussion about the future of Iraq, Abd al-Samad Nasir's callers tended toward the angry and negative. A Saudi caller warned against neglecting the Islamic dimension, while a caller from France demanded to know whether the Iraqi people "needed death and destruction . . . in order to get democracy from America," while others worried about further American interventions and blamed the invasion on Israel. A woman from Doha asked what future Iraq could possibly have when Donald Rumsfeld made jokes about the chaos in Baghdad being an example of Iraqis exercising their freedom. A woman from London expressed the view that "the American presence in Iraq is not about oil first. . . . All the Western leaders . . . have been very clear that it is a Crusader campaign aimed at preventing any unification under the flag of an Islamic caliphate."

The Arab response to the fall of Baghdad, then, was deeply shaped by preexisting convictions about the Iraqi opposition, by horror over the war, and by deep skepticism about American intentions. It was not, however, inevitably or uniformly hostile. A strong undercurrent could be heard of Arabs desperate for progressive change. Arabs keenly watched and publicly argued about every decision taken by the American authorities, with American deeds speaking far more loudly than words. The failure to establish order in Baghdad particularly baffled Arab observers who had difficulty crediting the explanation that an America able to defeat Iraq so handily could be too incompetent to provide basic infrastructure or protection.

The power of news coverage to shape these public arguments can be seen clearly in the topics, concerns, and fears that came up in these discussions—both in chosen topics and in unscripted phone calls. The reporting of the razing of the Baghdad Museum had a profound impact, with multiple callers invoking it as evidence for American lack of concern for anything other than oil. An April 14 program hosted by Ahmed Mansour focused on "the destruction of Iraqi civilization," for example, with Mansour offering few challenges or objections to guests or callers. A caller on April 16 explained his belief in American imperialist intentions in Iraq by noting that "we have seen on al-Jazeera the American flag raised more than once in Iraq." Other discussions brought the news coverage directly into question. On April 15, for example, Faisal al-Qassem asked a Kurdish analyst who seemed relatively sanguine about the course of events in Mosul about an al-Jazeera report featuring a woman screaming about an invading militia; the guest replied that "I imagine that this is greatly exaggerated."

Al-Jazeera itself came up repeatedly as a topic of discussion. Many callers began by thanking al-Jazeera for its coverage, and by expressing sympathy about Tariq Ayoub (the journalist killed in the American bombing of the al-Jazeera offices in Baghdad). But others attacked al-Jazeera, questioning its news coverage and its politics—again, live and uncensored. In an April 16 program, for example, the first caller was an Iraqi living in Syria, who began by complaining that "the Iraqi people suffered from a media blackout in the age of Saddam Hussein, and we hope that now after his fall you will bring our voices to the world and especially to the Arab people, . . . and we hope that your correspondents in Iraq open the arena to Iraqi citizens to express their feelings in your programs." Later the host read from a fax sent by an Iraqi living in the Gulf, who complained that "your program and the programs of the other Arab satellite stations increase differences and spread hatred among the Arab peoples." On April 17, a Saudi caller noted that "it is painful that all the Arabs remain unheard in their views, they have no opinions to be heard . . . except for a simple small voice on 'al-Jazeera's Platform.'" But another caller to the same program complained that "since the fall of Mosul there has been a harsh campaign by the Arab satellites to distort the image of Kurds, with no justification."

On April 18, a caller from London pointed out that al-Jazeera did not offer coverage of many of Iraq's provinces, so that viewers had no idea what was happening—for better or worse—in much of the country; he also argued—in what would become a common criticism of the media in general—that many good things were happening in Iraq that went uncovered by al-Jazeera, leaving too negative a picture of the new Iraq in the minds of its viewers. On April 19, a caller from Saudi Arabia complained that al-Jazeera had failed to cover a speech by Shaykh Ahmed Kabisi that had insulted the emir of Qatar by name, which he felt meant that al-Jazeera was losing its hard-won credibility. On April 20, a caller asked Faisal al-Qassem to comment on a story about Iraqi prisons reported on Abu Dhabi TV but which al-Jazeera had not reported. On April 22, a caller lambasted the Arab media, and especially al-Jazeera, for "conspiring with the occupation" by labeling its programs "Iraq after Saddam" or "Iraq after the War." A Kuwaiti caller on April 25 offered condolences to frequent al-Jazeera guest Abd al-Bari Atwan and to al-Jazeera for the loss of "their dear friend, Saddam Hussein."

While Iraqi critics often attacked al-Jazeera for inflaming sectarian and ethnic strife, the hosts of these programs generally tried to prevent rather than encourage such incitement. But the reality of such sentiments ensured that they would emerge in live, uncensored television. For example, on the April 12 program a caller from Qatar declared himself "saddened to hear in these difficult conditions for the Iraqi people as they pass into freedom such words as I just heard, words which encourage, which divide Sunnis and Shia." The studio guest weighed in to declare that "the truth is, there is a clear desire in the United States and in Britain to inflame Iraq's ethnic and religious divisions in order to justify an American military presence." When several callers complained about al-Jazeera's allowing such views to be aired, the host responded forcefully: "Of course, we listen to your opinion, just as we listened to [the caller] from Saudi Arabia, we respect all opinions and we provide them with our free platform, the al-Jazeera Platform [the name of the program]."

On an April 16 program, a woman from Holland went into a long, violent rant against the Kurds, blaming them for the fall of Iraq; Nasir allowed this to continue for some time before interrupting. But another caller urged all Iraqis of all political, ethnic, or religious roots to unite and to overcome their divisions for the greaer good. A Saudi caller on May 10 declared that Iraq's future would be guaranteed only if all the Shia would go back to Iran. On another program (April 17), the first caller, an Iraqi from Germany, began to denounce Shia and Kurds, and Jumana al-Namour firmly cut him off: "You are expressing a point of view, but in a negative and confrontational way, and we expect on our program that everyone will present their point of view without insulting anyone, without harming anyone. . . . I am sorry, but we cannot continue with your words, which are hateful and destructive." When another caller began to heap abuse on non-Kurdish Iraqis, Namour quickly intervened: "Most of our callers have affirmed that what Iraq needs now is unity and constructiveness and patriotism and looking to the future." On April 22, the host firmly instructed viewers that "in recent days some callers seem to be confused about the purpose of this program, . . . which is to present your views, not to be a platform for insults or poison or incitement or defamation of some individual or group."

From the perspective of the Arab order, blame for the fall of Baghdad spun in dangerous directions. For a Jordanian caller on April 16,

the fall of Iraq at American hands "was the result of the collective treason of all Arab rulers, and at their head Saddam Hussein, who did not
do what he needed to do to protect Iraq." From another direction, a
caller on April 18 complained that "when the tyrant was present, many
Arab regimes helped him . . . and did not give any real help to the Iraqi
people." On the same program, a caller from Austria declared that "I
am horribly saddened by the condition of all the Arab peoples, . . . and
I condemn intensely the position of all the Arab states, who cringed
and did not help Iraq, but put their land and their airspace at the service of the imperialist aggression against Iraq." A caller on April 25
yelled, "Our rulers are our real enemies. . . . America will not fall until
all these treasonous regimes fall."

Kuwaitis, as well as Iraqis (see below), had every opportunity to
be heard in these discussions. On April 21, a Kuwaiti caller urged al-
Jazeera to respect what Kuwait had been through and why it hated
Saddam. On April 22, Faisal al-Qassem hosted a discussion between
a member of the Kuwaiti Parliament, a political science professor
from Baghdad University, and an Egyptian journalist about the future
of Iraqi-Kuwaiti relations in which all parties frankly agreed that it
would be difficult for either side to easily forget about the past even
with Saddam gone. On April 28, former Kuwaiti Minister of Information Saad bin Taflah was invited to talk about Kuwaiti criticisms of
the Arab League. Bringing such contentious subjects into the public
sphere could easily inflame controversies and divisions, but at least the
problems were not avoided and neither position was silenced.

The programs made clear the enormous doubt and uncertainty
felt by many about Iraq's future. One caller on April 17 complained
that America spoke of freedom and democracy but brought death and
destruction, that many of the prominent figures in the Iraqi opposition had once been part of Saddam's regime, and that the opposition
and the Americans both wanted to divide Iraq into ethnic cantons.
An Egyptian caller urged the Iraqi people to come together: "This is
not a time for division, it is not a time for one group to be against
another, for we are all Muslims, and nobody can describe himself as
a Sunni or a Shia, for he is at the same time a Muslim." Several other
callers repeated this plea for unity. Another caller from Saudi Arabia
similarly urged the Iraqis to hold fast to their values and their unity,

and denounced the looters and thieves as "the greatest traitors to the Iraqi people." A Saudi caller stated simply, "I do not love Saddam, but I hate America, and any government in Iraq that it forms, no matter how it appears on the surface, on the inside is a lie." And another caller called on Iraqis to "wage war against America." But a caller on April 18 reminded viewers that "it is very early to judge America, whether it came in Iraq's interest or against it. . . . Perhaps America came for Iraq's oil, but what does it bring in exchange?" And, pointing to the disappearance of Saddam Hussein, he asked "Don't Arabs realize that this man was not a hero and not an Arab nationalist . . . that he did not work in the interests of his people?"

Iraqi Voices and the Iraqi Opposition

Iraqis, both inside Iraq and outside the country, were now frequent callers to the program, and the hosts repeatedly urged more Iraqis to phone in. The hostility expressed by many of these newly heard Iraqi voices toward the Arab public shocked and dismayed Arabs who had made sympathy for the Iraqi people central to their political identity.

The views of the Iraqi callers and guests spanned the range from enthusiastic support of the war to furious opposition. It was as common to hear callers, such as one on April 20, thanking George Bush and Tony Blair for liberating Iraqis from the tyranny as to hear another on the same day denouncing America for talking about democracy as it killed and maimed innocent Iraqis. The first caller to the April 21 program on the fate of Saddam Hussein, an Iraqi in London, declared his sympathy for all the martyrs in Iraq and Palestine, but then announced, "We must all hope that Saddam is gone, that the tyranny has ended, and everyone in the Arab world knew that he was a tyrant, and he is to blame for the Americans ending up in our country." An Iraqi caller on April 18 issued a heartfelt plea to Arab rulers: "I call on you in the name of Arabism and the name of Islam, as a humble Iraqi citizen, your family in Iraq is in desperate need of your support and your assistance, our hospitals lack even the most basic treatments … we do not need now more empty words." The first caller to an April 29 program on the formation of a temporary Iraqi government, an Iraqi in Germany, proclaimed his thanks that "the American administration has given us the chance for there to be a democratic patriotic [*watani*] government."

Another Iraqi caller on April 19 was more confrontational: "Where were the Arab states and the Arab leaders with their false tears? And those demonstrators who said we sympathize with the Iraqi people?" He blasted not only the Arabs, leaders and masses, but also the Arab media for trying to inflame conflict between Sunnis and Shia, Arabs and Kurds, and he attacked al-Jazeera for reporting on the Baghdad Museum but not sending a correspondent into the south to investigate the mass graves and to present Saddam's crimes to the Arab viewers. An Iraqi American calling on May 9 urged Arabs to realize the desperate need felt by all Iraqis to come together and avoid internal divisions and ethnic or religious violence, and blasted Arabs for treating Saddam as an "Arab nationalist hero" despite all of his crimes. On a May 10 program, caller after caller repeated their delight that "thirty-five years of Saddamist occupation" of Iraq had ended.

These programs encouraged Iraqis to share their stories of life under Saddam. On April 17, an Iraqi living in Sweden said that he had been a prisoner in an underground prison in Iraq, and Namour urged him to give details of his experience and the location of the prison, wanting him to share his experiences with an Arab audience. Later in the show another caller told a similar story about her brother, who had spent twenty-three years in one of Saddam's prisons. On April 20, Faisal al-Qassem patiently allowed an Iraqi women from Sweden to tell her story of her family being arrested in 1991, their houses destroyed, and many of her relatives killed. And on May 26, Jumana al-Namour hosted an emotional program about the mass graves, described below, which actively solicited stories about the horrors of life under Saddam.

While al-Jazeera (and the Arab public sphere more widely) actively sought out Iraqi voices, they remained hostile toward and contemptuous of the Iraqi opposition parties that quickly took center stage as the Iraqi face of the occupation. In the attempts to explain Arab attitudes toward the new Iraq, too little weight has been given to the impact of the American decision to rely heavily on an exiled Iraqi opposition with a long, negative history within the Arab public sphere. Seeing these hated, despised figures—who were widely considered to be American puppets—placed in positions of power and authority rankled the Arab public, who saw this as clear evidence that the United States did not really intend to create a democracy: how could a democratic system be created or led by manifestly unpopular figures such as Ahmed Chalabi?

Chalabi came in for particular abuse as a symbol of opportunism and American hypocrisy. The April 17 program hosted by Jumana al-Namour asked whether "Iraqis will accept that Chalabi's supporters monopolize leadership positions." The declaration by Mohammed Zubaydi, a colleague of Chalabi's, that he was in charge of Baghdad, though quickly terminated by the American forces, aroused howls of protest from Arabs already worried that Chalabi would be installed as an American puppet in Baghdad. For example, an Iraqi living in Romania responded derisively to a question about the Iraqi opposition (April 15): "If they are so brave, then why did they leave Iraq, disappear into America and Britain, and sit there talking about overthrowing Saddam and talking a lot?" Another caller mocked that "from the Gulf to the sea, everyone knows who is Ahmed Chalabi, who is Baqr al-Hakim, who is Iyad Allawi. . . . The truth is that they sold themselves cheaply."

Some callers even came to the defense of the Iraqi opposition, with one saying on April 17 that "anyone would be better than the police who ruled Iraq for thirty years. . . . Perhaps they have picked up some useful skills while living abroad, and learned a bit about democracy and humanity." On April 19, an Iraqi from Sweden described Chalabi as "a fighting man, one who has since 1991 defended the Iraqi issue, and better than those who have changed their loyalties in twenty-four hours," and urged all Iraqis and all Arabs to thank Bush for liberating Iraq from tyranny. But more typical was a caller from France on April 18: "The Iraqi opposition has come to Iraq, and it will be the real authorities in Iraq and will speak for the Iraqi people. . . . But the Iraqi people hate the opposition, this opposition which lived in London and in Washington and in Paris while the Iraqi people suffered under Saddam… . In truth they are traitors and American agents." Or, on April 20: "They come over Iraqi corpses and blood on American tanks, and whom should we trust? The criminal Ahmed Chalabi? They are all American agents." And on the same day, an Iraqi caller demanded to know "who is Ahmed Chalabi? . . . They do not represent the Iraqi people, the only ones who can represent the Iraqi people are those who suffered under the embargo. . . . Ahmed Chalabi will do the same thing as Saddam Hussein." Qassem challenged this caller: "Why do you have such expectations of someone who has been out of the country for decades, that you don't know anything about?" The Iraqi caller responded, "I only expect them to fail, for they are traitors. . . . The Iraqi people know very well who is Ahmed Chalabi."

Other opposition figures were treated with more respect. On April 12, Ghassan bin Jadu hosted a discussion about the Iraqi opposition with several members of different factions—but none from the Iraqi National Congress or the six parties that made up the American-backed opposition. All denounced Saddam Hussein's tyranny and blamed him for the suffering of the Iraqi people, but were sharply critical of the "six." Ibrahim Jaafari of the Dawa Party—which rejected participation in the American campaign, and which quickly emerged as the most popular political party in Iraq—defended his party's long struggle against Saddam, and warned that "the people who rejected Saddam Hussein, despite his dictatorship and long control, will reject any other occupation."

In an April 15 program, Faisal al-Qassem introduced the controversial Sunni tribal leader Mishaan Jabouri (allegedly an ex-Baathist with close ties to Saddam's intelligence services) as "a prominent opposition figure who led an Iraqi party and at the same time was one of the leading people beating the drum for the American project." Jabouri objected to the description, insisting that he had been beating the drum for an Iraqi national project, to overthrow Saddam Hussein for all time with or without American aid. When Jabouri criticized the Americans for failing to establish order, Qassem confronted him: "Before the war began, I asked you personally, will the Americans bring a democratic and development project to Iraq? And you were extremely enthusiastic. . . . So why do you now suddenly retreat from this and throw accusations at the Americans?" Jabouri responded that no honorable Arab could accept being a carrier of an American project, but that Iraq's national interest had agreed with the American national interest in overthrowing Saddam Hussein. Now, Jabouri insisted, the time had come to look out for Iraqi interests even if they conflicted with American policies. A few days later (April 18), a caller sympathetic to the Iraqi opposition blasted al-Jazeera for hosting Jabouri—"In Mosul there are professors and doctors and specialists who studied in Britain and America and France, but you interview only Mishaan Jabouri?"

The meeting held outside Nasiriya on April 16 to discuss a transitional regime received a great deal of attention, as Arabs struggled to divine American intentions for Iraq's future. Three al-Jazeera talk shows discussed the Nasiriya meeting over two days. In the first, Jordan's former Crown Prince Hassan bin Talal—who had sparked a media frenzy by appearing at an Iraqi opposition meeting in London the previous year—spoke generally about Iraq's future. Despite occasional interest in Washington over a Hashemite role in Iraq, however, Hassan inspired little interest within the Arabist public. More interesting were two call-in shows hosted by Abd al-Samid Nasir (April 16) and Jumana al-Namour (April 17). On April 16, a caller from Qatar dismissed the Iraqi opposition figures in Nasiriya as just wanting to rule Iraq, even if it meant allowing in American imperialism. Another caller mocked that "the Iraqi opposition can't do anything except on the backs of America and Israel. . . . It can't do anything for the Iraqi people, the first interest will always be that of America and Israel." A caller from France complained that "the meeting was called by Jay Garner, and Garner is well known for his warm relationship with Sharon, and I think that the Iraqi people are very close to the Palestinian people and won't be happy with this." Yet another caller declared that "I don't think that this meeting held by the opposition in Nasiriya will accomplish what the Iraqi people deserve, because the umma . . . because freedom which the Iraqi people deserve cannot come on the backs of American tanks." But another caller pointed out that while there were both negative and positive aspects of the meeting, it should not be forgotten that "a free Iraqi voice could speak on Iraqi land, and this is the first step toward change." Even this caller expressed disgust with the platform of "federalism and democracy and secularism and separating religion from politics," and worried that these ideas would lead to great differences and conflicts in the near future.

Several callers denounced the ethnic conception of Iraq embodied in the opposition's federalist vision, and rejected the idea that Iraqis should be described as Sunnis, Shia, Kurds, and other ethnic religious groups. A Jordanian caller described what had happened in Iraq as "just like what happened in Afghanistan and elsewhere at the hands of the criminal Bush. . . . But what is important is what we should do now." An Iraqi living in Norway said that "as an Iraqi citizen, personally, I reject this meeting. . . . How can one person, such as Jay Garner, I don't know his name, come and rule my country?" And, he went on, "I think that 99 percent of the opposition is from the mukhabarat (Iraqi intelligence). . . . How can there be an opposition outside of the country?"

On April 25, Namour hosted another discussion on what to expect from a new Iraqi government, in the light of Jay Garner's seeming preference of relying on the Iraqi opposition to oversee a transition to democracy. The first caller, an Iraqi from Germany, declared, "We don't know anything about these people, we have no way to evaluate them." Namour pushed him by quoting Garner's promise that the Iraqi people would choose their government, to which the caller responded dismissively: "The Iraqi people can't make this choice. . . . The Americans will choose. . . . They don't want democracy because it would not serve their interests." An Iraqi caller argued that Saddam had infiltrated the "clean" opposition with his agents, pointing fingers at Chalabi and other prominent opposition figures, and despaired that this "dirty" opposition was so well funded and had such support in the media that real opposition had little chance. Another denounced them as American and Zionist agents. But a Kurdish caller wanted to vouch for Garner, pointing to his assistance in building democratic institutions in northern Iraq in the 1990s. Garner's invitation to opposition figures the following week prompted yet another program, on April 28, discussing the appropriate role of the former opposition in the new Iraq. An Egyptian caller defended them, pointing out that even if they were forced to live in exile by Saddam they were still Iraqis and deserved to be treated with respect. Many of the callers were as offended by the American presumption to name Iraq's new leaders as by the composition of the meeting.

Toward a New Iraq?

These debates on al-Jazeera offer an extraordinary glimpse into the deep Arab uncertainty and fears after the fall of Baghdad, and the kinds of arguments and ideas that dominated Arab arguments. Contrary to conventional wisdom, there was no enforced conformity or single voice dominating these discussions. The al-Jazeera hosts generally tried to stay out of the way of the callers, rather than impose their own viewpoints, and the callers represented a diverse cross-section of Arabs from all over the world. Iraqis were well represented, and voices welcoming the overthrow of Saddam and expressing hopes for the future and thanks to America could be heard—even if they were significantly outnumbered by more pessimistic and critical views.

As insecurity mounted inside Iraq, however, and the occupation seemed unable to restore order or even basic services, opinion began to harden. The "wait and see" attitude evident in a significant middle ground of callers and guests gave way to a tangible disappointment with perceived failed American promises.

6

New Iraq, New Arab Public

Broadcasting against the Israeli forces in the West Bank, and perhaps soon against American forces in Iraq, the al-Jazeera satellite channel . . . will likely do the opposite of what its producers and reporters intend, by showing the hopelessness of opposing American power.

—Reuel Gerecht (2002)

We will see what al-Jazeera is reporting after we have defeated this regime and the United States and its coalition partners, working with others, working with the UN start to bring in humanitarian supplies, medical supplies, a reconstruction effort and put in place a better life for the people of Iraq. I hope al-Jazeera is going to be around to watch that and report that to the Arab public. And I think at that point, the Arab public will realize that we came in peace. We came as liberators, not conquerors.

—Colin Powell, March 2003[1]

The chaos that engulfed Iraq after the fall of Baghdad preempted the kind of public discussion of the American military triumph anticipated by Gerecht or reflections on the gratitude of happy Iraqis predicted by Powell. As the occupation of Iraq deteriorated, the welcoming attitude expressed by Gerecht and Powell toward the Arab media rapidly turned to outright hostility. American civilian and military officials alike complained bitterly about al-Jazeera's "lies" and "propaganda," and increasingly identified the Arab media as a key impediment to success in Iraq. As the insurgency escalated, these accusations became ever more focused and intense, with both Iraqi and American officials accusing the Arab media of creating an atmosphere supportive of the insurgency, or even actively collaborating in its terrorism.

The litany of such complaints is long. In July 2003, Deputy Defense Secretary Paul Wolfowitz accused al-Jazeera and al-Arabiya of incitement to violence against coalition forces. In September 2003, Mustafa Barzani (then holding the rotating presidency of the IGC) ordered the closure of al-Jazeera and al-Arabiya, and in December expelled al-Arabiya for two months for playing an audiotape from Saddam Hussein. In November, after the IGC raided al-Arabiya's offices and banned its broadcasts, Rumsfeld described al-Jazeera and al-Arabiya as "violently anti-coalition" and claimed to have seen evidence that the Arab stations were cooperating with insurgents. In January 2004, a senior CPA official warned al-Jazeera that it would be expelled from Iraq if it did not change its coverage. The first major military confrontation between American forces and Muqtada al-Sadr's Mahdi Army was triggered by the American decision to close down Sadr's newspaper *al-Hawza* for its alleged incitement. Dorrance Smith, who had been a senior CPA official responsible for the media, complained in the *Wall Street Journal* (without offering any evidence), "The collaboration between the terrorists and al-Jazeera is stronger than ever. While the precise terms of that relationship are virtually unknown, we do know this: al-Jazeera and the terrorists have a working arrangement that extends beyond a modus vivendi. When the terrorists want to broadcast something that helps their cause, they have immediate and reliable access to al-Jazeera."[2]

American military officials deeply resented their inability to control information from the battlefield, as in the battle of Falluja in April 2004, when al-Jazeera's team led by popular host Ahmed Mansour was the only news operation inside the besieged city. al-Jazeera and al-Arabiya correspondents on the ground reported severe harassment by Coalition forces, and several were arrested or killed while covering events in Iraq.[3] In November 2003, representatives of thirty media organizations—including CNN, ABC, and the *Boston Globe*—complained to the Pentagon about "an increasingly hostile reporting environment," including "numerous examples of US troops physically harassing journalists and, in some cases, confiscating or ruining equipment."[4]

The irony inherent in the fact that a free media proved the bete noir of the American occupation can be heard in one Iraqi's observation: "The biggest mistake the Americans made was allowing Iraqis to have satellite boxes. During Saddam's time, there was no satellite, so he could do what he wanted and nobody ever knew. Now even the little things the Americans do are played even bigger on Arabiya and Jazeera."[5] In April, the CPA instituted a "truth matrix" to track claims in the Arab media deemed to be inaccurate and then confront offending journalists in an effort to influence their output. To Khaled al-Haroub, the American position amounted to demanding that "the Arab media invent another Iraq, where security prevails and the occupation has everything under control. . . . Wolfowitz wants al-Jazeera to 'show the truth' in Iraq, the virtual American 'truth' that wants to give hope for things that never took place on the ground."[6] On July 15, 2004, Colin Powell told the U.S. Institute of Peace that "when a particular outlet, al-Jazeera, does such a horrible job of presenting the news and when it takes every opportunity to slant the news, present it in the most outrageous way . . . then we have to speak out, and we have."[7] Jihad Ballout of al-Jazeera pointedly responded that "we did not create these photos or these images. We are reporting what's on the ground, we are reflecting the reality." [8] As Maher Abdullah observed, "Blaming the messenger for bad news might help in hiding these [facts] from the public for a while. But it doesn't make them go away."[9] This chapter evaluates these arguments about the role of the Arab and Iraqi media in shaping the politics of postwar Iraq.

In chapter 2 I described the inherent limitations of a weak international public sphere, one able to mobilize a common identity and to shape public opinion but unable to translate its consensus into political outcomes. The situation in Iraq brutally exposed these limitations, posing a harsh challenge to the emerging, if tentative, self-confidence of Arab publics. As Ghassan bin Jadu put it, "The Intifada awakened the Arab elites, . . . but the Iraqi earthquake seems to have exposed to them that they lack any power to influence events."[10] This frustration contributed to the increasingly ugly, hostile tone of the Arab public sphere after the war, as well as to dramatically rising expressions of anti-Americanism. The aftermath of the Iraq war set in motion a profound debate about the Arab public sphere itself, with both external criticism and self-criticism pushing toward serious reflection on the nature of this public sphere phenomenon. In this final chapter I discuss the new Arab public's attitudes toward the new Iraq, as well as the trials and tribulations of both the Arab media and the Iraqi media in the period after Saddam's fall.

Perhaps the most profound shock to the Arab public after the war came not from Saddam's fall, but from the anger and resentment expressed by ordinary Iraqis toward the Arab world. Throughout the decade of public Arab debates about Iraq, the Iraqi people had largely lacked a voice of their own; neither the widely distrusted opposition in exile nor Saddam's regime could authentically speak for the Iraqi people, while Saddam's police state blocked access to any real free expression of their views. For Arabs whose very identity had come to be bound up in their support for the suffering Iraqi people, to suddenly hear themselves castigated by those self-same Iraqis for not being tougher on Saddam was genuinely disorienting and baffling. But it is vital to note a point that is often lost here: Arabs were exposed to these unsettling Iraqi views only because the Arab satellite stations gave them a platform and a voice. Al-Jazeera and al-Arabiya devoted an enormous amount of programming to Iraq, with programs covering all aspects of the new Iraq and putting Iraqis and Arabs into dialogue, exploring Iraqi views and opinions, and allowing them to speak for themselves for the first time.

An Iraqi Public Sphere?

Two months after the fall of the Baghdad, the Iraqi writer Abd al-Mana'am al-Aasim argued that the response to a problematic Arab media should be to "build an effective and credible Iraqi media, able to spread accurate information and to break the walls that have long encircled the minds of Arab citizens, which carry false and misleading information about Iraq and what is happening there."[11] Unfortunately, a combination of a growing insurgency and policy mistakes by the American occupation forces severely hindered the emergence of a credible, independent, and critical Iraqi public sphere. This failure allowed al-Jazeera and al-Arabiya, along with Hezbollah's al-Manar and Iran's al-Alam (the only foreign station available without a satellite dish), to become the most popular sources of information for Iraqis themselves.

After the fall of Saddam's regime, hundreds of newspapers began publishing, representing an enormous variety of political trends as well as many flavors of tabloid sensationalism. Some of these newspapers, such as Saad al-Bazzaz's *al-Zaman*, aspired to be respectable national dailies, while the vast majority were freewheeling tabloids and political party mouthpieces. Only *al-Zaman* and two established Kurdish newspapers reached a significant audience, however, as the tabloids appeared and disappeared routinely. The CPA established an official newspaper, *al-Sabah*, which had a large circulation but was widely perceived to be a mouthpiece for the occupation. Struggles between the Iraqi editorial staff of *al-Sabah* and the American occupation authorities ultimately led to the mass resignation of the entire staff in May 2004.

The CPA-run electronic media quickly came to be dismissed as "state media," reminiscent of Saddam's propaganda organs. The director of the Iraqi version of Radio Sawa, Ahmed Rikabi, quit in August 2003 in protest over Coalition interference, and started instead a popular independent radio station that offered a daily open platform for callers to air their views.[12] In line with the general disorganization and poor preparation that characterized the early days of the occupation, the CPA did not begin television broadcasting until May 13, and then only put out four hours a day of bare-bones presentations.[13] The Iraqi Media Network, run by the Florida-based Harris Corporation, which had no experience either in the media nor in the Arab world, produced an astonishingly dreary and unattractive product that reminded many Iraqis of Saddam's television, ran little news, and was largely ignored by Iraqis. Paul Bremer's weekly appearances on the IMN confirmed the impression that the station's only purpose was to be a mouthpiece for the occupation.[14] In November 2004, Jalal al-Mashtah, the general director of the Iraqi Media Network, resigned over complaints about Harris Corporation mismanagement.[15]

As a result, according to the assistant dean of Baghdad's College of Media, "al-Iraqiya is failing. It's technically backward. Its message is not convincing. It can't compete with other stations."[16] Al-Iraqiya was able to be received without difficulties at home by 84 percent of Iraqis—compared to 33 percent for the satellite stations—as late as April 2004.[17] But despite this advantage, a State Department survey in October found that of Iraqis with access to a satellite dish, 63 percent preferred either al-Jazeera or al-Arabiya, and only 12 percent al-Iraqiya.[18] Al-Hurra, designed to be broadcast over the air rather than by satellite in Iraq, nevertheless struggled—in April 2004, only 6 percent of respondents to a Gallup poll reported having viewed al-Hurra in the previous week.[19] In short, the Iraqi media under American occupation proved incapable of attracting an Iraqi audience, both because of professional shortcomings and because of tight political control, forcing Iraqis to look elsewhere. Saad al-Bazzaz did rather better with al-Sharqiya, the first privately owned satellite television station in Iraq, which quickly captured a significant audience with its focus on popular entertainment, music videos, reality TV shows, and soap operas.

Where the Arab media stood accused of exaggerating the violence and chaos in Iraq, the official Iraqi media under the CPA lost credibility by erring in the opposite direction. An Iraqi taxi driver described Coalition spokesman Brigadier General Mark Kimmett as "the lord of lies. . . . It is as though he gives opium to the people. He always talks about security and stability in Baghdad, and the happy life in Iraq, while the situation is [in reality] like hell."[20] As the insurgency escalated and personal security came to dominate the concerns of most Iraqi citizens, the CPA did little to establish the foundations of a healthy Iraqi public sphere. Even more, the Iraqi media largely failed to bring to the Iraqi public the kinds of information it would need to rationally and critically discuss the emerging political system.[21] In a July 2004 survey, for example, 52 percent of Iraqis said that they had heard nothing at all about recent UN recommendations on an interim government and 65 percent had heard nothing at all about plans to form an independent election commission.[22]

The CPA never fully resolved the inherent conflict between the concept of a free, independent, critical media and a concept of the media as a vehicle for conveying a particular political narrative. Nor did it resolve the tension between the military imperative of controlling information and the political imperative of creating a free and independent press. As Iraqis grew increasingly frustrated with the occupation—by May 2004, 80 percent of Iraqis surveyed lacked confidence in the CPA and 82 percent disapproved of the American military presence—their authentically expressed views grated on the beleaguered occupation authorities.[23] To the dismay of those who had wanted to believe in American democratic promises, the CPA took an ever more confrontational and even authoritarian attitude toward independent media—Arab and

Iraqi alike. A mid-June edict "prohibiting the local media from inciting attacks on other Iraqis and on the coalition forces" prompted one tabloid to declare that "Bremer is a Baathist!"[24] In late March 2004, the CPA triggered a major political crisis by shutting down Muqtada al-Sadr's newspaper *al-Hawza* for having "published articles that prove an intention to disturb general security and incite violence against the coalition and its employees."

As the insurgency escalated through 2004, journalism became exceptionally dangerous (Blake 2005). At least twenty-four journalists were killed in Iraq in 2004, and many more suffered harassment, threats, and intimidation.[25] It soon reached the point that Western journalists, like American administrators, were largely trapped in the Green Zone, reliant on Iraqi stringers to collect news. As translators and stringers became insurgency targets, even those sources began to dry up. On October 30, 2004, the al-Arabiya offices in Baghdad were the target of a horrific car bombing, and in December *al-Sharq al-Awsat* closed its Baghdad offices in the face of a credible insurgency threat. In short, both a deficient institutional framework and a spiraling insurgency mitigated against the evolution of a vibrant Iraqi public sphere.

The Occupation and the Former Iraqi Opposition

One of the most frequently aired complaints about al-Jazeera was its use of the term "occupation" rather than "liberation" to describe the American campaign against Iraq. Despite these attempts to police word choice in the Arab media, a year after the fall of Baghdad, 92 percent of Iraqis considered the United States to be an occupying force.[26] The failed hopes that Saddam's fall would lead quickly to a peaceful Iraqi democracy had far-reaching consequences for the evolution of Arab public opinion toward the new Iraq.

While explaining the course of the American occupation is beyond the scope of this book, the failure to establish basic services or to ensure personal security, turned many Iraqis against the American presence. Retired general Jay Garner entered Iraq expecting to rely heavily on the former Iraqi opposition, and based his plans on their advice that Iraqis would welcome the American forces as liberators.

Largely ignoring planning documents crafted in the State Department for the post-war scenario, Garner opted for a minimal American presence and a rapid political process based on the opposition returning from exile (Diamond 2004). But it quickly became clear that events in post-war Iraq bore little resemblance to what the Iraqi opposition had promised. Rampant looting, insecurity, and chaos interfered with all reconstruction plans, as Arabs and Iraqis alike wondered how and why the American military could be so incompetent in restoring order. The chaos and looting in Baghdad perplexed and terrified Arab observers, many of whom could not understand how the United States, with all its power and wealth, could be unable to prevent it. The increasingly confrontational relations between Iraqi citizens and American military personnel quickly overwhelmed early images of celebrating Iraqis. The growing bloodshed drove away whatever doubts Arabs might have otherwise felt about American power or intentions in Iraq. After an initial moment of uncertainty and shock, Arab attitudes hardened.

After less than a month, Garner was summarily replaced with Paul Bremer, who quickly and firmly moved to consolidate power within the CPA. Bremer's controversial decision to dissolve the Iraqi army sent tens of thousands of trained military personnel into the ranks of the insurgency. Operating out of one of Saddam's palaces in Central Baghdad, the CPA assumed a dominant position in all aspects of the occupation and reconstruction. Increasingly isolated from Iraqi society within the Green Zone as security concerns escalated, the CPA had little chance of reaching out to the Iraqi public.

Despite Bremer's contentious relationship with the former opposition exiles, they formed the core of the Interim Governing Council created in July 2003 to represent Iraqis and to form the nucleus for the presumed transition to an independent, democratic Iraqi government. The IGC proved unpopular and ineffective, however. Despite including several local Iraqis, the council was dominated by members of the former opposition in exile, whose in-fighting skills and comfort with American officials proved far more valuable in the new environment than local popularity or effectiveness at governing. A September 2003 survey found that 75 percent of Iraqis believed that the CPA controlled the council's policy decisions, with most opting to wait and see about its performance.[27] An October 2003 survey found that 69 percent or more had not heard enough about eighteen out of twenty-five members to have an opinion about them; only 38 percent said the same about Chalabi, but only 1 percent named him as the most trusted leader.[28] Between November 2003 and June 2004, the proportion of Iraqis expressing any confidence in the Interim Governing Council dropped from 63 percent to 28 percent.[29]

While the IGC was supposed to act as a conduit for Iraqi views to the CPA, "the IGC operate[d] from a building protected from its putative constituents by concertina wire and two U.S. military checkpoints" (Alkadiri and Toensing 2003). Reflecting the notorious internal conflicts and inability to cooperate that crippled the pre-war opposition, the IGC struggled to cooperate; for example, unable to choose a leader, the IGC settled on having a presidency that rotated every month. Members of the IGC were often out of the country, had few tangible accomplishments, and were almost invisible to Iraqi public opinion. Granted the power to appoint ministers for an interim "government," the IGC doled out positions to family members, tribes, business partners, and members of their political parties with little regard for local opinion. Above all, the IGC worked to ensure its own role in a future sovereign Iraqi government, jockeying with Bremer over all political arrangements and ultimately ensuring that all of its members were granted automatic positions in either the new Iraqi government (created on June 28, 2004) or the transitional parliament (as of August 2004). The "Iraqi National Conference" convened in August to put together a transitional parliament was brazenly manipulated by the five remaining core exile parties (with the INC excluded—see below).

The decision to grant leadership positions to these exiled opposition figures had far-reaching implications for the legitimacy of the new Iraq. Few of the exiles commanded any popular support inside Iraq, which gave them deep personal interests in delaying and minimizing the formation of real democratic institutions. Given their low standing with public opinion, the exiles had little incentive to push for rapid elections or for a more representative body—despite demands by figures such as Ayatollah Ali Sistani for early elections and a more democratic mechanism for choosing Iraqi leaders. An October 2003 U.S. State Department survey, for example, found that only 36 percent of Iraqis supported the inclusion of "formerly exiled politicians" in a future Iraqi government—compared to over 90 percent support for doctors, scientists, lawyers, judges, teachers, and professors and 75 percent support for religious leaders.[30] Despite these failings, the former opposition used their positions to effectively monopolize political power in the emerging Iraq. Iraqi National Accord leader Iyad Allawi was appointed transitional prime minister after the transfer of sovereignty at the end of June 2004, and the exiles virtually monopolized the transitional legislative body created by the Iraqi National Conference in August.

The Iraqi National Congress, in particular, proved to have little to no following inside Iraq, while its leader Ahmed Chalabi rapidly emerged as the single most unpopular politician in the new Iraq. In October 2003, his unfavorable rating of 35 percent was by far the highest of any active politician.[31] In a March 2004 public opinion survey, for example, Chalabi was named by 10 percent of Iraqis as the leader they "don't trust at all" (no other figure scored above 2 percent).[32] A June survey found only 0.3 percent who trusted him, and 42 percent of Iraqis who named a leader they did not trust at all listed Chalabi.[33] The determination of many American neoconservatives to see Chalabi emerge as the leader of the new Iraq clashed with commitments to build an Iraqi democracy. Nevertheless, in addition to his post on the governing council, Chalabi was placed in charge of de-Baathification, and given exclusive access to a wide range of potentially incriminating documents from the former regime.

Even the capture of Saddam—otherwise enormously popular with Iraqis—was tarnished by its exploitation by the former opposition. The ill-advised image of Ahmed Chalabi's visit to Saddam's jail cell, published in the INC newspaper *al-Mutamar*, along with the appointment of Chalabi's cousin Salem Chalabi to oversee Saddam's trial, reinforced the idea that a trial for Saddam had more to do with the Iraqi opposition's ambitions than with justice. As one observer put it, the IGC only "intermittently dealt with improving social welfare, the development of infrastructure, or the restoration of Iraqi self-rule. For the past eight months, the major theme has been the importance of exacting a suitable form of revenge on the leaders who tyrannised the country for thirty-five years."[34]

On June 30 the United States formally transferred sovereignty to a government headed by Iyad Allawi as prime minister, and the Sunni tribal leader Ghazi al-Yawwar as the symbolic president. In a public opinion survey conducted the month of the transfer of sovereignty, Yawwar was named by only 1.3 percent of Iraqis as their choice for president.[35] Allawi's rise to power came on the heels of Ahmed Chalabi's sudden, shocking fall from American good graces, as the CPA raided the INC leader's offices on the accusation of passing sensitive intelligence to Iran. Allawi's ascendance confirmed all of the worst expectations of the Arab public: rather than a liberal democrat, Allawi offered them the person of an ex-Baathist strongman, with no democratic credentials, little popular support, and an all-too-familiar enthusiasm for the use of force. While he gained some popularity inside of Iraq for his tough approach to the insurgency, his attitudes toward the media remained distinctly authoritarian. In August 2004 Allawi oversaw the creation of a "Higher Media Council", with wide-ranging powers to oversee and control the press, and over the subsequent months government officials routinely intimidated journalists.[36]

Iraqis and Arabs

FATHI [*from Iraq*]: al-Jazeera, you are all dogs, you are all dogs.
JUMANA AL-NAMOUR: Thank you. Ammad, from Doha.
AMMAD [*from Doha*]: . . . As Iraqis we feel that al-Jazeera is very biased in its coverage. . . . Al-Jazeera has an Arabist worldview, and Saddam Hussein's regime was once upon a time representing Arabism or at least a form of it, and al-Jazeera insists on this worldview and on hostility toward the regime that has followed Saddam.[37]

Your station is a symbol of evil and a transmitter of poison and sectarianism and hatred to the new Iraq, you support terrorism and kidnapping and you pray for the return of Saddam or the supporters of Saddam and you concealed every crime of Saddam against Iraq and the Iraqis, you are the station of Zarqawi and kidnapping and terror.
—An Iraqi open letter to al-Jazeera[38]

On July 5, 2003, Ghassan bin Jadu broadcast an episode of *Open Dia-logue* live from Baghdad.[39] The show, which brought Iraqis into direct dialogue with intellectuals from Cairo and Beirut, aired sensitive open wounds between Iraqis and Arab public opinion. The speakers and the host were all palpably aware that they were being asked to represent, to interpret, and to in some sense validate the Arab public sphere. One Iraqi, Hilal Idrisi, bluntly categorized Arab public opinion as following two trends: "The first trend didn't have reliable information about the internal situation in Iraq, and the second trend ignored the opinions of the Iraqi people and was part of the lobby defending the old regime." Iraqi after Iraqi attacked Arab public opinion for failing to distinguish between the Iraqi people and the Iraqi regime, for minimizing the ter-ror of life under Saddam, for ignoring or mischaracterizing the mass graves. They declared it an open secret that many Arab journalists and artists were on Saddam's payroll.

The Egyptians and Lebanese participants, for their part, were hurt and offended by these Iraqi accusations. Tariq al-Tahimi, of the Egyp-tian opposition newspaper *al-Wafd*, responded, "Egyptian public opinion was capable of distinguishing between the people and the re-gime, and the Egyptian people were capable of saying in their demon-strations in the streets that they demanded the lifting of the blockade of the Iraqi people, and no killing of Iraqis, that bombs don't make democracy, and at the same time they came out in the streets and said: 'we are with the Iraqi people and we are not with Saddam Hussein.'" Walid Barakat, speaking from Beirut, explained that "it may be true that public opinion didn't know everything about what went on inside Iraq, but it knew a lot. . . . It knew the extent of the oppression that the Iraqi people lived under. . . . We all knew about the mass graves and the oppression, . . . and we condemned it in every Arab country." But, he went on, "I think that the mass graves were for the million and a half Iraqis who died because of the American blockade."

Such angry exchanges featured prominently in the Arab public sphere's struggles to make sense of the new Iraq. On a December 2003 al-Jazeera program devoted to Arabs and the Iraqi issue, the Iraqi guests again aired their long-standing grievances with Arab official and popular silence toward Saddam's crimes, while Arab guests an-grily defended their long struggles on behalf of the Iraqi people.[40] A similar program that aired on al-Jazeera in April 2005 featured angry recriminations between the chief editor of Iraq's largest daily newspaper, journalists from Jordan and Egypt, and the editor in chief of al-Jazeera itself. The Iraqi complained that the Arab media failed to grasp the realities of Iraqi society today, refused to acknowledge that Iraq was not fully an "Arab" country, actively or tacitly supported the insurgency, and remained thoroughly corrupted by its prior support for Saddam Hussein.[41] The hostility directed toward the Arab media and toward the Arab world more generally by ordinary Iraqis stunned and confused the Arab public. In the Arab self-understanding, they had courageously rallied and organized and worked for years on behalf of the Iraqi people. They had demanded the lifting of the sanctions, condemned American bombings, and blasted their own regimes for failing to act—often at great personal risk. To now be accused by these very Iraqis clearly hurt them deeply.

But the anger was real. Mustafa Husseini, who traveled to Iraq in June 2003 with a group from the Arab Organization for Press Freedoms to see the condition of the Iraqi media, said that "the biggest surprise for me was the extent of hostility from Iraqis toward us. . . . Everybody said to us, where were you when Saddam Hussein was dealing with the Iraqi people by killing and torture."[42] In the typical words of one Iraqi writer, the Arab media "glorified the Iraqi regime" and deluded Arab viewers about the realities of Iraq under Saddam.[43] Ali al-Ghufli, writing in *al-Khaleej*, worried that a destructive and unfortunate "crisis of confidence" had opened up between the Arabs and Iraq.[44] An April 2004 public opinion survey of Iraqis found that 66 percent felt that Arab governments had been "too supportive" of Saddam's regime and only 11 percent "not too supportive."[45]

As the insurgency spiraled, many Iraqis blamed al-Jazeera and al-Arabiya (especially) for encouraging the violence, and accused both Arab states and the Arab people of doing too little to help. They complained about the choice of guests on the talk shows, especially on Faisal al-Qassem's *The Opposite Direction*, arguing that they were intervening in Iraqi politics by favoring some politicians and discrediting others.[46] The opinion pages of Iraqi newspapers, public opinion surveys, and interviews all confirm that anger with the Arab media went far deeper in the new Iraq than just among the former exiles. While Rumsfeld's accusations of active complicity by Arab journalists in attacks by insurgents seem exaggerated, the hyper-competitive Arab media did seek out compelling, graphic footage, as well as privileged access to insurgency sources.[47] While themselves drawn to these stations as the best source of information about their own country, many Iraqis became infuriated at how the Arab media portrayed events—to some degree because they felt that the coverage was inaccurate or exaggerated, to some degree because they feared that the coverage encouraged more violence, and to some degree because they worried that the coverage was warping Arab attitudes toward the new Iraq in unconstructive directions. With security the overwhelming priority of almost all Iraqis, critics denied that it was an issue of freedom of speech when—in their view—the broadcasts contributed to the killing of Iraqis.[48]

Sensing that the Arab media offered an easy and popular target emboldened the appointed Iraqi leadership—already deeply hostile to the Arab media from their days as exiled opposition—to attack. The INC in particular pursued a vendetta, seeking to settle old scores by brandishing documents allegedly seized from the former regime's archives to prove that their critics had been on Saddam's payroll. Then–IGC President Jalal Talabani explained his November 2003 closure of al-Arabiya in these terms: "We are not acting against legitimate and objective journalistic activities. We are taking steps to prevent psychological warfare and, more serious, incitement to murder. . . . That is not journalism; that is aiding, abetting, and encouraging criminal terrorist activity."[49]

The attack on the Arab media did indeed prove popular with some Iraqis.[50] In February 2004, an Iraqi Shia cleric blasted al-Jazeera during a Friday sermon and called on the IGC to permanently shut it down: "Al-Jazeera lies, and it creates divisions among the people," he complained.[51] Among his complaints were allegations that al-Jazeera was inaccurately reporting the size and scope of demonstrations in favor of early elections by Shias, and that Faisal al-Qassem during a talk show had displayed photographs of members of the IGC meeting with Israeli intelligence officials. In July Iraqi Foreign Minister Hoshyar Zebari accused the Arab media of "incitement" and of "one-sided" and "distorted" coverage of Iraq, warning that "the new Iraqi government will not tolerate these kinds of intentional breaches and violations." Almost immediately upon the transfer of sovereignty at the end of June, Zebari warned al-Jazeera to change its coverage or be shut down; in July, Prime Minister Iyad Allawi carried through this threat and shuttered the al-Jazeera offices for a month, with no protest from the American embassy. In late August, the police chief of Najaf rounded up at gunpoint all journalists covering the fighting there to lambaste them over their coverage—specifically al-Arabiya's (accurate) report of Ayatollah Ali Sistani's impending return to the city. And in August 2004, transitional prime minister Iyad Allawi ordered al-Jazeera's Baghdad offices closed down, a move described by Daoud al-Basri as "a sovereign decision that responds to the wishes of an Iraqi popular majority and . . . an appropriate and positive response."[52] In late November 2004, interim defense minister Hazem Sha'alan told *al-Sharq al-Awsat* that al-Jazeera was actively supporting the insurgency, claiming that its bureau chief was funneling money to Abu Musab al-Zarqawi's aide Omar Hadid (a claim later quietly retracted by another Iraqi official after al-Jazeera aired an exculpatory interview with the alleged Zarqawi conduit).[53]

The hostile Iraqi approach to the Arab media troubled many observers, who took it as evidence that the new Iraq would not be truly democratic. As Hazem Saghiye observed, "I am part of the Arab minority that is closer to accepting the present Iraqi situation than to accepting al-Jazeera. . . . That said, the recent decision by Baghdad to punish al-Jazeera is devoid of wisdom . . . [because] the only thing the current Iraqi regime is able to offer its Arab neighbors is its condition of freedom."[54] On an al-Jazeera talk show devoted to the closure, most callers interpreted the decision as a signal of encroaching Iraqi authoritarianism and American military frustration, as well as a wider American hope of "silencing the conscience of the Arab world."[55] Some Iraqi callers to that program defended the decision, however, on the basis of urgent security concerns. One underappreciated effect of the closure was that it shifted the incentives for al-Jazeera as a news organization: banned from covering official events, it no longer had much of an incentive—or opportunity—to convey the Iraqi interim government's perspective on events. Tellingly, however, when Hazem Sha'alan, Iraqi's interim defense minister and one of al-Jazeera's harshest Iraqi critics, wanted to launch an attack on political rival Ahmed Chalabi, he chose what he knew to be the most prominent and influential media outlet in Iraq: al-Jazeera.[56]

Beyond the implications for Iraqi governance and democracy, the prominence of these exiles proved devastating to relations between the new Iraq and the Arab world. As the pro-war writer Adnan Hussein witheringly complained, Arabs received a delegation from the IGC to Arab capitals "as if they were genies, or even devils. As if they were the historic enemy of the Arab *umma*, and also the Islamic *umma*. As if they were the cause of Arab disasters."[57] In August, the Arab League declined to recognize the IGC, insisting that only an elected government would be recognized (an ironic position for the Arab League, with its less-than-democratic membership roster). In a rare confluence, this position exactly mirrored the popular position taken by the majority of commentators on al-Jazeera.[58] But ultimately Arab states had little choice but to accommodate themselves to the new reality, and within a month (following a supportive Security Council resolution) Secretary-General Amru Musa announced that the Arab League would deal with the IGC as a practical matter of reality and allowed Iraq's provisional foreign minister, Hoshyar Zebari, to be seated as Iraq's representative at the Arab League. The "transfer of sovereignty" to the interim Iraqi government at the end of June 2004 made similarly little impact on Arab opinion, which largely considered such steps to be relatively meaningless; in a July online al-Jazeera poll with over 70,000 respondents, 81.5 percent said that the transfer was not the beginning of the end of the American occupation.

At the same time, Arab regimes offered only minimal support to the new Iraq, while Arab public opinion proved torn between hope for a return to normality and a kind of horrified admiration for the insurgency—which many viewed more in terms of its effectiveness against the American occupation forces than in terms of its impact on the future of Iraq. This infuriated Iraqis, who saw the Arab willingness to "sacrifice Iraqis in the name of fighting America" as identical with perceived Arab support for Saddam for the same reason in the past.[59] To some increasingly impaients observers, the Arab position toward the new Iraq appeared to be motivated more by the expressive concerns of Arab identity than by any clear strategic logic.

The hostility expressed by many Iraqis toward the Arab world led some to wonder whether the very Arab identity of Iraq was in danger.[60] These fears were reinforced by the insistence on federalism, the high profile of

Kurdish parties in the emerging Iraqi government, and some advocacy of the idea by prominent American neo-conservative backers of the war. The announcement of a new Iraqi flag—which replaced the traditional Arab colors with a blue closely resembling that of Israel's flag—fueled the fears. Some Kurdish and Turkoman (and other) Iraqi writers argued that imposing an Arab identity on the new Iraqi state recalled the Baathist tyranny.[61] At the same time, Iraqis—and some Arabs—marveled at how little the Arab world had done to help the new Iraq.[62] In an Arab public sphere increasingly dominated by identity politics, such a debate over Iraq's Arabness was inevitable, and not necessarily destructive. If such a debate forced a rethinking of what it meant to be Arab, as hoped by many Arab liberals and American backers of the war, it could prove salutary. But for the most part the debate instead turned into one critical of the new Iraq rather than critical of Arab identity.

The Iraqi elections of January 2005 offer one final vignette of the interaction between the Arab media and the Iraqi arena. Al-Jazeera, al-Arabiya, and most of the new media covered the elections extensively, positively, and constructively. Despite the continuing ban on official operations in Iraq, al-Jazeera lavished the elections with saturation coverage.[63] Rather than highlighting the negatives, as many had expected, they broadcast uplifting footage of delighted Iraqi voters and broadcast numerous talk shows discussing the possibilities and pitfalls facing a post-election Iraq. Many commentators worked over the contradictions of having democratic elections under conditions of occupation, and a number of influential figures seemed skeptical, but this did not prevent saturation coverage of the elections themselves. Coverage differed from station to station, of course, with one Lebanese critic observing that the stations had become political parties in Iraq in their own right—al-Arabiya backing Allawi and cheerleading for the election, and al-Jazeera worrying about the Sunni boycott and a Shia-dominated government.[64] Even interim prime minister Iyad Allawi, usually a fierce critic of the Arab media, acknowledged the constructive role it had played in the elections: "Arabic satellite TV stations such as al-Arabiya were obviously excited and inspired by the sight of real democracy in the heart of the Arab world. By reporting fairly on the elections, they in turn inspired their Arab audience across the Middle East and beyond."[65]

Arguing the Insurgency

In July 2003 Ghassan bin Jadu introduced a hotly contested program broadcast from Baghdad on the resistance: "One hundred days have passed since the fall of Baghdad. . . . Some considered it a war of liberation and its result freedom, others called it an aggression and its result occupation. In Iraq there is a consensus or a near consensus that the fall of the Saddam Hussein regime was good for Iraq and Iraqis and the region. . . . And so the question for our *Open Dialogue*: is the choice of resistance a good one?"

The Arab public sphere struggled with how to best respond to the Iraqi insurgency. A morbid fascination with a "successful" resistance mixed uneasily with a despairing hope for normality. On the one hand, many were gratified with the successful campaign against the American occupation, and took some vicarious thrill from seeing American forces struggle. But others were worried by its increasingly violent and nihilistic turn, and worried that such an insurgency's effects would not disappear with the American occupation forces. In November, al-Arabiya's news director Salah al-Qullab declared bitterly that "the only thing worse than the occupation is this resistance."[66] In the summer of 2004, in a series of provocative articles asking who exactly was fighting in Iraq and why, the influential Egyptian columnist Fahmy Huwaydi called to "liberate the Iraqi resistance" from those who would hijack a legitimate national independence movement for its own aims. On al-Jazeera, one of the first programs to deal with the insurgency—a May 2, 2003, program focusing on Falluja—marveled that resistance to American occupation might still be possible. But by March 2004, an *Open Dialogue* was focusing instead on "the blind violence in Iraq" (with Ibrahim Jaafari and Yusuf al-Qaradawi among the guests), while an August 2004 program asked bluntly whether the bombings in Iraq should be considered resistance or terrorism.[67]

The horrific introduction of the practice of videotaping the beheading of hostages challenged the Arab public sphere. While transfixed by the images, many Arabs worried that they contributed little to any legitimate goals. The beheading videos seemed to embody a helpless despair, a nihilistic failure of hope. Ahmed al-Rubai declared "shame on the Arab satellites for broadcasting these tapes. . . . Nobody knows their goals or their intentions, whether they have a just cause or are just thieves."[68] In contrast to the reception to similar attacks on the Arab media, some prominent Arabists—who had opposed the war and conditionally supported the insurgency—agreed with Rubai's sentiments. An online al-Jazeera poll, surprisingly, found only 54.8 percent out of almost 50,000 respondents disagreeing with the claim that the Arab satellite stations were inciting resistance against the occupation—a less than overwhelming show of support from al-Jazeera's own viewers.[69] But, driven by market pressures and by political imperatives, the Arab media continued to broadcast the images.

The revelation of the sexual torture of Iraqi prisoners in the Abu Ghraib prison had a devastating effect on the American image with the Arab public, confirming many of their worst fears and allegations. Perhaps surprisingly, however, the Arab media (including al-Jazeera and al-Arabiya) did not particularly dwell on this scandal.[70] This low profile can be partly explained by the relentless American pressure on the Arab media during this period, which left these stations more cautious than usual. Still, even underplayed the story of Abu Ghraib proved devastating to the American narrative for Iraq; as one analyst noted, "Arabs who had given Washington the benefit of the doubt and hoped for a new beginning in Iraq instead saw a tragedy of errors being committed by the U.S. and its representatives. . . . In live call-in programs, viewers with no apparent political affiliations wondered how the world's superpower could allow such inhumane practices to take place."[71] As former Jordanian ambassador Adnan Abu Odeh observed, the Abu Ghraib revelations bought al-Jazeera some "breathing space," deflecting the American public relations campaign against al-Jazeera, which remained "the most honest reflection of Arab public opinion and its most powerful shaper."[72] Interestingly, the highest profile response in the Arab public sphere came with an episode of *The Opposite Direction* that focused not on Abu Ghraib, but on torture in Arab prisons.

The disparity between Arab and Iraqi priorities can be seen clearly in the response to the capture of Saddam Hussein in December 2003. Hostility to Saddam was overwhelming among most Iraqis outside the Sunni hard-core of the Baathist regime, as the memories of decades of tyranny and repression had seared horrific scars on the collective Iraqi psyche. The revelations of mass graves confirmed the worst fears and experiences of Iraqis, and the newly free press gave ample opportunity for Iraqis to share their stories of suffering and dispossession. As documented in chapter 5, al-Jazeera programs such as Jumana al-Namour's *al-Jazeera's Platform* frankly and emotionally argued about the mass graves and their implications. American observers failed to appreciate the undercurrent of anti-American feeling beneath this hatred of Saddam, however. The enormous suffering of the Iraqi people under sanctions had not simply been Saddam's propaganda, and every Iraqi knew of the American and British role in sustaining the sanctions. Indeed, the rapid American military victory paradoxically confirmed for many Iraqis (and Arabs) a widely held conspiracy theory that the United States had secretly preferred to maintain Saddam in power.

Saddam was far less central to Arab concerns than to Iraqi or American concerns, however. Many Americans hoped that capturing Saddam Hussein and broadcasting images of the disheveled former dictator far and wide would deflate the insurgency, and convince Arab public opinion of the inevitability of a successful transition to a new Iraqi regime. But the impact disappointed on both counts. The insurgency continued unabated, fueled far more by competition over future power in Iraq and deepening resentment of the American presence than by the former dictator. Despite much-circulated jokes about other leaders such as Bishar al-Assad and Moammar Qaddafi rushing to avoid Saddam's fate, the shock of seeing the deposed leader disheveled and in chains provided only a momentary pause. Because the Arab consensus about Iraq had long been more about the Iraqi people than about supporting Saddam Hussein, few were particularly exercised by his fate. One of the first al-Jazeera programs to deal with his capture concentrated on whether Saddam should be treated as a war criminal or as a prisoner of war, with SCIRI's Hamid al-Bayati one of the guests.[73] In a predictable development, lawyers from all over the Arab world offered to lead his defense, and American and Iraqi officials began to have nightmares of a Milosevic-style trial giving the deposed leader a forum to air his views and, perhaps, to reveal embarrassing details.

In the summer and fall of 2004, the interaction between the insurgency and the Arab media became a topic of intense concern on

all sides (al-Marashi 2004). In addition to its wider campaign of terrorism, suicide bombings, and targeting of Iraqi "collaborators," the
Iraqi insurgency began kidnapping a wide range of people, especially foreign aid workers, and releasing videotapes of the hostages
and—sometimes—their graphic beheading. As Jon Alterman (2004)
observed, the Arab media became an integral part of the insurgency
strategy: "Many of these kidnappings and beheadings are best thought
of as made-for-television events; a calculated set of actions and images directed toward influencing a mass audience." Such "collaboration"—whether intentional or not—was a primary justification for
the controversial decision by interim prime minister Iyad Allawi to
close al-Jazeera's Baghdad bureau and ban it from officially covering
events in Iraq. These videos, just like Osama bin Laden's videotaped
statements, posed an impossible dilemma for the satellite stations. On
the one hand, they were clearly newsworthy, and in the face of fierce
competition for market share not even the pro-American al-Arabiya
felt comfortable declining to air them. On the other hand, airing the
videos clearly played in to the insurgency's strategy, leaving the satellite television stations vulnerable to charges of at least tacit collusion.
In Allawi's pungent phrase, "The terrorists feed on the oxygen of propaganda—we cut this off, they will die."[74]

Many Iraqis, as well as a number of Arab and Western critics,
took these hostage videos as a decisive indictment of al-Jazeera and
the other Arab media. In an influential *Washington Post* article, Mamoun Fandy complained, "As I scanned Arab satellite television channels and Arabic newspapers, I found a lot of reporting on the brutal
attacks, but very little condemnation and a widespread willingness
to run the stomach-turning video and photos again and again."[75]
Al-Jazeera management, for its part, bitterly denied that it had ever
aired a video of a hostage being beheaded, at one point even offering
a $10,000 reward to any critic who could document such a broadcast.
But the overall criticism clearly hit home: did al-Jazeera and the rest of
the Arab media help to create a political and normative environment
that encouraged such atrocities? If they did, how could they possible
contribute to a meaningful reform of the Arab world?

Al-Jazeera itself, like other stations, clearly saw the importance of
the debate over airing the hostage videos, and openly debated its own

coverage. No less than four different al-Jazeera programs discussed the kidnappings in a two-week span in September. On September 6, *al-Jazeera's Platform* held an open call-in discussion on the topic of "kidnapping foreigners in Iraq." On September 21, *The Opposite Direction* hosted a fierce argument between Tala'at Ramih and the Iraqi Karim Badr. This episode left a bad taste in the mouths of many, as Ramih offered a defense of the beheadings that struck many critics as morally repugnant.[76] At the same time, it is clear that such views existed in the Arab world, and exposing them to public scrutiny can be seen as an important service—particularly given that Ramih was held up to considerable scorn as the evening wore on. Finally, on September 24 Sami Haddad hosted a more general discussion of the future of Iraq given the horrors besetting the country. Far from stacking the deck with hostile commentators, Haddad invited Entifadh Qanbar, former spokesman for the Iraqi National Congress, former opposition leader Wafiq al-Samarrai, Iraqi politician Abd al-Amir Alwan, and the conservative American analyst Patrick Clawson of the Washington Institute for Near Eastern Affairs. On several occasions, al-Jazeera even actively intervened to plea for the release of particular hostages.

On September 20, Yusuf al-Qaradawi's al-Jazeera program *Sharia and Life* discussed the kidnappings and executions, with Qaradawi endorsing the Iraqi's people right to resist military occupation but sternly denouncing the targeting of civilians. The context of this program is particularly interesting. Qaradawi had recently been accused of issuing a *fatwa* authorizing the killing of American civilians in Iraq, a charge he hotly denied and of which considerable evidence suggests he was innocent.[77] Nevertheless, Qaradawi's alleged *fatwa* became a cause célèbre, with a leading al-Jazeera critic, Shakir al-Nabulsi, leading a petition drive for him to be brought before the International Criminal Court for supporting terrorism. Ironically, even as Qaradawi became the object of an intensely hostile campaign in the United Kingdom and in the Arab world, his refusal to sanction the killing of innocents in Iraq simultaneously brought the wrath of Abu Musab al-Zarqawi. In November 24, Zarqawi released a statement denouncing the "sultans of the airwaves"—especially Qaradawi: "You have betrayed us in the darkest circumstances. . . .You have left the mujahadeen alone to confront the biggest enemy." Munir Shafiq argued that Qaradawi's condemnations of the beheadings and hostage-taking, broadcast regularly on al-Jazeera and widely disseminated in the Islamic world, evidently had had some impact on Zarqawi's standing and strategy, prompting this unusual and bitter open attack.[78] Qaradawi and other moderate *ulema* "weaken the forces of extremism in Islam," according to Shafiq, by rejecting their right to carry out atrocities or to pass judgment on other Muslims. The controversy over Qaradawi, and al-Jazeera's crucial role in amplifying his influence, goes to the heart of the debates central to this book.

Many Americans expressed surprise with the enthusiastic coverage of the elections by al-Jazeera, al-Arabiya, and the rest of the new media.[79] They should not have. As this book has amply documented, the new Arab public has long been intensely interested in elections and the prospects for democratic reform. For all their suspicion of the American project in Iraq, the new media largely shared the ambitions for creating a democratic Iraq, and for bringing greater democracy to the rest of the region. The Iraqi elections allowed many Americans, perhaps for the first time, to appreciate the potentially positive role for al-Jazeera that its Arab defenders had seen all along.

The Arab Public Sphere: Criticism and Self-Criticism

The Arab media today is worse than the media in 1967, because it is not objective and it is not impartial.

—Abd al-Rahman al-Rashed[80]

Mamoun Fandy argued in April 2003 that the Iraq war would have the same impact on the Arab satellite television stations as the 1967 War had had on Egypt's Voice of the Arabs: discrediting them and destroying their reputation once the contrast between their rhetoric and reality became painfully clear. While the Arab media has seriously debated the implications of its performance in the war (see below), it has not suffered any such lapse in credibility, however, and has remained as popular and influential as before.

Rather than being discredited by the sudden collapse of Baghdad, the new media were buttressed by the rapid shift to a new storyline of a struggling American occupation and an emerging Iraqi insurgency, as well as by the American failure to find Iraqi weapons of mass destruction or evidence of ties between the Iraqi regime and al-Qaeda. Competition among the Arab satellite television stations tended to push toward more radical and explicit reporting, while Arab audiences continued to tune in with morbid fascination at the unfolding events in Iraq. American criticism of al-Jazeera (and to a lesser extent al-Arabiya) enhanced the credibility and popularity of those stations. Finally, many Arab viewers agreed with al-Jazeera's Washington bureau chief Hafez al-Mirazi: "Was the Arab media right from the beginning? . . . The Arab world did not believe and denied from the beginning the questing of WMD and it saw the American presence in Iraq as an occupation, so why should it back down now?"[81]

It would be wrong to say that the new public sphere went on as before, however. The Arab public is extraordinarily self-conscious, and there was a powerful and urgent self-critique of the news coverage and of Arab public opinion in general. As Khaled al-Haroub noted, the Arab criticism of the satellite television networks was, if anything, more intense and more hostile than the criticism from the West.[82] Prompted not only by American allegations of bias and incitement, but also by the rage expressed by many Iraqis toward their erstwhile Arab supporters and by the dissatisfaction of many Arab elites with their coverage of Iraq, the Arab public sphere looked inward. The launch of the American satellite station al-Hurra in February 2004 sparked another (rather more self-satisfied) round of reflection and discussion of the Arab media's strengths and weaknesses.

In the face of intense American and internal Arab criticism, al-Jazeera took the unusual step of establishing an honor code to govern its programming. Program after program on al-Jazeera and al-Arabiya dissected the performance of the Arab media during and after the war, with fierce critics of al-Jazeera routinely invited onto that station's programs to present their case. In a typical move, Faisal al-Qassem invited one of his own fiercest critics, Shaker al-Nabulsi, onto his program to present his criticisms. Opinion pages of Arab newspapers filled with ruminations on the quality of the Arab media and the validity of the critiques. These intense internal debates are, ironically, powerful evidence of its own existence as a public sphere: self-referential, self-critical, and aware of its role in the Arab political system.

In a July 17, 2004, episode of *Open Dialogue* tied to the second annual al-Jazeera Media Forum, Ghassan bin Jadu brought together prominent critics and defenders of the new Arab media to discuss these questions: "What is the dividing line between the media function and propaganda?" asked bin Jadu, and "Had the Arab media crossed that line? Has our Arab media discourse erred in overemphasizing nationalist or ideological dimensions or political over professional ones or objectivity or credibility? Has propaganda triumphed over professionalism. . . . Or are the criticisms themselves only propaganda from the outside?" *Al-Hayat* journalist Hazem al-Amin complained that "during the war we all contributed in the Arab media to deceiving viewers with dreams which led to the state of general Arab frustration today. . . . We did not feel our responsibility to the viewers or readers, we gave false information which contributed to creating a general atmosphere which continues to have implications." Bin Jadu objected to Amin's accusations: "When you accuse the Arab media of distortion this is a great problem, as if it were an intelligence agency or a political one or a propaganda organ and part of everything that happened, as if it were like Mohammed Said al-Sahhaf."

Most of the guests agreed that the Arab media discourse was primarily inwardly directed rather than addressing the West. Since most in the West do not speak Arabic, argued Azzam Tamimi, the Arabic language broadcasts could only be really directed to those who speak Arabic—wherever they might happen to live. While bin Jadu pointed out that Western decision makers followed the Arabic media closely, and used it as a window into Arab public opinion, Mahmoud Shimam pointed out that Western leaders had other sources of information; while the Arab media might have this as a secondary function, its primary purpose was clearly to address and to inform Arab public opinion. Why, then, did Western leaders object so strenuously to the Arab media, asked bin Jadu? Several guests hypothesized that the problem was the flow of graphic images from al-Jazeera and al-Arabiya coverage of Afghanistan and Iraq into the Western media. But others placed the blame on the United States, which insists on controlling the interpretation of world events and the flow of information, and therefore "does not want us to have an honest free media."

Over the course of 2004 the critics of the Arab media stepped up their attacks, reinforcing American accusations of incitement and complicity in the Iraqi chaos. The Saudi newspaper *al-Sharq al-Awsat*—along with writers associated with the former Iraqi opposition—stood out for the severity of its criticism. Its editor, Tareq Alhomayed, argued that "our greatest crisis is the Arab media. What al-Jazeera has done in its broadcasts from Falluja, alone, is baffling. What we see is not reporting but wails and tears. This is not the role of the media."[83] Daoud Basri accused al-Jazeera of waging a "war of sectarianism and terror."[84] Another Iraqi writer cried out that "the inciting media is murdering the dreams of an emerging Iraq."[85] Kuwaiti writer Ahmed al-Rubai called on the Gulf Cooperation Council to sign a joint declaration "in order to stop media incitement to terrorism and murder. It is clear that there are Gulf stations funded by Gulf money that specialize in incitement to violence and terrorism and that are spreading a culture of killing. . . . These stations celebrate violence in Iraq."[86] Mamoun Fandy claimed that there were no real journalists in the Arab world, arguing that anyone who thinks that Arab satellite television might play a constructive role "is at best deceived and at worst a liar or ignorant."[87]

And what was the effect of the Arab media? Abd al-Bari Atwan worried that its newfound independence from oppressive state censorship might be one of the first casualties of the American concerns, which would be an ironic and depressing outcome of a campaign allegedly fought in the name of spreading democracy.[88] Al-Jazeera struggled to meet the intensely competing demands of its American critics, both directly and through indirect pressure on the Qatari government, its vocal Arab critics, and its mass audience. Its honor code, issued in the spring of 2004, aimed at deflecting attacks on its "professionalism," although such a document alone did little to assuage its critics. Its coverage of Iraq became somewhat more cautious, although it is difficult to know the extent to which this reflected a response to pressure or its own reflection on its political role. In 2005 reports began to circulate that al-Jazeera would be privatized, allegedly under American pressure, which many feared would lead to the silencing of the station under a new (presumably Saudi) ownership. Al-Arabiya, for its part, over the course of 2004 aligned itself closely with the Allawi interim government (including airing an extremely positive documentary about

Allawi shortly before the Iraqi elections and airing a large number of his campaign commercials) and a general pro-American agenda, to increasingly positive reviews in the West (Shapiro 2005).

And so the debate raged. For its defenders, al-Jazeera and the other satellite stations continued to widen the margin of freedom in Arab discourse, to challenge Western hegemony in the media sphere, and to inform and mobilize the Arab public. Others pointed to the failures of the American media during the war, and defended the Arab media's performance as standing up rather well by comparison. But above all, the Arab public sphere continued to engage with Iraq as Arabs deeply concerned with the future of that country and of the Arab world.

The Arab Public Sphere Beyond Iraq

There is little in this book to support hysterical claims that al-Jazeera was "Jihad TV" or "killers with cameras," actively collaborating with insurgents.[89] The Arab public sphere's engagement with Iraq was far more ambiguous and conflicted than its broad-brush caricatures would suggest. There was genuine disagreement, open argument, and at key moments profound uncertainty about how to interpret events and about the appropriate "Arab" response. But what about the Arab media beyond Iraq? What about its coverage of Palestine, of Osama bin Laden and the war on terror, of political reforms, of America? What is its wider significance to the dynamics of Arab politics? Has it reached its limits, and as such demonstrated wider structural problems with international public spheres? In this concluding section, I touch on several of these questions and argue for the potentially positive role of the new Arab public sphere.

Even at the height of the criticism and self-criticism of the Arab media, even during the most difficult days of the insurgency in Iraq, al-Jazeera and the rest of the new Arab public remained the premiere site for reformist discourse in the Arab world. The simple fact that the most widely viewed television stations in the Arab world dedicated themselves urgently to criticizing the repressive status quo and demanding fundamental change cannot be overemphasized. The period of the run-up to the Iraq war, the war itself, and the immediate aftermath was perhaps the least reform-oriented in the history of this new Arab public. Rather than immediately sparking a discussion about democratic reform, the invasion of Iraq sparked intense suspicion and fear of the United States, and drove reform and democracy temporarily off the public agenda. But the intense demand for internal reform was deeply central to the identity and the agenda of the new Arab public, regardless of American policies. Over the course of 2004, the op-ed pages of *al-Hayat* and *al-Sharq al-Awsat* and a dozen other Arab newspapers, just like the talk shows of al-Jazeera and al-Arabiya and a half-dozen other satellite television stations, filled with debates about the pros and cons of particular reform proposals. Most Arab arguments insisted on distance from the American reform promotion agenda, with a typical formulation being something along the lines of "we need to change, even if the Americans say so."

Al-Jazeera remained the cutting edge of reform talk. As early as September 30, 2003, Faisal al-Qassem stepped away from Iraq to examine "political and governmental reforms in the Arab states," asking specifically whether the Arab states were sincere in their recent public calls for such reform; in the accompanying online poll, 84 percent of al-Jazeera viewers said that the Arab regimes were not sincere, and not capable of reforming themselves. By the winter of 2003, the Arab public sphere had returned with a vengeance to the question of reform. Most notably, on December 6, Ghassan bin Jadu hosted a remarkable episode of *Open Dialogue* on the topic of "political reform in the Arab world," featuring two of the most prominent public intellectuals in the Arab world, Saad Eddin Ibrahim and Fahmy Huwaydi.

American reform programs, from the still-born Greater Middle East Initiative to the 2004 "Forum for the Future," sparked endless rounds of debate. On February 20, 2004, Sami Haddad hosted American conservative Patrick Clawson, radical Arabist Muta Safadi, liberal human rights activist Haytham Muttaa, and Islamist Abd al-Wahhab al-Affendi to discuss the Greater Middle East Initiative. A week later, Ghassan bin Jadu hosted a discussion of "calls for change in the Arab world," featuring (among others) former Iraqi dissident and now official in an American democracy promotion program Layth Kubba. Four different programs in March discussed the abortive Tunis Arab summit to discuss these American proposals. The

G-8 summit in June dedicated to pushing Arab reform similarly generated great interest. In late September, Ahmed Mansour hosted a program about "American demands on the Arab states" that featured highly skeptical views about American intentions: "imposing American values on the Middle East," "Arab oil and American economic hegemony," "the invasion of Iraq and serving Israeli interests" were among the main topics discussed. But six weeks later (November 5), after the reelection of George W. Bush, Sami Haddad hosted a fascinating discussion between the leading Arabist journalists Abd al-Bari Atwan, the deputy director of Egypt's Al-Ahram Center Mohammed el-Sayid Sa'id, and the prominent American neo-conservative strategist Reuel Gerecht.

While American initiatives received considerable attention and publicity in the new Arab public, the impetus toward reform came very much from within. Al-Jazeera, and much of the rest of the new public, explicitly cast Arab leaders and Arab governments as obstacles rather than as allies in the pursuit of Arab interests and Arab identity. Consider some representative al-Jazeera programs between the spring of 2004 and early 2005: "corruption and unemployment in the Arab world" (April 29); "reform projects and the Arab position toward them" (May 4); "Arab prisons" (May 18, after Abu Ghraib); "the future of reform projects" (May 25); "reform in the Arab world" (interview with Israeli Arab leader Azmi Bishara, June 14); "corruption in Arab countries" (September 25); "the reality of change in Arab countries" (December 4); "Arab elections" (December 7); "The Great Leader" (mocking Arab cults of personality, December 21); "the Arab future and the issue of reform" (January 1, 2005); "dangers that threaten freedom of opinion in the world" (January 12); "religious and intellectual freedom" (with Yusuf al-Qaradawi, January 30). When George W. Bush indicated that he had been inspired by a book by Natan Sharansky, a former dissident and now Israeli politician, al-Jazeera responded by interviewing Sharansky about his book and how it might apply to the Arab world (January 27).

In short, al-Jazeera and the new Arab public have been consistently and forcefully insistent on discussing reform in the Arab world, putting almost every issue—social, economic, cultural, political—and every regime under fierce public scrutiny.

Kefaya: The New Arab Public Moves

The Kefaya movement, which galvanized Egyptian politics with a series of increasingly bold public demonstrations against extending Hosni Mubarak' regime for a fifth term, can be seen as the quintessential expression of this new Arab public. Composed of a diverse coalition of oppositional movements—from new Islamists (the leading figures of the al-Wasat party), liberals (Ayman Nour), Nasserists, and Arabists—the Kefaya movement revolved around a core demand for change from below. Its slogan of "enough" articulated exactly the frustrations of the new Arab public described in this book: enough weakness, enough apathy, enough impotence, enough corruption. The Kefaya movement expertly worked with the new Arab media, especially al-Jazeera (where many of its leading figures had long been regular guests). It maintained a popular Web site, which laid out the movement's agenda, reproduced articles and analysis from around the Arab media, and announced future protests and demands. Beginning in 2003, the movement's demands for change focused on the 2005 presidential referendum, in which Hosni Mubarak looked set either to stand for a fifth term or hand off power to his son Gamal.

The roots of the Kefaya movement lay in precisely the contentious politics described in this book. Its organizers began to form into a network, and to develop their approach to demonstrations, through engagement in the protests against the sanctions on Iraq and the Palestinian uprising in the late 1990s. The first identifiable Kefaya protest came in March 2003, when a protest against the invasion of Iraq turned into an unprecedented anti-Mubarak demonstration.[90] Kefaya's narrative was that of the new Arab public, a restless, impatient demand for an end to the exhausted, incompetent Arab order combined with a fierce resentment of American foreign policy. Their modus operandi was television-friendly protests, at first quite small but soon escalating into larger and more dramatic demonstrations and spreading out of Cairo into the provinces. And their arguments clearly resonated with the wider Arab public: in a late February 2005 online al-Jazeera poll, over 90 percent of respondents opposed a fifth term for Mubarak.

In 2004, Ayman Nour, the leader of the new opposition party Hizb al-Ghad, was arrested on the floor of the Egyptian parliament and his immunity from prosecution stripped on a technicality. Nour's arrest became a cause célèbre in the West and the Arab media alike. The Arab media, including al-Jazeera and to a lesser extent al-Arabiya, covered it heavily, keeping a steady focus on Egyptian political repression and giving a regular platform to Kefaya activists. These stations sent cameras to even the smallest early protests, magnifying their presence and legitimating their demands as part of the wider Arab agenda. Americans also took note, and in 2005 Condoleeza Rice bluntly informed the Egyptian regime of the need to release Nour and to begin political reforms. Shortly thereafter, Nour was released (though he still faced charges), and then Mubarak stunned the Egyptian political world by announcing his decision to change article 76 of the constitution and allow multiparty presidential elections.

While this was claimed as a success of American diplomacy, or even as a positive spinoff of the Iraqi war, most Egyptians saw it as a triumph for the new Arab public, which had been demanding exactly such changes for years. The Kefaya movement strongly opposed American foreign policy, including the occupation of Iraq, and pointedly rejected any relationship with the American embassy. Even Ayman Nour complained of being tarred by association with the United States and insistently distanced his party from the American reform agenda.[91]

The Kefaya movement demonstrates both the strengths and the limitations of the new Arab public. The combination of a focused, courageous, and dedicated domestic social movement with the magnifying power of the new Arab media proved capable of transforming the political environment. Kefaya pointed a way toward overcoming the inherent limitations of the weak Arab public sphere, by adding the hard organizational and mobilizational work on the ground that the media alone could not offer. Multiparty presidential elections and the constitutional change were not small developments. The simple fact of ongoing, regular political demonstrations and protests aimed inwardly rather than at Iraq or Palestine revolutionized the political balance. On the other hand, the limits on this change were painfully apparent. Kefaya demonstrations faced continuing repression and harassment, and as the months went on experienced ever-greater physical risks at the hands of security forces. Ayman Nour and Hizb al-Ghad, like all other opposition parties, were subjected to legal and extralegal harassment, and no observer seriously doubted that Mubarak's National Democratic Party would dominate whatever elections were held. The government arrested hundreds of members of the still-banned Muslim Brotherhood, including its most popular leader, Essam el-Erian. When terrorism against tourists reared its ugly head, with attacks in Khan al-Khalil in April and against several tourist sites in May, many Kefaya activists worried that the government would take the excuse of terrorism to clamp down on what new tolerance existed. During the national referendum over changing the Constitution on May 25, regime thugs brutally attacked opposition protestors, singling out women for abuse.

The new Arab public moved throughout the Arab world in the spring of 2005, with mixed results. Probably the most visible of these movements came from the "Cedar Revolution" in Lebanon, after the assassination of former prime minister Rafik Hariri. In the aftermath of his murder, vast crowds appeared seemingly spontaneously demanding a full investigation. Their demands soon extended to the withdrawal of Syrian troops, a goal achieved by the end of April. These protests demonstrated phenomenal media savvy, playing to the television cameras and carefully "branding" the social movement to highlight its youthfulness, idealism, and attractiveness. The Arab media again proved vital to the success of the movement, directly conveying the excitement and drama of those crowds to a vast Arab audience. When Bashar al-Asad, president of Syria, complained that the Arab media was exaggerating the size of the protests and demanded that the cameras "zoom out" to reveal their true size, the protestors enthusiastically embraced his demand, turning "zoom out" into their own frequently chanted demand. The protestors tapped in to the primal Arabist narrative—of a popular movement for change against an oppressive status quo—even as they won over American audiences attracted to their idealistic rhetoric (and attractive young Lebanese girls). In an online al-Jazeera survey, over 80 percent of respondents sided with the Lebanese protestors, rejecting Syrian claims to be an embattled, targeted Arab state. Still, when Hezbollah mounted a massive counter-rally in central Beirut, al-Jazeera and the Arab media covered it on equal terms, which complicated any simple narrative of a united Lebanese public opinion.

Beyond Egypt and Lebanon, stirrings of this new Arab public could be seen, albeit less dramatically. The Jordanian opposition pushed back fiercely against plans by the government of Faisal al-Fayez to restrict the political activities of the professional associations. Clearly learning from the Lebanese and Egyptian experiences, Jordanian activists pointedly flew the national flag and tried to ensure coverage on al-Jazeera and the other satellite stations. The Jordanian government proved equally sensitive to those lessons, taking special efforts to bar satellite television coverage of the protests. In early April, King Abdullah replaced Fayez's government with the "reformist" Adnan Badran, at least in part in an attempt to prevent these domestic disturbances from getting out of hand. Bahrain similarly witnessed a series of remarkable demonstrations, including a series of heavily covered protests over the arrest of a human rights campaigner and other demonstrations demanding constitutional reforms. In all, the ferment of Arab politics in these months—dubbed an "Arab spring" by many onlookers—had less to do with Iraq than with this gathering force of the new Arab public.

Beyond Politics: Popular Entertainment and the Culture Wars

This book has focused on the political dimension of the new Arab media. It is worth mentioning, at least in passing, one other important component of this new Arab media: a cultural revolution sparked by popular entertainment. Alongside the news and politics stations on the satellite television packages are a wide range of popular entertainment stations. These stations make Western and Arab movies, television serials and soap operas, and other kinds of entertainment programming widely available. While there have been few studies to date of its effects, it seems potentially important that Arab viewers now have such ready access to everything from *Friends* to the National Basketball Association to *Buffy the Vampire Slayer*.

One of the most popular formats on these entertainment stations has been reality television, and indeed anything that includes a participatory, interactive component. An Arabic version of *Who Wants to Be a Millionaire?* proved wildly popular for a time, and indeed was aired directly opposite Faisal al-Qassem's *The Opposite Direction* in an evident attempt to take away some of his audience. Even more popular have been music competition programs such as *Super Star* and *Star Academy*, which featured live contests between singers from all over the Arab world where voters could phone in their choices to determine the outcome. These programs contributed to the growing sense of shared Arab identity, even as singers emerged as the "national" champions of particular Arab countries: Moammar Qaddafi called in to one program to cheer on a Libyan finalist, for example. The Saudi government banned the use of cell phones for voting on *Star Academy* in January 2005, declaring it an un-Islamic activity, but this did not prevent a Saudi contestant from winning that year's contest (he was later arrested by the Saudi morality police for spreading corruption when he was mobbed by adoring female fans at a shopping mall). And in 2004, MBC was forced to end production of an Arabic version of *Big Brother* by Islamist protests in Bahrain, where it was being filmed.

Finally, music video clips have emerged as a particularly hotly contested cultural form in recent years. Music videos featuring aggressively sexy young musicians such as Nancy Ajram, Haifa Wehbi, Ruby, and Elissa aired on a growing number of satellite television stations to great effect. As these young singers, with their skimpy clothes and provocative lyrics, rose to cultural prominence, they sparked a growing backlash. In January 2005, Kuwait's minister of information was driven from office, in part because of Islamist anger at his permitting these singers to perform in the country; a similar controversy had hit Bahrain the previous year. A lawsuit was filed in the UAE in February 2005 against a satellite television station for airing music videos that clashed with Islamic values. In March 2005, Egyptians protested against overly erotic music videos, while the Egyptian government banned several of them from the airwaves. When Shaaban Abd al-Rahim, who came to be seen as "voice of the Arab street" with his incendiary political hits such as "I Hate Israel" and "Attack on Iraq," came out with a video endorsing the re-election of Hosni Mubarak in April 2005, political observers had to take his influence (and his acumen in reading the popular mood) seriously indeed.

Some Final Lessons

The Lessons of Iraq

The experience of Iraq has hardly been a positive one for the Arab world. But in one important way, the Arab public sphere's intense focus on Iraq offers real promise. In both 2001 and 2002, roughly one-third of all al-Jazeera talk shows focused on Palestine; in 2003, almost 45 percent focused instead upon Iraq. Almost all Arabs agree about Palestine, meaning that these talk shows almost always reinforced an existing consensus—but in an area where positive progress seems unlikely.

Iraq, as this book has demonstrated, has been an issue that brings out the most intense disagreements in the Arab public sphere. Rather than a firm consensus, the arguments over Iraq have revealed uncertainties, disagreements, and a multiplicity of perspectives—all within the same self-defined Arab identity. Arguing over Iraq may be ugly, but the very intensity of these arguments suggests an openness to disagreement and to public argument. And, while at the time of writing it may seem unlikely, events in Iraq could well develop in a more positive direction, allowing the Arab public sphere to participate in a more constructive manner than in Palestine. The January 2005 elections, for example, generated mostly positive coverage, and rare optimistic views from a generally deeply worried Arab public.

Expectations of a "democratic domino effect," as Iraqi freedom spills over into neighboring countries, have been vastly overstated; if anything, the chaos and horrors of Iraq have acted as a sobering example of the risks of change. But since most of the new Arab public demands reform for their own reasons, not because of American interests or American pressure, the very act of arguing about Iraq could help to increase the pressures on Arab regimes to respond . . . especially if the United States proves willing to hold its own allied regimes, such as Egypt, Jordan, and Saudi Arabia, accountable to its own liberalizing rhetoric.

A REAL PUBLIC SPHERE . . . The new Arab public sphere is a genuine public sphere, characterized by self-conscious, open, and contentious political argument before a vast but discrete audience. Al-Jazeera call-in shows were particularly distinctive in this regard, as almost any voices could potentially be heard and individuals were placed into unscripted, uncensored dialogue over which hosts could exercise only some control. Al-Jazeera was only one part of this evolving public sphere, however, as competing television stations, the press, and the Internet offered a plethora of platforms for these public arguments.

These public arguments are plainly consequential, shaping not only political attitudes but also conceptions of political identity and the strategies of all political actors. Reform has been a consistent obsession of this new public, a constant topic of intense public argument in the op-ed pages and on the talk shows.

... BUT A WEAK PUBLIC The Arab public sphere remains cut off from any viable means of directly influencing policy outcomes. This generates frustration and anger, but also offers a curious empowerment. By virtue of not being beholden to states, the Arab public sphere has the opportunity to construct a more reasoned and authentic public opinion, which can in turn challenge the political status quo. But such freedom can also lead to an absence of accountability, encouraging dramatic declarations of principle over pragmatic discussion of competing alternative policies.

A POPULIST PUBLIC OR A LIBERAL PUBLIC? Vocal criticism by some Arab liberals highlights the very real possibility that even as the Arab public gains visibility and influence it may have decidedly nonliberal characteristics. The emphasis on identity—and particularly on a narrative of collective suffering and disenfranchisement—runs counter to liberal presuppositions. The political impact of the new Arab public sphere rests heavily, I would argue, on whether it evolves in a liberal or a populist direction.

Prior to the invasion and occupation of Iraq, most signs pointed toward a liberal evolution, as the new Arab public challenged the repressive status quo, demanding reform and action and accountability. Rather than spurring democratization in the region, as some Americans had hoped, the occupation of Iraq has undermined the liberal qualities of the Arab public sphere and strengthened its populism. This could stand as one of the greatest unrecognized tragedies of the war. But even here, the urgent imperative toward open dialogue and the celebration of disagreement mitigate against any notion that al-Jazeera and the new Arab public simply celebrate a "competing authoritarianism" (Rubin 2002). As noted in chapter 2, this celebration of argument and internal publicity offers a frank challenge to Osama bin Laden and al-Qaeda, just as it challenges Arab dictators and American foreign policy. The new Arab public will not soon lose its populism: its celebration of Arab identity, its confrontational attitudes toward the West, its support for Arab causes in Palestine and elsewhere, its caustic dismissiveness toward Arab rulers. But such populism is not in itself incompatible with progressive change.

A Call for Dialogue

Many supporters of the invasion of Iraq agreed with Reuel Gerecht that a show of American power in Iraq would increase respect for the United States. A key element of the neo-conservative argument for war rested on the belief that Arabs respected force, not reason, and—oddly adopting the analysis of Osama bin Laden—would flock to "the stronger horse." This has not happened. The invasion and occupation of Iraq generated enormously greater anti-American sentiment throughout the Middle East. Rather than dealing a decisive blow against Islamist extremism, it seems to have significantly encouraged its spread and strengthened al-Qaeda and its sympathizers. And rather than offering a decisive demonstration of an irresistible American power, the occupation of Iraq has shown Arabs an unpopular, ineffective, and illegitimate occupying power, one increasingly equated with the hated Israeli occupation of the West Bank and Gaza.

The new Arab public sphere offers an unprecedented platform for an Arab public opinion deeply critical of the authoritarian status quo. The urgent calls for reform and insistent critique of the Arab status quo in much of the new Arab media accords well with American hopes for the region. Given the intense interest al-Jazeera had always shown in democratic reform, an eventual transition to democracy in Iraq would likely receive positive coverage in the Arab public sphere.

The chaos and insecurity of post-war Iraq, particularly when viewed through the lens of the intense pre-war fears and antagonisms, pushed coverage and commentary in a more critical direction, however. The hope that America might change the Arab world through the "demonstration effect" of an occupied Iraq was deeply misguided. I would like to conclude this book by arguing for a very different approach to the new Arab public.

The Bush administration's approach to the Arab public sphere treated it as either an enemy to be defeated (in a "war of ideas") or as an object to be manipulated (via public relations). Between its harsh attacks on the Arab satellite stations and its decision to launch an Arabic language satellite television station (al-Hurra) in order to have its own (controllable) voice in the Arab arena, American policy has seemed designed to marginalize and weaken the Arab public sphere as an effective political voice. But these policies have largely failed. Anti-American attitudes have skyrocketed, al-Hurra has failed to capture an audience, and Arab public opinion remains suspicious.

Given the urgency of fighting effectively against radicalism in the struggle against terror, these failures offer a powerful incentive to contemplate a real dialogue with the Arab public sphere. The most effective approach would be for the United States to enter more directly into the Arab public sphere and to engage with it as a public sphere, relying on reasoned argument rather than power (Lynch 2003a; Eickelman 2002). Instead of pressuring al-Jazeera, the United States should embrace the opportunity it offers to reach a vast Arab audience preconditioned to yearn for change. Instead of wasting vast sums of money on a satellite television station nobody watches, the United States should enter the Arab public sphere as it really exists.

This would not offer a miracle solution to the problems of the Middle East. But it would hold out the unique opportunity for the United States to align itself with a new Arab public that in many ways wants the same things America claims to want. Opinionated, well-informed, and proud of their identity, these Arabs tend to be offended by American propaganda and highly suspicious of American motives. But at the same time they overwhelmingly support demands for comprehensive reforms in the Arab world, and have little patience for the entrenched, repressive status quo. By treating them as enemies, the

United States not only risks losing a powerful potential ally for change, but also pushes these influential voices into a hostile camp. These Arab voices oppose key American policies in the Middle East, particularly with regard to Israel and Iraq. Dialogue is unlikely to change this in the near term.

But opposition to American policies should not be equated with irrational "anti-Americanism," nor should rationally articulated opposition be dismissed as "extremism." The new Arab public is open to argument and committed to public debate. If the United States proves willing to engage seriously with the new Arab public sphere, changing policies where appropriate, that public could prove receptive. Such real dialogue with the new Arab public offers a route toward a coalition for moderation and for genuine progressive change in the Arab world.

Notes

1. Iraq and the New Arab Public

1. *The Opposite Direction*, al-Jazeera, August 30, 2003.

All quotes from al-Jazeera, unless otherwise noted, are this author's translation of the official transcript as published on the al-Jazeera Web site (http://aljazeera.net).

2. Poll conducted by Zogby International for Shibley Telhami, June 2001.

3. Fadhil Fudha, "Al-Jazeera and the Declining Arab Media," *Elaph,* May 5, 2004.

4. "The Third Gulf War," *al-Ahram,* May 2002; and in *al-Ahram Weekly* 612, November 7, 2002. Author interview, Cairo, May 2002.

5. Mamoun Fandy, "Perceptions: Where al-Jazeera and Co. Are Coming From," *Washington Post,* March 30, 2003, B01.

6. Quoted by Ibrahim Ghurayba, http://www.aljazeera.net, August 24, 2003.

7. *Al-Sharq al-Awsat,* February 19, 2002.

8. Hazem al-Amin, *al-Hayat,* July 19, 2004.

9. *Al-Hayat,* May 18, 2003.

10. It is impossible to quantify the damage done by partisan translation services such as the Middle East Media Research Institute, which have consistently misled American audiences about the real distribution of opinion and argument in the Arab media.

11. The five are *The Opposite Direction, More Than One Opinion, Open Dialogue, al-Jazeera's Platform* [Minbar al-Jazeera], and *No Limits;* I exclude *Sharia and Life* because of its subject material.

12. Mohammed Sid-Ahmed, *al-Ahram Weekly* 503, October 12–18, 2000.

13. Fawzia Abu Khalid, "Reading the Reaction of the Arab Street Against the American Aggression on the Iraqi People," *al-Hayat,* January 10, 1999.

14. Zogby International public opinion survey, April 2002, available at http://www.zogby.com/news/ReadNews.dbm?ID=564.

15. Ipsos-Stat, National Opinion Poll Survey/Jordan (28/02/2003 BBC).

16. Mahmoud Bounab, *al-Quds al-Arabi*, February 3, 2000.

17. Salah al-Nasrawi, *al-Hayat*, July 10, 2003.

18. Hazem Sha'alan, interviewed in *al-Sharq al-Awsat*, November 23, 2004.

19. *New York Post*, June 21, 2004.

20. Rumsfeld quoted in the *New York Times*, February 8, 2004.

21. House hearing, April 18, 2002.

22. House hearing, April 18, 2002; and author interview, Washington D.C., August 2002.

23. *Washington Post,* August 14, 2002, A29.

24. Quoted in Rania Abouzeid, "Jazeera's Iraq Coverage Hits U.S. Raw Nerve," Reuters, May 18, 2004.

25. *Al-Jazeera's Platform*, al-Jazeera, November 24, 2003.

26. *Open Dialogue*, al-Jazeera, December 2, 2003.

27. Mihna al-Habil, "The Democratic Republic of al-Jazeera," http://al-jazeera.net, January 18, 2004.

2. *The Structural Transformation of the Arab Public Sphere*

1. Hazem Saghiyeh, "But Is There Really and Is It Possible For There to Be . . . 'Arab Public Opinion'?" *al-Hayat*, July 2, 2004; author phone interview, July 19, 2004.

2. Michael Dobbs, "Envoy to 'Arab Street' Stays Hopeful," *Washington Post*, June 9, 2003.

3. Palestinian Center for Survey and Policy Research, Public Opinion Poll no. 43, September 2–4, 1999 (http://www.pcpsr.org/survey/cprspolls/99/poll43a.html).

4. *Al-Jazeera's Correspondents*, al-Jazeera, May 5, 2004.

5. *The Opposite Direction*, al-Jazeera, July 27, 2003.

6. "Reporters Without Borders: Yemen Report," December 28, 2004.

7. "Democracy in Jordan" annual surveys conducted by the Center for Strategic Studies at the University of Jordan. http://www.css-jordan.org/polls/democracy/2003/index.html .

8. http://www.css-jordan.org/polls/democracy/2003/index.html.

9. Palestinian Center for Survey and Policy Research, Public Opinion Poll no. 43, September 2–4, 1999 (http://www.pcpsr.org/survey/cprspolls/99/poll43a.html), and Public Opinion Poll no. 47, February 24–26, 2000 (http://www.pcpsr.org/survey/cprspolls/2000/poll47a.html).

10. See Fallows 2003 for a skeptical evaluation of this event; in terms of Arab perceptions, however, these questions hardly matter.

11. *Al-Quds al-Arabi*, April 6, 2002.

12. Ibrahim al-Aris, "Who Draws the Picture of the Arab Mind?" *al-Hayat*, February 13, 2004.

13. As quoted by Ian Urbina, *Asia Times*, March 1, 2003.

14. Ian Urbina, *Asia Times*, March 1, 2003.

15. Interview, Abd al-Rahman al-Rashed, al-Arabiya, August 3, 2004, available at http://www.alarabiya.net/Articlep.aspx?P=5458.

16. Abd al-Rahman al-Rashed, interviewed in *al-Riyadh* (Saudi Arabia), as reported on al-Arabiya, May 19, 2005; and Rashed quoted in the The *Economist*, February 24, 2005.

17. As quoted in "Arab TV Stations Debate Use of Videos Supplied by Camera-Toting Militants," Associated Press, August 10, 2004.

18. Arab Advisors Group survey, reported in *Arab News*, September 10, 2004.

19. Arab Advisors Group, survey released January 26, 2005, http://www.menareport.com/en/business/179353.

20. Arab Advisors Group, January 2005; survey available at http://tbsjournal.com/ArabAdvisors.html.

21. See *al-Ahram Weekly*, July 10, 2004, for details.

22. Tarek Atia, "Aiming for Extinction," *al-Ahram Weekly*, October 14, 2004.

23. As quoted by Rania Abouzeid, Reuters, May 18, 2004.

24. As quoted by Nicholas Kristof, "Al-Jazeera: Out-Foxing Fox," *New York Times*, July 3, 2004.

25. Yasir Abu Hilala, *al-Rai*, October 7, 2003.

26. *No Limits*, al-Jazeera, January 4, 2003.

27. *No Limits*, al-Jazeera, September 6, 2000.

28. Aida Dabbas, author interview, Amman, May 21, 2002.

29. Faisal al-Qassem, author phone interview, March 1, 2004.

30. *Open Dialogue*, al-Jazeera, December 2, 2003.

31. On al-Jazeera, January 13, 2002.

32. *Open Dialogue*, al-Jazeera, July 17, 2004.

33. Khaled Haroub, "Sociology of the Arab Media," *Wajhat* (UAE), January 10, 2005.

34. Yusuf Nur Awadh, *al-Quds al-Arabi*, June 3, 1999.

35. Munir Shafiq, *al-Dustour*, February 1, 2004.

36. *Open Dialogue*, al-Jazeera, December 2, 2003.

37. *The Iraqi Scene*, al-Jazeera, April 24, 2005.

38. *The Opposite Direction*, al-Jazeera, February 4, 2004.

39. *The Opposite Direction*, al-Jazeera, July 27, 2003.

40. Anti-Defamation League's Arab Anti-Semitism Watch.

41. *No Limits*, al-Jazeera, August 28, 2002.

42. On al-Jazeera, January 7, 2002.

43. "The Arab Media to Where?" al-Jazeera, January 13, 2002.

44. *The Opposite Direction*, October 21, 2000.

45. On al-Jazeera, January 13, 2002.

46. *Wall Street Journal*, November 21, 2002. Also see Brumberg's Congressional testimony, October 8, 2002.

47. *Al-Hayat*, August 17, 2002.

48. *Al-Hayat*, April 16, 2003.

49. *Al-Jazeera's Platform*, al-Jazeera, October 21, 2002.

50. *Al-Sharq al-Awsat*, July 13, 2004.

51. Marie Colvin, "How Saddam's Agents Targeted al-Jazeera," *Sunday Times of London*, May 12, 2003. The role of the Iraqi National Congress in delivering these documents makes their authenticity difficult to determine.

52. On January 3, the Associated Press reported that this videotape showed then al-Jazeera station director Mohammed Jassem al-Ali saying to Uday Hussein that "al-Jazeera is your channel." On January 9, the AP retracted the story as a mistranslation.

53. These specific allegations are from Daveed Gartenstein-Ross and Eric Stakelbeck, "Uday's Oil-for-News Program," *Weekly Standard*, May 16, 2005.

54. Abd al-Bari Atwan, author phone interview, July 8, 2004.

55. Salama Nima'at, author interview, Amman, May 2002; also see Brand 1995.

56. David Pallister, "Media Mogul Accused of Running Saudi-Funded Propaganda Campaign," *The Guardian*, January 26, 2005.

57. Abd al-Bari Atwan points out that for all the INC's efforts, no evidence has been produced of any Iraqi payments to *al-Quds al-Arabi* (author phone interview, July 8, 2004). It is worth noting that during the research for this book, I was told with great authority by well-informed people that *al-Quds al-Arabi* was financed alternately by Qatar, by Saddam Hussein, by independently wealthy Palestinians, and by others. Whatever the truth, such opacity invites speculation and political questioning.

58. Quoted by Tarek Atia, "Horsing Around," *Cairo Live*, http://www.cairo-live.com/newcairolive/critic/hurra.html.

59. Mustafa Hamarneh, Center for Strategic Studies, author interview, Amman, May 21, 2002.

60. Abd el-Monem Said, *al-Ahram Weekly*, October 30, 2003; author interview, Cairo, May 2002.

61. Nawaf Obayd, "What the Saudi Public Really Thinks," *Daily Star*, June 24, 2004; *Washington Post*, June 30, 2004.

62. Mustafa Hamarneh, author interview, May 21, 2002.

63. Tharya al-Shahri, *al-Sharq al-Awsat*, May 18, 2004.

64. *Open Dialogue*, al-Jazeera, May 21, 2003.

65. Ragheda Dergham, *al-Hayat*, January 15, 1999.

66. Alterman 1999.

67. Muta Safadi, *al-Quds al-Arabi*, August 10, 1998.

68. Layth Shubaylat quoted in *al-Quds al-Arabi*, January 29, 1998.

69. *Al-Hayat*, June 6, 2000.

70. *Al-Ahram Weekly*, May 2, 2002.

71. *Daily Star*, February 28, 2002.

72. Bilal al-Hassan, in *al-Hayat*; as quoted by *Mideast Mirror* 14.197 (October 12, 2000).

73. John Kifner, "The New Power of Arab Public Opinion," *New York Times Week in Review*, November 11, 2001.

74. Roscoe Suddarth, "Take Account of Arab Opinion and Keep a Cool Watch on Saddam," *Washington Post*, December 9, 1997, 8.

75. Makiya remarks to American Enterprise Institute, "The Day After: Planning for a Post-Saddam Iraq," October 3, 2002.

76. This excludes important special-interest programs such as *Sharia and Life* (Islam) and *Under Blockade* (Palestine)—which would bias the sample toward overemphasizing those themes—as well as the plethora of programs devoted to Iraq beginning in 2003 (see chapter 5 for details).

77. Faisal al-Qassem, author phone interview, March 1, 2004.

78. Jumana al-Namour, *Minbar al-Jazeera,* al-Jazeera, June 27, 2002.

79. *The Opposite Direction*, al-Jazeera, April 16, 2002.

80. *Al-Quds al-Arabi*, April 19, 2002.

81. See Musa Kaylani and Walid Said articles, *Jordan Times*, August 12, 2002.

82. *Washington Post*, November 4, 2002.

83. *Los Angeles Times*, February 4, 2003.

84. Arab Press Freedom Watch Annual Reports of 2001 and 2002.

85. Yusuf al-Qaradawi, *Sharia and Life*, al-Jazeera, July 11, 1999.

86. Yusuf al-Qaradawi, "Dialogue between Islam and Christianity," *Islam Online* 2001. My translation.

87. "Muslims and the West . . . Dialogue or Clash?" September 10, 2002, http://qaradawi.net.

88. Hazem al-Amin, *al-Hayat*, July 19, 2004; Shakir al-Nabulsi, *Elaph*, July 2004.

3. The Iraqi Challenge and the Old Arab Public

1. Personal correspondence, William Rugh, U.S. Ambassador to the UAE, 1992–1995.

2. Quoted in Deutsche Presse Agentur, March 5, 1997.

3. *Al-Quds al-Arabi*, February 17, 1994.

4. Akeel Sawwar in *Akhbar al-Khaleej*, February 21, 1994; see *Mideast Mirror* 8.35 (February 21, 1994), 8.36 (February 22, 1994), and 8.38 (February 24, 1994) for details.

5. *Akhbar al-Khaleej*, March 5, 1997; and *Mideast Mirror* 11.45 (March 5, 1997).

6. Abd al-Bari Atwan, the editor of *al-Quds al-Arabi*, says that at the time his newspaper was the only one, other than a few Jordanian papers, to challenge the sanctions. Author phone interview, July 8, 2004.

7. Hafez al-Shaykh, in *Akhbar al-Khaleej*, May 11, 1997; as quoted in *Mideast Mirror* 11.90 (May 12, 1997).

8. Quoted in *Mideast Mirror* 7.138 (July 20, 1993).

9. Kamaran Karadaghi, *al-Hayat*, November 23, 1993, and March 21, 1994.

10. Salim al-Nashi, *al-Qabas*, April 13, 2002.

11. *Al-Quds al-Arabi*, November 29, 1993.

12. http://www.fao.org/documents/show_cdr.asp?url_file=/DOCREP/004/W6519E/W6519E00.HTM.

13. Richard Garfield, author interview, March 2001.

14. Dennis Halliday's resignation speech, September 30, 1998.

15. Comprehensive Report of the Special Advisor to the DCI on Iraq's WMD, September 30, 2004, http://www.cia.gov/cia/reports/iraq_wmd_2004/chap1.html.

16. Salama Ahmad Salama, *al-Ahram*, March 22, 1994; as quoted in *Mideast Mirror* 8.56 (March 23, 1994).

17. *Mideast Mirror* 8.205 (October 24, 1994).

18. Gamal Mattar, *al-Hayat*, June 22, 1994.

19. Warren Christopher, as quoted in *Mideast Mirror* 8.89 (May 11, 1994); and interview with *USA Today*, quoted in Deutsche Presse Agentur, October 24, 1994.

20. Indyk quoted in "Coalition Against Iraq Starts to Fray," *Baltimore Sun*, April 15, 1994, 12A.

21. Ragheda Dergham (*al-Hayat*, April 25, 1997) argued that Iraq understood this to be American policy.

22. *Al-Quds al-Arabi*, April 7, 1997; as reported in *Mideast Mirror* 11.66.

23. Quoted in *Mideast Mirror* 8.219 (November 11, 1994).

24. Author interviews: Martin Indyk, Washington D.C., September 28, 2001; Robert Pelletreau, Washington D.C., March 23, 2000; Kenneth Pollack, Washington, D.C., September 27, 2001. Anthony Lake, author phone interview, November 5, 2001.

25. Thomas Pickering, Under-Secretary for Political Affairs, testimony before the Senate Foreign Relations Committee, May 21, 1998; author interview, Washington, D.C., October 25, 2001.

26. Samuel Berger, National Security Adviser, remarks on Iraq, Stanford University, December 8, 1998. http://www.state.gov/www/regions/nea/981208_berger_iraq.html.

27. Tareq Aziz, quoted by Barbara Crossette, *New York Times*, April 15, 1995.

28. Abd al-Rahman al-Rashed, editor of *al-Sharq al-Awsat*, as quoted in *Mideast Mirror* 9.73 (April 18, 1995); Hazem Saghiya in *al-Hayat*, as quoted in *Mideast Mirror* 10.20 (January 29, 1996).

29. Ragheda Dergham in *al-Hayat*, as quoted in *Mideast Mirror* 9.76 (April 21, 1995).

30. Yasser Za'atra in *al-Quds al-Arabi*, as quoted in *Mideast Mirror* 9.156 (August 15, 1995).

31. For details on Saddam's use of the oil-for-food program, see the first interim report of the Independent Inquiry Committee into the United Nations Oil-For-Food Program, chaired by Paul Volcker (February 3, 2005), available at http://www.iic-offp.org/documents.htm.

32. Comprehensive Report of the Special Advisor to the DCI on Iraq's WMD, September 30, 2004, http://www.cia.gov/cia/reports/iraq_wmd_2004/chap1.html.

33. *Mideast Mirror* 10.28 (February 9, 1996). Interviews with Lake (November 5, 2001) and Pelletreau (March 23, 2000).

34. Ragheda Dergham in *al-Hayat*, as quoted in *Mideast Mirror* 10.39 (February 23, 1996).

35. On these events, see Hiro 2001: 107, and Cockburn and Cockburn 2000.

36. UN press release GA/9113 (October 2, 1996).

37. Ragheda Dergham, *al-Hayat*, January 31, 1997.

38. Salamah Nimaat, author interview, Amman, May 9, 2002; Lynch 1998/99.

39. *Jordan Times* (September 26, 1998); Abd al-Hadi al-Majali, speaker of the House of Representatives, author interview, Amman, May 5, 2002.

40. Salem al-Nahass, author interview, Amman, April 29, 2002.

41. Ahmed al-Qadiri, president of Professional Associations, author interview, Amman, May 2002.

42. Bassam al-Dajani, author interview, Amman, April 20, 2002.

43. Author interviews: Sulayman Arar, Amman, July 10, 1997, and Hakem al-Fayez, Amman, April 30, 2002.

44. Hamza Mansour, author interview, Amman, May 6, 2002.

45. Aida Dabass, author interview, Amman, May 21, 2002.

46. Salem al-Nahass, quoted in *Jordan Times* (January 27, 2000). Also see reports in *Jordan Times* (October 31, 1999); *Jordan Times* (February 27, 2000); *Jordan Times* (May 17, 2000).

47. Author interviews: Hisham Bustani, Amman, May 7, 2002; and Salem al-Nahass, Amman, April 29, 2002.

48. Communique published in the *Jordan Times* (October 29, 1997).

49. Inter-Press Service, January 23, 1997.

50. Fuad Zakaria, *al-Hayat*, February 4, 1994.

51. Faryal Ghazul, author interview, Cairo, May 15, 2002.

52. Iraqi News Agency, March 22, 1995 (BBC SWB ME/2258/MED); for other examples, Cairo-MENA, November 14, 1998 (FBIS-NES-98-318).

53. Nabil Fahmy, author interview, October 18, 2000; Gehad Awda argues that the lines between the Egyptian state and civil society are so blurred that it would be nearly impossible to sharply distinguish between what was government and what was private in this context (author interview, May 15, 2002).

54. Cairo-MENA, December 27, 1997 (FBIS-NES-97-36227); Cairo, al-Musawwar, January 23, 1998 (FBIS-NES-98-023).

55. Faryal Ghazul, author interview, May 15, 2002.

56. SANA News Agency, November 6, 2000 (BBC SWB).

57. On al-Thani, see chapter 2, figure 18 of the Comprehensive Report of the Special Advisor to the DCI on Iraq's WMD, September 30, 2004, available at http://www.cia.gov/cia/reports/iraq_wmd_2004/chap2.html.

58. Faryad Ghazul, "What After the Sadness?" *Nur* 17 (2001): 10.

59. Faryal Ghazul, author interview, Cairo, May 16, 2002.

60. Naguib Mahfouz, quoted in Iraqi weekly *Alif Baa*, September 9, 2000.

61. Author interviews: Hakem al-Fayez and Sami Awadallah, Amman, May 1, 2002.

62. Bassem al-Dajani, president of Arab Conference of Professional Associations for Solidarity with Iraq, author interview, Amman, April 30, 2002.

63. Assam Namaan, chairman of the Arab Nationalist Conference, on al-Jazeera, May 7, 2003.

64. Huda Husseini, in *al-Sharq al-Awsat*; as quoted in *Mideast Mirror* 10.32 (February 14, 1996).

65. In *al-Hayat* and in *al-Ahram*; as quoted in *Mideast Mirror* 10.89 (May 8, 1996).

66. In *al-Ahram*; as quoted in *Mideast Mirror* 10.94 (May 15, 1996); *Mideast Mirror* 10.100 (May 23, 1996).

67. Usama al-Baz, interviewed on Cairo-MENA, June 11, 1996 (FBIS-NES-96-114); Hosni Mubarak, in *Mideast Mirror* 10.111 (June 10, 1996).

68. Author interviews with senior British and French officials at the United Nations, 2000–2001, and with Antonio Monteiro, chair of the Sanctions Committee, July 12, 2000.

69. BBC Summary of World Broadcasts, January 9, 1996.

70. January 27, 1996 (FBIS-NES-96-019).

71. Quoted in *Jordan Times*, February 10, 1996.

72. Ismat Abd al-Meguid, interviewed in *al-Quds al-Arabi*, November 29, 1994.

73. Omani Minister of State for Foreign Affairs Yusuf bin Alawi bin Abdullah, September 10, 1995 (FBIS-EE/D2406/ME).

74. *The Opposite Direction*, al-Jazeera, January 12, 1999.

75. Ghassan Attiyah, in *al-Malaf al-Iraqi*; as quoted in *Mideast Mirror* 7.126 (July 2, 1993).

76. Iraqi News Agency, March 3, 1995 (BBC SWB ME/2293/MED).

77. Nabil Fahmy, Egyptian Ambassador to the United States, author interview, Williamstown, MA, October 18, 2000.

78. *Al-Quds al-Arabi*, June 27, 1993.

79. For example, Abderrahim Omar, in *al-Rai* (Jordan), June 27, 1993; as quoted in *Mideast Mirror* 7.122 (June 28, 1993).

80. For example, Salama Ahmed Salama, in *al-Ahram*, July 13, 1993; as quoted in *Mideast Mirror* 7.134 (July 14, 1993).

81. Jihad al-Khazen, *al-Hayat*, June 28, 2003.

82. *Al-Ahram* leader and column by Salama Ahmed Salama, June 28, 1993; both quoted in *Mideast Mirror* 7.123 (June 29, 1993).

83. *Al-Quds al-Arabi*, June 27, 1993.

84. *Mideast Mirror* 10.174 (September 6, 1996) quotes *al-Quds al-Arabi* and *al-Bayan* (UAE); *Mideast Mirror* 10.177 (September 11, 1996) quotes Tareq Masarweh in *al-Quds al-Arabi* and Salama Ahmed Salama in *al-Ahram*.

85. *Sada al-Usbou* (Bahrain); in *Mideast Mirror* 7.116 (June 18, 1993).

86. Deputy Prime Minister Sheikh Sabah al-Ahmad, address to Kuwaiti National Assembly; quoted in *Mideast Mirror* 7.124 (June 30, 1993).

87. Mohammed al-Rumayhi, *al-Hayat*, July 19, 2003.

88. Abd al-Wahhab Badrakhan, *al-Hayat*, June 21, 1993.

89. *Mideast Mirror* 7.118 (June 22, 1993).

90. *Mideast Mirror* 7.227 (November 23, 1993).

91. Kingdom of SA TV1, December 12, 1993 (BBC SWB ME/1880/MED).

92. United Press International, January 27, 1994.

93. *Mideast Mirror* 8.33 (February 17, 1994).

94. Associated Press, April 27, 1994.

95. Deutsche Presse Agentur, September 18, 1994.

96. United Press International, November 8, 1994.

97. *Riyadh Daily*, October 30, 1994.

98. GCC communique, October 10, 1994.

99. Ali Sayyar, in *Sada al-Usbou'* (Bahrain); as quoted in *Mideast Mirror* 8.237 (December 7, 1994).

100. Shafik Ghubra, in *al-Watan* (Kuwait); as quoted in *Mideast Mirror* 8.247 (December 21, 1994).

101. Mahmoud Shammam, in *al-Watan*; as quoted in *Mideast Mirror* 8.222 (November 16, 1994).

102. *Al-Quds al-Arabi*; as quoted in *Mideast Mirror* 8.244 (December 16, 1994).

103. *Mideast Mirror* 8.247 (December 21, 1994).

104. Kuwait TV, December 23, 1994 (BBC SWB ME/2186/MED).

105. Amr Mousa, Cairo-MENA, December 20, 1994 (BBC SWB ME/2183/MED).

106. *Al-Ahram*, September 30, 1994; as quoted in *Mideast Mirror* 8.189.

107. Associated Press—Salah Nasrawi, January 11, 1995; Omani statement in Radio Monte Carlo, January 30, 1995 (BBC SWB ME/2214/MED); Qatari statement quoted in *Mideast Mirror* 9.44 (February 13, 1995).

108. UPI—Faisal al-Matheri—March 14, 1995.

109. King Hassan, quoted in *New York Times*, March 12, 1995.

110. Saudi Radio, March 22, 1995 (BBC SWB ME/2258/MED).

111. *Mideast Mirror* 9.68 (April 7, 1995).

112. Dilip Hiro, Inter-Press Service, October 22, 1995.

113. Dilip Hiro, Inter-Press Service, January 2, 1996.

114. *Mideast Mirror* 10.233 (November 28, 1996) quotes UAE Foreign Minister Rashed Abdallahal Nu'aimi.

115. Al-Sayyid Zahra, in *al-Akhbar al-Khaleej* (Bahrain); as quoted in *Mideast Mirror* 10.234 (November 29, 1996).

4. The al-Jazeera Era

1. *Sharia and Life*, al-Jazeera, December 20, 1998.

2. *More Than One Opinion*, al-Jazeera, January 5, 1999.

3. *The Opposite Direction*, al-Jazeera, February 2, 1999.

4. *More Than One Opinion*, al-Jazeera, March 8, 1999.

5. *The Opposite Direction*, al-Jazeera, August 24, 1999.

6. *The Opposite Direction*, al-Jazeera, December 12, 2000.

7. *Behind Events*, al-Jazeera, May 7, 2003.

8. There has been much speculation as to whether the Bush administration had intended to invade Iraq prior to 9/11. My point here refers only to the American public agenda, not to the president's private deliberations.

9. *The Opposite Direction*, al-Jazeera, June 12, 2001.

10. *Al-Quds al-Arabi*, August 1, 2001.

11. *The Opposite Direction*, al-Jazeera, October 16, 2001; *No Limits*, al-Jazeera, November 28, 2001; *The Opposite Direction*, al-Jazeera, December 4, 2001.

12. For example, Ghassan Attiyah, *al-Hayat*, October 9, 2001; Tareq Masarweh, *al-Quds al-Arabi*, October 8, 2001.

13. Ragheda Dergham, *al-Hayat*, April 25, 1997.

14. *More Than One Opinion*, al-Jazeera, September 17, 1999.

15. *More Than One Opinion*, al-Jazeera, September 17, 1999.

16. Saoud al-Samakha, *al-Qabas*, March 20, 2002.

17. For example, Abdullah al-Biyari, vice president of Kuwaiti Democratic Forum, on *More Than One Opinion*, al-Jazeera, August 4, 2000. Some Kuwaitis did dismiss Iraqi suffering: Ayad al-Manaa (*The Opposite Direction*, al-Jazeera, December 12, 2000) claimed, "I asked many Iraqis, how bad is the problem? And they said what problem? We have food, medicine. . . . The problem there is not so great . . . except what is imposed from the inside." But this was very much the exception to the rule.

18. *The Opposite Direction*, al-Jazeera, August 24, 1999.

19. *Al-Hayat*, May 29, 2002.

20. *Today's Encounter*, al-Jazeera, January 13, 2000.

21. *Today's Encounter*, al-Jazeera, February 18, 2000.

22. Khadija bin Qanah, another female presenter, challenged Iraqi Oil Minister Omar Rashid on the same point (*Today's Encounter*, al-Jazeera, March 9, 2000).

23. *The Opposite Direction*, al-Jazeera, August 24, 1999.

24. *More Than One Opinion*, al-Jazeera, November 5, 1999.

25. *More Than One Opinion*, al-Jazeera, August 4, 2000.

26. *No Limits*, al-Jazeera, June 28, 2000.

27. I exclude *al-Sharq al-Awsat*, which would have tilted the numbers below into a more anti-Saddam, pro-Saudi direction, as well as the less widely read *al-Arab*, which tilted toward a Libyan, critical line.

28. Madeleine Albright, *al-Hayat*, August 2, 2000.

29. *The Star* (Amman), "An Arab Stand on Iraq," May 23, 1996, p. 4 (FBIS-NES-96-101).

30. Agence France Presse, October 19, 2000.

31. Amr Musa, author interview, Cairo, May 2002.

32. *The Opposite Direction*, al-Jazeera, December 12, 2000.

33. *More Than One Opinion*, al-Jazeera, May 19, 2000.

34. Haroun Mohammed, *al-Hayat*, May 28, 2001, and Maan Bashour, *al-Hayat*, May 31, 2001.

35. Mohammed al-Rumayhi, *al-Hayat*, January 6, 1999.

36. Mohammed al-Rumayhi, *al-Hayat*, August 16, 2000.

37. Mohammed al-Rumayhi, *al-Hayat*, December 12, 2001.

38. Salim Zubaydi, on *Sharia and Life*, al-Jazeera, December 20, 1998.

39. For example, *The Opposite Direction*, al-Jazeera, February 2, 1999.

40. *Al-Quds al-Arabi*, August 15, 2000; Mohammed al-Musaffir, *al-Quds al-Arabi*, August 30, 2000.

41. *The Opposite Direction*, al-Jazeera, September 12, 2000.

42. Zuhair Qusaybati, *al-Hayat*, August 21, 1999.

43. Amar Najib, *al-Quds al-Arabi*, March 6, 2000.

44. Yusuf Nur Awadh, *al-Quds al-Arabi*, February 5, 1998.

45. Lead editorial, *al-Quds al-Arabi*, February 22, 1999; Maher Athman, *al-Hayat*, March 3, 1999; Ragheda Dergham, *al-Hayat*, March 12, 1999; *al-Quds al-Arabi*, May 1, 1999; *al-Quds al-Arabi*, June 22, 1999; *al-Quds al-Arabi*, August 18, 1999.

46. Burhan al-Jalabi, *al-Quds al-Arabi*, March 9, 1999.

47. Burhan al-Jalabi, *al-Quds al-Arabi*, October 27, 1999.

48. Ahmed al-Rubai, *al-Qabas*, January 6, 2002.

49. Amad al-Sayf, *al-Qabas*, January 21, 2002.

50. *Al-Quds al-Arabi*, February 21, 1998.

51. Subhi Hadidi, *al-Quds al-Arabi*, February 5, 1999.

52. Al-Jazeera online poll ending January 2, 2003.

53. Abd al-Wahhab al-Affendi, *al-Quds al-Arabi*, February 9, 2002.

54. Abdullah al-Hourani, *al-Quds al-Arabi*, February 9, 2000.

55. Adil al-Qayar, *al-Quds al-Arabi*, August 3, 2000.

56. Fahd al-Fanik, *al-Rai*, February 7, 2002.

57. Mohammed Abd al-Hakim Diyab, *al-Quds al-Arabi*, January 30, 1999.

58. Mohammed Abd al-Hakim Diyab, *al-Quds al-Arabi*, April 18, 1999; see Tetreault 2000 for the Kuwaiti debates about Arab identity.

59. Ihsan Ali Buhaliqah, *al-Hayat*, January 13, 1999.

60. Khalid al-Shami, *al-Quds al-Arabi*, August 11, 1999.

61. Biyan Jabar, SCIRI, on *Behind Events*, al-Jazeera, May 7, 2003.

62. Mahmoud Attallah, on *More Than One Opinion*, al-Jazeera, January 5, 1999.

63. Ragheda Dergham, *al-Hayat*, November 6, 1999; also see Dergham, *al-Hayat*, June 4, 1999.

64. Mohammed Abd al-Hakim Diyab, *al-Quds al-Arabi*, December 12, 1998.

65. Joseph Samaha, *al-Safir*, August 9, 2004.

66. *First Wars*, al-Jazeera, March 6, 2002.

67. Ala al-Lami, *al-Quds al-Arabi*, June 14, 2000.

68. Joseph Samaha, *al-Hayat*, January 22, 1999.

69. Subhi Hadidi, *al-Quds al-Arabi*, February 5, 1999; Ibrahim al-Habib, *al-Quds al-Arabi*, April 9, 1999; Haroun Mohammed, *al-Quds al-Arabi*, April 27, 1999; Abd al-Husayn Shabaan, *al-Hayat*, May 18, 1999.

70. Ala al-Lami, *al-Quds al-Arabi*, July 14, 1999; Jassem Murad, *al-Zaman*, February 2, 2001.

71. Abd al-Wahhab al-Affendi, *al-Quds al-Arabi*, April 18, 1998.

72. Makiya to American Enterprise Institute, October 3, 2002. "The Final Report on The Transition to Democracy in Iraq," the final version of the working document of the Conference of the Iraqi Opposition, November 2002, section 8.2.1 (p. 95), says Iraq would no longer be an "Arab" state.

73. Mohammed al-Musaffir, *al-Quds al-Arabi*, February 26, 2002.

74. Assam al-Yasri, *al-Quds al-Arabi*, July 18, 2002.

75. Ala al-Lami, *al-Quds al-Arabi*, November 27, 1998.

76. Bashir Musa Nafii, *al-Quds al-Arabi*, November 25, 1998, and Adli Sadeq, *al-Quds al-Arabi*, November 30, 1998.

77. For good examples, see Ghassan Attiyah, *al-Quds al-Arabi*, January 7, 1999; *al-Hayat*, June 30, 1999; *al-Hayat*, July 29, 1999; *al-Hayat*, October 7, 1999. Also see Salah al-Nasrawai, *al-Hayat*, May 25, 1999; Haroun Mohammed,

al-Quds al-Arabi, April 27, 1999; Haytham al-Nahi, *al-Quds al-Arabi*, July 4, 1999; Mohammed Bahr al-Uloum, *al-Hayat*, July 14, 1999.

78. Abd al-Halim al-Rahimi, *al-Hayat*, November 19, 2001.

79. *More Than One Opinion*, al-Jazeera, November 6, 1999.

80. *Al-Quds al-Arabi*, November 12, 1999.

81. *Al-Hayat*, October 29, 1999.

82. *Al-Mutamar*, February 16, 2002, p. 12. Al-Jazeera hosts applied this rule consistently, not singling out Iraqi opposition voices for censure.

83. Kanan Makiya, "The Day After: Planning for Post-Saddam Iraq," panel discussion, American Enterprise Institute, Washington, D.C., October 3, 2002. Transcript available at http://www.aei.org/events/filter.,eventID.72/transcript.asp

84. See the frank discussion on *Behind Events*, al-Jazeera, May 12, 2003.

85. Ghassan Attiyah, *al-Hayat*, September 7, 2001.

86. Mohammed Bahar al-Aloum, *al-Hayat*, March 17, 2002.

87. Hazem Saghiyeh, *al-Hayat*, January 13, 1999.

88. *Al-Quds al-Arabi*, August 7, 1998.

89. Barzan al-Tikriti, Iraq's representative to the UN in Geneva, interviewed in *al-Wasat*, December 10, 1996 (BBC SWB ME/D2793/MED, December 12, 1996).

90. Tariq Aziz, Iraqi TV, February 24, 1998 (BBC SWB, February 25, 1998).

91. Several American officials, including Pollack and Indyk, told me that Iraqi propaganda got better over time, although Saddam still could be counted on to sabotage himself under pressure.

92. Tariq Aziz, speech to visiting Jordanian delegation, Iraqi TV, Baghdad, September 28, 2000 (BBC SWB, September 29, 2000).

93. Ghassan Attiyeh, *al-Quds al-Arabi,* February 4, 1998.

94. Mahfouz al-Ensari, chief editor for MENA, commentary on Cairo-MENA, December 29, 1998 (FBIS-NES-98-363).

95. *Al-Quds al-Arabi*, January 21, 2001.

96. National Assembly statement quoted on Iraqi TV, October 23, 2000 (BBC SWB ME/D3980/MED, October 25, 2000).

97. Salim Nassar, *al-Hayat*, September 4, 1999; Salah Nasrawi, *al-Hayat*, October 7, 1999; *al-Quds al-Arabi*, March 24, 2000; Sabah Ali al-Shahir, *al-Quds al-Arabi*, May 16, 2000; Salim Nassar, *al-Hayat*, March 16, 2002.

98. *Al-Quds al-Arabi*, January 31, 2001.

99. For example, *al-Quds al-Arabi*, September 30, 1998, and October 3, 1998.

100. Ali Hussein, *al-Quds al-Arabi*, January 16, 2001.

101. *Al-Ayyam* (Ramallah), January 20, 1998 (FBIS-NES-98-020). Mohammed Krishan, *al-Quds al-Arabi*, June 1, 1998.

102. Abdullah al-Ashaal, *al-Hayat*, March 21, 2002; Mohammed Sid Ahmed, *al-Khaleej*, March 21, 2002.

103. For example, Zayd Hamza, *al-Rai* (Jordan), March 17, 2002.

104. Mohammed al-Musaffir, *al-Quds al-Arabi*, March 5, 1999.

105. Ghassan Attiyah, *al-Hayat*, May 2, 2000.

106. Mutaa Safadi, *al-Quds al-Arabi*, December 10, 2001.

107. Fahd al-Fanik, *al-Rai*, March 19, 2002.

108. *Al-Hayat*, March 19, 2002.

109. Kuwaiti foreign minister to press conference, as quoted in *al-Qabas*, March 20, 2002.

110. Ahmed al-Rubai, *al-Qabas*, March 18, 2002.

111. Said al-Shihabi, *al-Quds al-Arabi*, March 20, 2002.

112. Khalid al-Shami, *al-Quds al-Arabi*, March 19, 2002.

113. Abd al-Bari Atwan, *al-Quds al-Arabi*, March 11, 2002.

114. For example, Awni al-Qalmaji, *al-Quds al-Arabi*, January 14, 1998.

115. *Al-Sharq al-Awsat*, August 5, 1998 (FBIS-NES-98-217).

116. Adli Sadeq, *al-Quds al-Arabi*, January 27, 1998.

117. Mohammed Abd al-Hakim Diyab, *al-Quds al-Arabi*, January 31, 1998.

118. Muta Safadi, *al-Quds al-Arabi*, February 9, 1998.

119. *Al-Quds al-Arabi*, January 29, 1998.

120. Mohammed Abd al-Hakim Diyab, *al-Quds al-Arabi*, February 28, 1998.

121. Editorial, *al-Quds al-Arabi*, February 21, 1998.

122. Muta Safadi, *al-Quds al-Arabi*, March 23, 1998.

123. Ghassan Attiyah, *al-Hayat*, September 7, 2001.

124. Muta Safadi, *al-Quds al-Arabi*, February 16, 1998.

125. *Al-Quds al-Arabi*, February 24, 1998; Mohammed Abd al-Hakim Diyab, *al-Quds al-Arabi*, February 28, 1998.

126. Ghassan Attiyah, *al-Quds al-Arabi*, March 5, 1998.

127. Ghassan Attiyeh, *al-Quds al-Arabi*, February 4, 1998.

128. *Christian Science Monitor*, November 17, 1998, p. 1.

129. Hasan al-Khashif, *al-Ayyam* (Ramallah), November 12, 1998 (FBIS-NES-98-318).

130. Fawzia Abu Khaled, *al-Hayat*, January 10, 1999.

131. Hamad Abd al-Aziz al-Kawari, *al-Hayat*, January 5, 1999.

132. Hamad Abd al-Aziz al-Kawari, *al-Hayat*, February 4, 1999.

133. Amin Huwaydi, *al-Hayat*, January 26, 1999.

134. Yusuf Nur Awadh, *al-Quds al-Arabi*, January 14, 1999.

135. Clovis Maksoud, *al-Hayat*, January 7, 1999.

136. Abdullah Iskander, *al-Hayat*, January 11, 1999.

137. Ragheda Dergham, *al-Hayat*, January 15, 1999.

138. Abd al-Bari Atwan, on *More Than One Opinion*, al-Jazeera, January 5, 1999.

139. Mohammed Dalbah, *al-Quds al-Arabi*, January 29, 1999.

140. *More Than One Opinion*, al-Jazeera, June 28, 1999.

141. Associated Press report, August 16, 2000.

142. Stephen Farrell, "UN Officials Round on Americans," *The Times* (London), February 21, 2001.

143. *More Than One Opinion*, al-Jazeera, October 4, 1999.

144. Raghed al-Saleh, *al-Hayat*, 3 June 1999.

145. *Al-Quds al-Arabi*, April 10, 2000.

146. *More Than One Opinion*, al-Jazeera, October 4, 1999.

147. Mohammed al-Musaffir, *al-Quds al-Arabi*, February 8, 2000.

148. *Al-Quds al-Arabi*, April 23, 1997.

149. Salah al-Nasrawi, *al-Hayat*, October 18, 2000.

150. UN press release SC/6833, March 24, 2000.

151. Independent Inquiry Committee into the United Nations Oil-For-Food Program, chaired by Paul Volcker (February 3, 2005), available at http://www.iic-offp.org/documents.htm.

5. Baghdad Falls

1. Zogby International public opinion survey, April 2002; http://www.zogby.com/news/ReadNews.dbm?ID=564.

2. Pew Research Center for the People and Press, "A Year After the Iraq War," March 16, 2004. Available at http://people-press.org/reports/display.php3?ReportID=206.

3. Rashid Khalidi, *Washington Post*, April 11, 2002.

4. Patrick Tyler, *New York Times*, April 8, 2002.

5. As quoted in the *New York Times*, April 3, 2002.

6. Shibley Telhami, *Christian Science Monitor*, April 15, 2002.

7. As quoted in the *New York Times*, April 16, 2002.

8. For example, see the discussion on *al-Jazeera's Platform*, al-Jazeera, January 16, 2003.

9. *Al-Jazeera's Platform*, al-Jazeera, February 24, 2003.

10. *More Than One Opinion*, al-Jazeera, November 19, 2002.

11. *From Washington* and *More Than One Opinion*, al-Jazeera, January 24, 2003.

12. Fatahallah Arslan, *Behind Events*, al-Jazeera, April 26, 2003.

13. *More Than One Opinion*, al-Jazeera, January 24, 2003.

14. *Al-Quds al-Arabi*, March 15, 2002.

15. Faisal al-Qassem, author phone interview, March 1, 2004; also see Qassem's "Letter to America," *al-Sharq*, March 21, 2004.

16. *The Opposite Direction*, al-Jazeera, November 5, 2002.

17. *Al-Jazeera's Platform*, al-Jazeera, August 22, 2002.

18. *Issue of the Hour*, al-Jazeera, January 19, 2003.

19. *Al-Jazeera's Platform*, al-Jazeera, February 20, 2003. I have heard variations on these claims from several civil society activists in Jordan and in Egypt who must remain anonymous.

20. *Al-Jazeera's Platform*, al-Jazeera, February 20, 2003.

21. Quoted in *Washington Post*, March 14, 2003 (Michael Dobbs reporting).

22. *Jordan Times*, March 29, 2003.

23. *Jordan Times*, May 15, 2003.

24. *The Guardian*, March 28, 2003.

25. For discussions of the tight control over information at CENTCOM, see Michael Massing, "The Unseen War," *New York Review of Books*, May 29, 2003.

26. Zainab Hefni, *Arab News,* April 22, 2003.

27. Abd al-Hadi tells this story on *Behind Events*, al-Jazeera, April 20, 2003.

28. Mohammed el-Nawawy, "Whose 'Truth' Is Being Reported?" *Christian Science Monitor*, April 8, 2003.

29. Nawawy, *Christian Science Monitor*, April 8, 2003.

30. *Al-Jazeera's Platform*, al-Jazeera, April 11, 2003.

31. *Behind Events*, al-Jazeera, April 13, 2003.

6. New Iraq, New Arab Public

1. Colin Powell, interview with National Public Radio, March 25, 2003; http://www.state.gov/secretary/former/powell/remarks/2003/19052.htm.

2. *Wall Street Journal,* April 25, 2005

3. Two al-Arabiya journalists were killed on March 18, 2004; an al-Jazeera reporter was killed on May 21.

4. Mark Jurkowitz, *Boston Globe*, November 13, 2003.

5. As quoted by Hannah Allam, Knight Ridder, May 5, 2004.

6. Khaled al-Haroub, *al-Hayat*, November 11, 2003.

7. Reuters, July 15, 2004.

8. As quoted by Rania Abouzeid, Reuters, May 18, 2004.

9. Maher Abdullah, *The Guardian*, August 11, 2004.

10. *Behind Events*, al-Jazeera, April 26, 2004.

11. Abd al-Mana'am al-Aasim, *al-Zaman*, June 24, 2003.

12. Agence France Presse, June 21, 2004; for early conflicts between Rikabi and American officials, see Peter Slevin, *Washington Post*, May 26, 2003.

13. Sam Jaffe, "Dead Air," *New Republic*, June 9, 2003.

14. Walter Pincus, *Washington Post*, October 29, 2003.

15. Reported in *al-Safir*, November 19, 2004.

16. As quoted by Alan Sipress, *Washington Post*, January 8, 2004.

17. *USA Today* public opinion survey, April 29, 2004.

18. *Washington Post*, January 8, 2004.

19. CNN/*USA Today*/Gallup Poll, available at http://i.a.cnn.net/cnn/2004/WORLD/ meast/04/28/iraq.poll/iraq.poll.4.28.pdf.

20. As quoted by Aqil Jabbar, "U.S. Army Press Chief Riles Locals," *IWPR Iraqi Crisis Report* 73, July 13, 2004.

21. IIACSS survey, May 14–23, 2003.

22. International Republican Institute survey, July 2004; http://www.iri.org/09-07-04-IraqPoll.asp.

23. Confidential CPA public opinion survey discussed by Thomas Ricks, *Washington Post*, May 13, 2004.

24. Ilene Prusher, *Christian Science Monitor*, June 19, 2003.

25. Borzou Daraghi, "The Nightmare That Is Media Work in Iraq," *Arab Reform Bulletin* 2.11, December 2004.

26. Associated Press report on a confidential CPA public opinion survey, June 15, 2004.

27. Gallup Poll, September 23, 2003.

28. Office of Research, U.S. Department of State, October 31, 2003.

29. IIACSS survey, May 13–23, 2004.

30. Office of Research, U.S. Department of State, October 21, 2003 (M-151-03).

31. Office of Research, U.S. Department of State, October 31, 2003.

32. ABC News poll, March 15, 2004; also 10 percent in the Oxford Research International February 2004 poll.

33. Oxford Research International poll, June 2004.

34. Glen Rangwala, "Iraq's Former Exiles Need This Trial," *The Guardian*, December 16, 2003.

35. Oxford Research International poll, June 2004.

36. Monroe Price, "Reimposing Controls on the Iraqi Press," *International Herald Tribune*, October 9, 2004; also see the coverage of Iraq by the Committee to Protect Journalists, report of journalist harassment by the *Iraqi Crisis*

Report 108 (February 1, 2005); http://www.iwpr.net/index.pl?archive/irq/irq_108_1_eng.txt.

37. *Al Jazeera's Platform*, al-Jazeera, November 24, 2003.

38. *Sawt al-Iraq*, August 8, 2004.

39. *Open Dialogue*, al-Jazeera, July 8, 2003.

40. *The Iraqi Scene*, al-Jazeera, December 28, 2003.

41. *The Iraqi Scene*, al-Jazeera, April 24, 2005.

42. *From Washington*, al-Jazeera, July 1, 2004.

43. Siyar al-Jamil, *al-Zaman*, May 4, 2003.

44. Ali al-Ghufli, *al-Khaleej*, July 12, 2004.

45. *USA Today*, April 29, 2004.

46. Abd al-Manaam al-Aasam, *al-Zaman*, May 7, 2003.

47. While such allegations of collaboration with the insurgency were a staple of American and Iraqi criticism, it is worth noting that American government inquiries have failed to produce even a single publicly reported incident of such collaboration despite serious attempts to find such evidence. For an example of the ongoing allegations, see former CPA media advisor Dorrance Smith's essay, "Al-Jazeera Is the Enemy," *Wall Street Journal*, April 25, 2005.

48. For example, the Iraqi weekly *Kul al-Iraq* accused al-Jazeera of inciting violence, August 12, 2004.

49. Jalal Talabani, *Washington Post*, December 4, 2003.

50. Aziz al-Haj described the closure as "a small step in the right direction" (*Elaph*, August 8, 2004).

51. As reported on al-Jazeera, February 13, 2004.

52. Daoud al-Basri, *Elaph*, August 9, 2004.

53. Hazem Saghiye, *al-Hayat*, August 10, 2004.

54. Sha'alan interviewed in *al-Sharq al-Awsat*, November 23, 2004; see also interview with Falah al-Naqib, *al-Sharq al-Awsat*, December 21, 2004.

55. *Al-Jazeera's Platform*, al-Jazeera, August 9, 2004.

56. Interview on al-Jazeera, January 26, 2004.

57. *Al-Sharq al-Awsat*, Sept 3, 2003.

58. *Al-Zaman*, September 7, 2003.

59. Mahmoud Hassan Abass, *al-Zaman*, April 4, 2004.

60. Ghassan al-Imam, *al-Sharq al-Awsat*, September 16, 2003.

61. Sardar Abdullah, *al-Zaman*, September 7, 2003; Abd al-Jabar Mandil, *al-Zaman*, September 7, 2003.

62. Salah Hemeid, *al-Ahram Weekly*, September 3, 2003.

63. *Al-Sharq al-Awsat*, November 26, 2003.

64. Zaynab Yaghi, *al-Safir*, January 31, 2005.

65. Hassan Fattah, "Voting, Not Violence, is the Big Story on Arab TV," *New York Times*, January 30, 2005.

66. Iyad Allawi, "The Task Ahead," *Wall Street Journal*, February 28, 2005.

67. *Al-Jazeera's Platform*, May 2, 2003; *Open Dialogue*, March 6, 2004; *Al-Jazeera's Platform*, August 2, 2004.

68. *Al-Sharq al-Awsat*, July 25, 2004.

69. Al-Jazeera online poll concluding August 2, 2004.

70. As the perceptive Arab media critic Khaled Haroub put it, "where were the torture pictures?" *al-Hayat*, May 21, 2004.

71. Badran Badran, "The U.S. and the Arab Media: A Reversal of Fortune," *Daily Star*, June 8, 2004.

72. Adnan Abu Odeh, "Thanks to Abu Ghraib, al-Jazeera Has Gained Some Breathing Space," *Daily Star*, May 24, 2004.

73. *The Iraqi Scene*, al-Jazeera, January 11, 2004.

74. As quoted by Paul Majendi, Reuters, October 1, 2004.

75. Mamoun Fandy, "Where's the Arab Media's Sense of Outrage?" *Washington Post*, July 4, 2004, B04.

76. Youssef Ibrahim, "Al-Jazeera Boosts Beheadings," *Gulf News*, September 27, 2004.

77. Fahmy Huwaidy, *al-Sharq*, September 14, 2004. Also see Qaradawi's September 26 *fatwa*, available at http://www.islam-online.net/English/News/2004–09/26/article06a.shtml. In April 2005 Qaradawi sued *al-Itthad*, the newspaper that had broken the story, for defamation.

78. Munir Shafiq, *al-Hayat*, December 6, 2004.

79. The extensive coverage on its Web site may be found here: http://www.aljazeera.net/NR/exeres/A4C51088-5950-410F-9BAB-709B5FE2C106.htm.

80. *Al-Sharq al-Awsat*, April 1, 2003.

81. *From Washington*, al-Jazeera, July 1, 2004.

82. Khaled al-Haroub, *al-Hayat*, July 17, 2003.

83. *Al-Sharq al-Awsat*, April 12, 2004. Alhomayed established a media criticism page in *al-Sharq al-Awsat*, and his newspaper published a series of inflammatory allegations about al-Jazeera's relations with the former Iraqi regime and with the insurgency.

84. *Elaph*, November 13, 2004.

85. Bidour Zaki Mohammed, *al-Sharq al-Awsat*, December 24, 2004.

86. *Al-Sharq al-Awsat*, May 3, 2004.

87 *Al-Sharq al-Awsat*, April 6, 2004.

88. *Al-Quds al-Arabi*, July 23, 2003.

89. Walid Phares (*National Review Online*, March 26, 2003) called it "Jihad

TV . . . the global madrassa"; Ralph Peters, "Killers with Cameras," *New York Post*, June 21, 2004.

90. Dan Murphy, *Christian Science Monitor*, March 31, 2005.

91. Nour interviewed in *al-Araby*, April 10, 2005; see also Lina Atallah, "Traitors, Spies, and Democrats," *Cairo Magazine*, April 4, 2005.

Bibliography

Abedi, Mehdi, and Michael Fischer. 1993. "Thinking a Public Sphere in Arabic and Persian." *Public Culture* 6: 220–229.

Abu Lughod, Leila. 1993. "Finding a Place for Islam: Egyptian Television Serials and the National Interest." *Public Culture* 5: 493–513.

al-Affendi, Abd al-Wahhab. 1993. "The Eclipse of Reason." *Journal of International Affairs* 47.1: 163–193.

———. 2002. "Rationality of Politics and Politics of Rationality." In A. Tamimi and J. Esposito, eds., *Islam and Secularism in the Middle East*, 151–169. New York: New York University Press.

Ajami, Fouad. 1991. *The Arab Predicament: Arab Political Thought and Practice Since 1967*. 2d ed. New York: Cambridge University Press.

———. 1998. *Dream Palaces of the Arabs*. New York: Pantheon.

———. 2001. "What the Muslim World Is Watching." *New York Times Magazine* (November 18), 48–53, 76–78.

———. 2003. "Iraq and the Arabs' Future." *Foreign Affairs* 81.1.

Alkadiri, Raad, and Chris Toensing. 2003. "The Iraqi Governing Council's Sectarian Hue." *Middle East Report Online* (August 20).

Alterman, Jon B. 1998. "Transnational Media and Regionalism." *Transnational Broadcasting Studies* 1. http://www.tbsjournal.com.

———. 1999a. "Transnational Media and Social Change in the Arab World." *Transnational Broadcasting Studies*. http://www.tbsjournal.com.

———. 1999b. *New Media, New Politics*. Washington, DC: Washington Institute for Near East Policy.

———. 2002. "Slouching Toward Ramallah." *Opinion Journal* (November 21). http://www.opinionjournal.com.

————. 2004. "The Information Revolution and the Middle East." In Dan By-man and Nora Bensahel, eds., *The Future Security Environment in the Middle East*, 224–251. Washington, DC: RAND.

Anderson, Jon. 2003. "New Media, New Publics: Reconfiguring the Public Sphere of Islam." *Social Research* 70.3: 887–906.

Anderson, Jon, and Dale Eickelman, eds. 1999. *New Media in a Changing Middle East*. Bloomington: Indiana University Press.

Anonymous ("A Special Correspondent"). 1987. "'A Policeman on My Chest, A Scissor in My Brain': Political Rights and Censorship in Jordan." *Middle East Report* 149: 30–34.

"Are We Listening to the Arab Street?" 2002. Hearing of the National Security, Veterans Affairs, and International Relations Subcommittee of the House Government Reform Committee (October 8).

Armbrust, Walter. 2000. *Mass Meditations: New Approaches to Mass Culture in the Middle East and Beyond*. Berkeley: University of California Press.

Ayalon, Ami. 1995. *The Press in the Arab Middle East: A History*. New York: Oxford University Press.

Ayish, Mohammed. 2001. "American-Style Journalism and Arab World Television: An Exploratory Study of News Selection at Six Arab World Satellite Television Channels." *Transnational Broadcasting Studies* 6. http://www.tbsjournal.com.

————. 2004. "News Credibility During the Iraq War: A Survey of UAE Students." *Transnational Broadcasting Studies* 12. http://www.tbsjournal.com.

al-Azm, Sadiq Jalal. 2000. "The View from Damascus." *New York Review of Books* 47.10 (June 15), 70–77.

Bahlul, Raja. 2003. "Toward an Islamic Conception of Democracy: Islam and the Notion of Public Reason." *Critique* 12.1: 43–60.

Baker, Raymond. 2003. *Islam Without Fear*. Cambridge, MA: Harvard University Press.

Baram, Amatzia. 2000. "The Effect of Iraqi Sanctions: Statistical Pitfalls and Responsibility." *Middle East Journal* 54: 194–223.

Barnett, Michael N. 1998. *Dialogues in Arab Politics: Negotiations in Regional Order*. New York: Columbia University Press.

Barnett, Michael N., and Shibley Telhami, eds. 2003. *Identity and Foreign Policy in the Middle East*. Ithaca, NY: Cornell University Press.

Bayat, Asef. 2003. "The 'Street' and the Politics of Dissent in the Arab World." *Middle East Report* 226: 10–17.

Bennett, W. Lance. 2003. "Operation Perfect Storm: The Press and the Iraq War." *Political Communication Report* 13.3. http://www.ou.edu/policom.

———. 2004. "Global Media and Politics: Transnational Communication Regimes and Civic Cultures." *Annual Review of Political Science* 7: 125–148.

Bennett, W. Lance, and Robert M. Entman, eds. 2001. *Mediated Politics*. Cambridge: Cambridge University Press.

Bishri, Tareq. 1996. The Islamist-Secularist Dialogue [in Arabic]. Cairo: Dar al-Sharouq.

Blake, Mariah. 2005. "From All Sides." *Columbia Journalism Review* (March/April): 16–18.

Bohman, James. 1998. "The Globalization of the Public Sphere: Cosmopolitan Publicity and the Problem of Cultural Pluralism." *Philosophy and Social Criticism* 24.2/3: 199–216.

———. 1999. "Citizenship and Norms of Publicity: Wide Public Reason in Cosmopolitan Societies." *Political Theory* 27: 176–202.

———. 2000. "The Public Spheres of the World Citizen." In James Bohman and Matthias Lutz-Bachmann, eds., *Perpetual Peace*, 179–200. Cambridge, MA: MIT Press.

Bourdieu, Pierre. 1979. "Public Opinion Does Not Exist." In Armand Mattelart and Seth Siegelaub, eds., *Communication and Class Struggle*. UK: International General.

———. 1998. *On Television*. Stanford: Stanford University Press.

Bowen, John. 2003. *Islam, Law, and Equality in Indonesia*. Cambridge University Press.

Boyd, Douglas. 2001. 1993. *Broadcasting in the Arab World*. 2d ed. Ames: Iowa State University Press.

———. 2002. "Saudi Arabia's International Media Strategy." In Hafez 2001.

Bradley, John R. 2004. "Will al-Jazeera Bend?" *The Prospect* 97 (March 25). http://www.selvesandothers.org/article6502.html.

Brand, Laurie A. 1995. *Jordan's Inter-Arab Relations*. New York: Columbia University Press.

Brumberg, Daniel. 2002. "Arab Public Opinion and U.S. Foreign Policy: A Complex Encounter." Testimony prepared for the Congress of the United States, House of Representatives, Committee on Government Reform, Subcommittee on National Security Veterans Affairs, and International Relations, October 8, 2002.

———. 2003. "Liberalization Versus Democratization." Carnegie, Democracy and Rule of Law Project Working Paper 37 (May).

Brunkhorst, Hauke. 2002. "Globalising Democracy Without a State: Weak Public, Strong Public, Global Constitutionalism." *Millennium* 31.3: 675–690.

Buck-Morss, Susan. 2003. *Thinking Past Terror: Islamism and Critical Theory on the Left.* New York: Norton.

Bunt, Gary R. 2003. *Islam in the Digital Age: E-Jihad, Online Fatwas, and Cyber Islamic Environments.* London: Pluto Press.

Burkhart, Grey E., and Susan Older. 2003. *The Information Revolution in the Middle East and North Africa.* Santa Monica, CA: RAND National Defense Research Institute.

Byman, Daniel. 2000a. "A Farewell to Arms Inspections." *Foreign Affairs* 79.1: 119–132.

——. 2000b. "Proceed with Caution: U.S. Support for the Iraqi Opposition." *Washington Quarterly* 22.3: 23–38.

Byman, Daniel, Kenneth Pollack, and Gideon Rose. 1999. "Can Saddam Be Toppled?" *Foreign Affairs* 78.1: 24–41.

Calhoun, Craig. 1988. "Populist Politics, Communications Media, and Large-Scale Social Integration." *Sociological Theory* 6: 219–241

——. 1992. *Habermas and the Public Sphere.* Cambridge, MA: MIT Press.

——. 2002. "The Class Consciousness of Frequent Travelers: Towards a Critique of Actually Existing Cosmopolitanism." *South Atlantic Quarterly* 101: 869–897.

——. 2004. "The Democratic Integration of Europe." *Eurozine* (June 21).

Carapico, Sheila. 1998. *Civil Society in Yemen: The Political Economy of Activism in Modern Arabia.* New York: Cambridge University Press.

Chambers, Simone. 2003. "Deliberative Democracy Theory." *Annual Review of Political Science* 6: 307–326.

"Changing Minds, Winning Peace: A New Strategic Direction for U.S. Public Diplomacy in the Arab and Muslim World." 2003. Report of the Advisory Group on Public Diplomacy for the Arab and Muslim World to the Committee on Appropriations, U.S. House of Representatives.

Chatterjee, Partha. 2004. *The Politics of the Governed: Reflections on Popular Politics in Most of the World.* New York: Columbia University Press.

Cockburn, Andrew, and Patrick Cockburn. 2000. *Out of the Ashes: The Resurrection of Saddam Hussein.* New York: Perennial.

Cortright, David, and George Lopez. 2000. *The Sanctions Decade.* Boulder, CO: Westview Press.

Diamond, Larry. 2004. "What Went Wrong in Iraq." *Foreign Affairs* 83.5: 34–44.

Ebert, Barbara. 1992. "The Gulf War and Its Aftermath: Evolving Arab Responses." *Middle East Policy* 1: 77–94.

Eickelman, Dale F. 2000. "Islam and the Languages of Modernity." *Daedalus* 129: 119–136.

———. 2001. "Kings and People: Information and Authority in Oman, Qatar, and the Persian Gulf." In J. Kechichian, ed., *Iran, Iraq, and the Arab Gulf States*, 193–209. New York: Palgrave, Macmillan.

———. 2002. "Bin Laden, the Arab Street, and the Middle East's Democratic Deficit." *Current History* (January): 36–40.

Eickelman, Dale F., and Armando Salvatore. 2002. "The Public Sphere and Muslim Identities." *Arch. europ. social.* 43.1: 92–115.

Elbendary, Amina. 2001. "TV Meets the Madding Crowd." *Al-Ahram Weekly Online*, June 14–20.

Emirbayer, Mustafa, and Mimi Sheller. 1998. "Publics in History." *Theory and Society* 27: 727–779.

Fallows, James. 2003. "Who Shot Mohammed al-Durra?" *Atlantic Monthly* (June), 49–56.

Fandy, Mamoun. 2000. "Information Technology, Trust, and Social Change in the Arab World." *Middle East Journal* 54.3: 378–394.

Fraser, Nancy. 1992. "Rethinking the Public Sphere." In Craig Calhoun, *Habermas and the Public Sphere*, 109–142. Cambridge, MA: MIT Press.

Gamson, William A. 2001. "Promoting Political Engagement." In W. L. Bennett and R. M. Entman, eds., *Mediated Politics: Communication in the Future of Democracy*, 56–74. New York: Cambridge University Press.

Garnham, Nicholas. 1993. "The Mass Media, Cultural Identity, and the Public Sphere in the Modern World." *Public Culture* 5: 251–265.

Gerecht, Reuel M. 2002. "Better To Be Feared Than Loved, cont." *Weekly Standard* (April 29).

Ghadbian, Najib. 2001. "Contesting the State Media Monopoly: Syria on Al-Jazira Television." *Middle East Review of International Affairs* 5.2: 75–87.

Ghareeb, Edmund. 2000. "New Media and the Information Revolution in the Arab World: An Assessment." *Middle East Journal* 54.3: 395–418.

Gonzalez-Quijano, Yves. 2003. "The Birth of a Media Ecosystem: Lebanon in the Internet Age." Trans. Dale F. Eickelman and William F. P. Raynolds. In *New Media in the Muslim World: The Emerging Public Sphere*, 61–79. Indiana: Indiana University Press.

Gourevitch, Alex. 2003. "Exporting Censorship to Iraq." *American Prospect* (October 1).

Graham-Brown, Sarah. 1999. *Sanctioning Saddam: The Politics of Intervention in Iraq*. London: I. B. Tauris.

Habermas, Jurgen. 1989. *Structural Transformation of the Public Sphere*. Cambridge, MA: MIT Press.

———. 1996. *Between Facts and Norms: Contributions to a Discourse Theory of Law and Democracy*. Cambridge, MA: MIT Press.

———. 1999. *On the Pragmatics of Communication.* Cambridge, MA: MIT Press.

Hadj-Moussa, Ratiba. 2003. "New Media, Community, and Politics in Algeria." *Media, Culture, and Society* 25.4: 451–468.

Hafez, Kai, ed. 2001. *Mass Media, Politics, and Society in the Middle East.* Cresskill, NJ: Hampton Press.

Hafez, Sabry. 2000. "The Novel, Politics, and Islam." *New Left Review* 5: 117–141.

Hayes, Stephen. 2003. "Al Jazeera: 'Fair,' 'Balanced,' and Bought." *Weekly Standard,* May 28.

———. 2004. "Saddam's Cash." *Weekly Standard,* January 30.

Herbst, Susan. 1993. *Numbered Voices.* Chicago: University of Chicago Press.

Hiro, Dilip. 2001. *Neighbors, Not Friends: Iraq and Iran After the Gulf Wars.* New York: Routledge.

Hirschkind, Charles. 2001. "Civic Virtue and Public Reason: An Islamic Counterpublic." *Cultural Anthropology* 16.1: 3–34.

Human Rights Watch. 1997. *Jordan: Clamping Down on Critics.* HRW/Middle East 9.12.

Ibrahim, Saad Eddin. 2004. "Thoughts on Arab Satellite Television, Pan-Arabism, and Freedom of Experssion." *Transnational Broadcasting Studies* 13. http://www.tbsjournal.com.

Ismael, Tareq, and Jacquie Ismael. 1993. "Arab Politics and the Gulf War." *Arab Studies Quarterly* 15: 1–11.

Jabar, Faleh. 2001. "Assessing the Iraqi Opposition." *MERIP Press Information Notes* 51 (March 23).

Jamai, Aboubakr. 2005. "Morocco Still Shoots the Messenger." *Arab Reform Bulletin* 2.12.

Joffe, George. 1993. "Middle Eastern Views of the Gulf Conflict and Its Aftermath." *Review of International Studies* 19: 177–199.

Jorisch, Avi. 2004a. "Al-Manar: Hizbullah TV, 24/7." *Middle East Quarterly* (winter): 17–31.

———. 2004b. *Beacon of Hatred: Inside Hezbollah's al-Manar Television.* Washington, DC: Washington Institute for Near East Policy.

Judah, Tim. 2003. "The Fall of Baghdad." *New York Review of Books* (May 15), online edition.

Kalathil, Shanthi, and Taylor C. Boas. 2003. "Technology and Tradition in the United Arab Emirates, Saudi Arabia, and Egypt." In *Open Networks, Closed Regimes: The Impact of the Internet on Authoritarian Rule,* 103–134. Washington, DC: Carnegie Endowment for International Peace.

Kalb, Marvin, and Jerome Socolovsky. 1999. "The Emboldened Arab Press." *Harvard International Journal of Press/Politics* 4.3: 1–4.

al-Kallab, Salih. 2003. "The Arab Satellites—the Pros and Cons." *Transnational Broadcasting Studies* 11. http://www.tbsjournal.com.

al-Kasim, Faisal. 1999. "Crossfire: The Arab Version." *Harvard International Journal of Press/Politics* 4.3: 93–97.

Katovsky, Bill, and Timothy Carlson. 2003. *Embedded: The Media at War in Iraq.* Guilford, CT: Lyons Press.

Katulis, Brian. 2004. "Women's Rights in Focus: Egypt." Freedom House (October 19).

Kerr, Malcolm H. 1971. *The Arab Cold War: Gamal Abd al-Nasir and His Rivals, 1958–1970.* 3d ed. New York: Oxford University Press.

Khazen, Jihad. 1999. "Censorship and State Control of the Press in the Arab World." *Harvard International Journal of Press/Politics* 4.3: 87–92.

Kohler, Martin. 1998. "From the National to the Cosmopolitan Public Sphere." In Daniele Archibugi et al., *Re-Imagining Political Community.* Stanford: Stanford University Press.

Kraidy, Marwan M. 2000. "Transnational Television and Asymmetrical Interdependence in the Arab World: The Growing Influence of the Lebanese Satellite Broadcasters." *Transnational Broadcasting Studies* 5. http://www.tbsjournal.com.

Kull, Steven, et al. 2003. "Misperceptions, the Media, and the Iraq War." Program on International Policy Attitudes, University of Maryland, October 2. http://www.pipa.org/OnlineReports/Iraq/Media_10_02_03_Report.pdf.

Kuran, Timur, and Cass Sunstein. 1999. "Availability Cascades and Risk Regulation." *Stanford Law Review* 51: 683–768.

Kurzman, Charles. 2003. "Pro-U.S. Fatwas." *Middle East Policy* 10.3: 155–166.

Kuttab, Daoud. 2003. "The Arab TV Wars." *New York Times,* April 6, 2003.

Lewis, Justin. 2001. *Constructing Public Opinion.* New York: Columbia University Press.

Lucas, Russell. 2003. "Press Laws as a Survival Strategy in Jordan, 1989–1999." *Middle Eastern Studies* 39.4: 81–98.

Lynch, Marc. 1998/99. "Abandoning Iraq: Jordan's Alliances and the Politics of State Identity." *Security Studies* 8.2/3: 347–388.

———. 1999. *State Interests and Public Spheres: The International Politics of Jordan's Identity.* New York: Columbia University Press.

———. 2000a. "The Dialogue of Civilizations and International Public Spheres." *Millennium* 29.2: 307–330.

———. 2000b. "The Politics of Consensus in the Gulf." *Middle East Report* 215: 20–23.

———. 2001. "Smart Sanctions: Rebuilding Consensus or Maintaining Conflict?" *MERIP Press Information Note* 62 (June 28).

———. 2002a. "Why Engage? China and the Logic of Communicative Engagement." *European Journal of International Relations* 8.2: 187–230.

———. 2002b. "Jordan's King Abdullah in Washington." *MERIP Press Information Note* 94 (May 9).

———. 2002c. "Using and Abusing the UN, Redux." *Middle East Report* 225: 8–13.

———. 2003a. "Taking Arabs Seriously." *Foreign Affairs* 82.5: 81–94.

———. 2003b. "Beyond the Arab Street: Iraq and the Arab Public Sphere." *Politics and Society* 31.1: 55–91.

———. 2003c. "Irrelevance Lost." *Middle East Report Online* (March 18).

———. 2004a. "The Arab Media Environment." In Bill Rugh, ed., *Engaging the Arab/Islamic World*. Washington, DC: Public Diplomacy Institute.

———. 2004b. "Not the Enemy: The Arab Media and American Reform Efforts." *Arab Reform Bulletin* 2.4.

———. 2004c. "Shattering the Politics of Silence: Satellite Television and the Transformation of Arab Political Culture." *Arab Reform Bulletin* 2.11.

———. 2005. "Dialogue in an Age of Terror." *Global Society* 19: 5–28.

MacArthur, John R. 1992. *Second Front: Censorship and Propaganda in the Gulf War*. Berkeley: University of California Press.

Makiya, Kanan. 1995. *Cruelty and Silence*. New York: Norton.

al-Marashi, Ibrahim. 2004. "Iraq's Hostage Crisis: Kidnappings, Mass Media, and the Iraqi Insurgency." *MERIA* 8.4.

Massing, Michael. 2004. *Now They Tell Us*. New York: New York Review Press.

McCollam, Douglas. 2004. "How Chalabi Played the Press." *Columbia Journalism Review* (July/August). http://www.cjr.org.

Mernissi, Fatima. 2004. "The Satellite, the Prince, and Scheherezade: The Rise of Women as Communicators in Digital Islam." *Transnational Broadcasting Studies* 12. http://www.tbsjournal.com.

Miles, Hugh. 2003. "Watching the War on Al Jazeera." *London Review of Books* 25.8 (April 17), online edition.

———. 2005. *Al-Jazeera: The Inside Story of the Arab News Channel That Is Challenging the West*. New York: Grove Press.

Minear, Larry, David Cortright, Julia Wagler, George Lopez, and Thomas Weiss. 1998. *Toward More Humane and Effective Sanctions Management: Enhancing the Capacity of the United Nations System* (Watson Institute Occasional Papers 31). Providence, RI: Thomas J. Watson Institute for International Studies, 1998.

Mneimneh, Hassan. 2003. "The New Intra-Arab Cultural Space in Form and Content: The Debates Over an American 'Letter.'" *Social Research* 73.3: 907–930.

Mohammadi, Ali, and Annabelle Sreberny Mohammadi. 1994. *Small Media, Big Revolutions*. Minneapolis: University of Minnesota Press.

Moustafa, Tamir. 2004. "Protests Hint at New Chapter in Egyptian Politics." *Middle East Report Online* (April 9).

Muravchik, Joshua. 2003. "Listening to Arabs." *Commentary* 116.5: 28–33.

Mutz, Diane. 1998. *Impersonal Influence*. New York: Cambridge University Press.

Nabulsi, Shaker. 2003. The Arab Street [in Arabic]. Beirut: Arab Institute for Studies and Publications.

Najjar, Fauze. 1998. "Islamic Fundamentalism and the Intellectuals." *British Journal of Middle Eastern Studies* 25.1: 139–168.

Nanz, Patrizia, and Jens Steffek. 2004. "Global Governance, Participation, and the Public Sphere." *Government and Opposition* 39: 314–335.

el-Nawawy, Mohammed, and Adel Iskander. 2002. *Al Jazeera*. Boulder, CO: Westview.

Nisbet, Erik C., Matthew C. Nisbet, Dietram A. Sheufle, and James E. Shanahan. 2004. "Public Diplomacy, Television News, and Muslim Opinion." *Press/Politics* 9.2: 11–37.

Parenti, Christian. 2004. "Al Jazeera Goes to Jail." *The Nation* (March 29).

Pipes, Daniel. 2002. "A New Round of Anger and Humiliation: Islam After 9/11." In Wladyslaw Pleszczynski, ed., *Our Brave New World: Essays on the Impact of September 11*, 41–61. Stanford: Hoover Institution Press.

Pollack, Kenneth M. 2002. *The Threatening Storm: The Case for Invading Iraq*. New York: Random House.

Pollock, David. 1992. *The "Arab Street"? Public Opinion in the Arab World*. Washington, DC: Washington Institute for Near East Policy.

al-Qaradawi, Yusuf. 1981/2002. "Extremism" (1981), as translated in Charles Kurzman, *Liberal Islam: A Source Book*. New York: Oxford University Press, 2002.

Risse, Thomas. 2000. "Let's Argue! Communicative Action in World Politics." *International Organization* 54: 1–39.

Rouleau, Eric. 1995. "America's Unyielding Policy Towards Iraq: The View from France." *Foreign Affairs* 74.1: 59–72.

Rowat, Colin. 2000. "UN Agency Reports on the Humanitarian Situation in Iraq." http://www.cam.ac.uk/societies/casi.

Roy, Olivier. 2004. *Globalized Islam: The Search for a New Ummah*. New York: Columbia University Press.

Rubin, Barry. 2003. *The Tragedy of the Middle East*. Cambridge: Cambridge University Press.

Rugh, William. 2004a. *Arab Mass Media*. New York: Praeger.

——, ed. 2004b. *Engaging Arab and Islamic Worlds Through Public Diplomacy*. Washington, DC: Public Diplomacy Institute.

Saeed, Abdel Moneim. 2003. "The Arab Satellites—Some Necessary Observations!" *Transnational Broadcasting Studies* 11. http://www.tbsjournal.com.

Saghiyeh, Hazem. 2004. "Al Jazeera: The World Through Arab Eyes." http://www.opendemocracy.net (June 17).

Sakr, Naomi. 2001a. "Contested Blueprints for Egypt's Satellite Channels: Regrouping the Options by Redefining the Debate." *Gazette* 63.2–3: 149–167.

——. 2001b. *Satellite Realms*. New York: St. Martin's.

Salvatore, Armando. 1997. *Islam and the Political Discourse of Modernity*. London: Ithaca Press.

Salvatore, Armando, and Dale Eickelman. 2004. *Public Islam and the Common Good*. London: Brill.

Samhat, Nayef, and Rodger Payne. 2003. "Regimes, Public Spheres, and Global Democracy." *Global Society* 17.3: 273–295.

Schanzer, Jonathan. 2003. "The Iraq War: How It Was Seen in the Middle East." *Middle East Quarterly*.

Schemm, Paul. 2003. "Egypt Struggles to Control Anti-War Protest." *Middle East Report Online* (March 31).

Schleifer, S. Abdallah. 1998. "Media Explosion in the Arab World: The Pan-Arab Satellite Broadcasters." *Transnational Broadcasting Studies* 1. http://www.tbsjournal.com.

——. 2001. "Looks Are Deceiving: Arab Talk Shows and TV Journalism." *Transnational Broadcasting Studies* 6. http://www.tbsjournal.com.

Schuessler, Alexander. 2000. *A Logic of Expressive Choice*. Princeton: Princeton University Press.

Schulze, Reinhard. 2000. *A Modern History of the Islamic World*. Trans. A. Azodi. London: Tauris.

Schwedler, Jillian. 2003. "More Than a Mob: The Dynamics of Political Demonstrations in Jordan." *Middle East Report* 225: 18–23.

Scott, James. 1986. *Domination and the Arts of Resistance*. New Haven: Yale University Press.

Shapiro, Samantha. 2005. "The War Inside the Arab Newsroom." *New York Times Magazine* (January 2), 26–33.

Sreberny, Annabelle. 2001. "Mediated Culture in the Middle East: Diffusion, Democracy, Difficulties." *Gazette* 63.2–3: 101–119.

Sunstein, Cass. 2003. "The Law of Group Polarization." In James Fishkin and Peter Laslett, eds., *Debating Deliberative Democracy*, 80–137. New York: Oxford University Press.

Tajbakhsh, Kian. 2003. "Media in the Islamic World: Introduction." *Social Research* 73.3: 869–876.

Tarrow, Sidney, Charles Tilly, and Douglas McAdam. 2002. *The Dynamics of Contentious Politics*. New York: Cambridge University Press.

Tayler, Jeffrey. 2004. "The Faisal Factor." *Atlantic Monthly* (November).

Taylor, Philip. 1992. *War and the Media: Propaganda and Persuasion in the Gulf War*. New York: St. Martin's.

Telhami, Shibley. 1993. "Arab Public Opinion and the Gulf War." *Political Science Quarterly* 108.3: 437–452.

———. 2002. *The Stakes*. Boulder, CO: Westview Press.

———. 2005. *Reflections of Hearts and Minds: Media, Opinion, and Identity in the Arab World*. Washington, DC: Brookings Institution.

Tessler, Mark. 2003. "Arab and Muslim Political Attitudes." *International Studies Perspectives* 4.3: 175–180.

Tetreault, Mary Ann. 2000. *Stories of Democracy: Politics and Society in Contemporary Kuwait*. New York: Columbia University Press.

Umanksy, Eric. 2004. "Dangerous Science: Why a Mob Attacked the Most Rational Man in the Middle East." *Columbia Journalism Review* (January). http://www.cjr.org.

Van de Steeg, Marianne. 2002. "Rethinking the Conditions for a Public Sphere in the European Union." *European Journal of Social Theory* 5.4: 499–519.

Warner, Michael. 2002. *Publics and Counterpublics*. New York: Zone Books.

Wedeen, Lisa. 1998. *Ambiguities of Domination*. Chicago: University of Chicago Press.

———. Forthcoming. *Peripheral Visions: Political Identifications in United Yemen*.

Woodward, Bob. 2004. *Plan of Attack*. New York: Simon and Schuster.

"Words Have Consequences: The Impact of Incitement and Anti-American and Anti-Semitic Propaganda on American Interests in the Middle East." 2002. Hearing before the subcommittee on the Middle East and South Asia of the Committee on International Relations, House of Representatives (April 18).

Wright, Lawrence. 2004a. "Web of Terror." *New Yorker* (August 2).

———. 2004b. "The Kingdom of Silence." *New Yorker* (January 5), 48–73.

Yamani, Mai. 2000. *Changed Identities: The Challenge of a New Generation in Saudi Arabia*. London: Royal Institute for International Affairs.

Zakaria, Fareed. 2004. "Islam, Democracy, and Constitutional Liberalism." *Political Science Quarterly* 119: 1–20.

Zayani, Mohamed, ed. 2005. *The al-Jazeera Phenomenon: Critical Perspectives on New Arab Media.* London: Pluto Press.

Zednick, Rick. 2002. "Inside al-Jazeera." *Columbia Journalism Review* (April 5). http://www.cjr.org.

Index